The Admiral's Son

Hank Miller

Greenbrae, CA

© 2007 by Lulu Press

All rights reserved.

ISBN: 978-0-6151-6505-9

Library of Congress Control Number: 2007937327

Printed in the United States of America.

Preface

If you want to read something like "Winds of War" and the Henry family put this book down immediately. If you want to read the story of "The Great Santini" then put this book down immediately, if not sooner. This is a series of short stories about growing up as a Navy Junior and eventually becoming a Naval Aviator and all of the shenanigans associated thereunto.

This is about life and living it to the fullest - some of it good and some bad. Nonetheless, I am alive and thankful for that albeit a little bit loony at times. So be it. One cannot be normal and be a pilot flying off aircraft carriers. Proceed with caution and with a sense of exploration and discovery. I think you will have a fun journey only I repeat only if you don't take it too serially.

The primary reason for my including the Personnel Fitness Reports, otherwise known as performance evaluations, is to provide a time line for when I was gung-ho, full of piss and vinegar, ready to take on the entire Vietnamese bad guys to one of complacency rapidly evolving into utter contempt for the commands to which I was attached. It got so bad while I was assigned to Treasure Island Naval Base, San Francisco, my commanding officer wrote a letter that is included in the fitness reports outlining my daily work schedule. Where I could go, where I could eat, when and how I could leave the building. I considered it a badge of honor at the time. Maverick, not a team player, sort of a big royal screwup to the military. My complacency was so bad I failed to appear at the Playboy Club in San Francisco for my retirement party and acceptance of a plaque made with my name inscribed on the brass nameplate.

The inclusion of the fitness reports is critical to this book. As you continue to read you will understand what I mean.

My father was a career Naval officer attaining the rank of Rear Admiral prior to his death in 1993. He was a true sailor. The MAIN difference between us is that he was the trainer of General Doolittle's Raiders for the 30 Seconds Over Tokyo mission that helped to change the direction of World War II. My legacy is that I was thrown out of at least 30 bars in Japan during the liberty I spent on her shores. His history was recorded in books and film. Mine was recorded in the Shore Patrol logs.

I suppose my interest with the Navy began as a result of DNA and a desire for travel and adventure more so than flying. As a matter of fact I had no interest in flying other than becoming one of those handsome Blue Angels one sees at the Officers Club. Women flocked around them like flies so that appealed to me big time. I knew Vietnam was around the corner during my senior year at Auburn University, so I took the written, oral, and physical exams and passed much to my amazement since I was hung over during all three evaluations. Then, off to U.S. Naval School Pre-Flight, in Pensacola, FL and then Corpus Christi, TX where I earned my Aviator Wings of Gold in 1966.

My involvement with the Vietnam Conflict began in 1966 after completing the training at Naval Air Station Lemoore, California and reporting to Attach Squadron 152, Alameda Naval Air Station, California as directed by orders from Navy Bureau of Personnel. This was considered to be an honor for propeller-trained pilots as most were relegated to long haul cargo or anti-submarine patrol aircraft. Being assigned to an attack squadron meant one thing: You were going to Vietnam, simple as that.

I was a junior aviator soon to become a seasoned attack pilot flying the A1 H/J model Skyraider, better known as the Spad. McDonnell Douglas produced this aircraft for the Korean War and it proved to be formidable then and in the Vietnam Conflict. The H/J type had a single seat for a solo pilot, four - bladed propeller with a 3350 horsepower reciprocating engine capable of sustained flight and carrying nearly its own weight in armament. The Vietnamese communist ground forces feared this aircraft since they had virtually no impending warning of its arrival overhead. We flew low, slow, and very quietly. We could deliver lethal weaponry on target most of the time unlike faster and higher flying jets who announced their arrival and had trouble hitting the broadside of a barn with their bombs.

We deployed aboard USS Oriskany, CVA - 32, in early June, 1967, and spent the following seven months on station in Tonkin Gulf and various liberty ports of call. Tonkin Gulf borders all of North and South Vietnam and provided the platform for the numerous air strikes flown off aircraft carriers to eradicate the supply lines up and down the Ho Chi Minh Trail as well as other targets. When not in action we were either enroute or in various ports of call for both recreation and for overhauling the carriers' systems. Ports such as Subic Bay, Philippines, Sasebo and Yokosuka, Japan, and Hong Kong provided me with relaxation, shopping, and photographic opportunities.

The images I took using my Nikkormat FT were mostly as a result of using my camera as a distraction from the action and the stark fear I experienced while flying. Rather than totally freak out, I would open the shutter and start snapping images to take my mind off the fact I may get shot down or crash. It also provided an unemotional shield between people who I either knew or strangers rather than having to socialize with them. In other words the camera acted as some sort of a barrier. Some of the images were taken before my deployment to Vietnam. These photos are of persons with whom I shared a personal relationship. Those times, those friends, and those memories are precious to me to this day.

The overlayment of the images was a result of a suggestion by someone who saw an image I had printed as a large mural. People commented about how I should consider using my Vietnam images in an art form. I had my slides, negatives and prints scanned by a high school buddy, also an Air Force pilot and a Vietnam veteran. The images could then be manipulated and layered into the final art project. The project took six months from inception to completion. Now I could use Photoshop and layer them into what I remember and wanted to convey about the subjects artistically. Ultimately the project evolved into an exhibition held at San Francisco City Hall, 2001.

BOOK ONE contains stories about my youth mostly spent with my maternal grandparents and cousins Rego Stevie and Carol Rue in Opp, Alabama. Those were wonderful summers that broke the loneliness I felt during the other nine months in various schools across the country.

BOOK TWO continues of the first book with episodes during high school in Manila and Washington DC then as a student at Auburn University, Alabama.

BOOK THREE is the meat market of the matter. Tales of "fright school", dating before and during the Summer of Love San Francisco style, then across the pond to Vietnam as an attack pilot in both the war and in the various ports of call. That seems like an eternity ago. 40 years has passed since we departed Alameda for the western Pacific. The book ends with Notes and my observations about why things were going "South" with this war called Conflict. Must be a McNamara kind of thing.

I dedicate this book to all Vietnam combatants and their survivors living and dead.

Hank Miller

LT USNR

VA-152

Lckt13, "Non Hankus Pankus"

You are not even a pawn. Your death will not make the world safe for your children. Your death means no more than if you had died in your bed, full of years of respectability, having begotten a tribe of young. Yet by your courage in tribulation, by your cheerfulness before the dirty devices of this world, you have won the love of those who have watched you. All we remember is your living face, and that we loved you for being of our clay and spirit.

Magnicourt-sur-Canche, France 21 October 1916

<u>A Passionate Prodigality</u>

Guy Chapman

Touch Me - A Soliloquy

Touch me. Don't be afraid. I can't hurt you. Go ahead and touch my smooth surface. Feel the cold, glass-like smoothness and the crevices and lines that make me what I am. Use both hands if you wish. We are more similar than you dare to believe.

Touch my face. Yes, I have a face like yours. It has weathered the centuries as yours has the years. My face portrays my evolution. Yours, the birth and death of a generation. My face has aged like yours as we have endured together the testimony of earth's elements.

I have eyes like yours. My inscriptions stare out at you as I search for the meaning of why we are here. I look into your eyes and see who you are. Who am I? I was formed millions of years past and now you see the results of my evolution.

I can feel your hands and the sweat from your palms flow into the countless combination of the letters that make me. I know you. I have known you since I was able to breathe in the air as my smoothness began to take shape and my color matured along with natural flaws. You have known me since the days when you came to take me from my mother.

You cannot hear me. I am static and unmoving. But, I can hear your murmurs and your cries of pain and sadness. Your sons and daughters ask why? There are no answers.

I am very old. I have seen everything and I am none the wiser for the pain and suffering I have witnessed since I rose from the bowels of the earth. I have witnessed the conflict, the death, the civilizations, and the societies that have come before you. Yet I remain mystified about this day.

I feel sad yet alive with a purpose. I have come to know those who are now an integral part of the reason for my being here at this place and time. That purpose has become apparent as I stand before you on this day while your brethren gather to witness my reflections and the changes of light that mirror your soul.

I am a reflection of you.

I am all of you . . .

I am your spirit . . .

I am The Wall.

"All we remember is your living face . . ."

Hank Miller

The Boswain's Mate Piped the Old Man Ashore

Henry L. Miller, born in Fairbanks, Alaska, on 18 July 1912 died on 25 January 1993 and was buried in Arlington National Cemetery on 3 February, with full military honors. He was an Annapolis graduate, Class of '34, who served with distinction in three wars. He trained General Doolittle's Army pilots for the carrier launch from USS Hornet, and was a member of the exclusive 30 Seconds over Tokyo Raiders. In addition, he commanded Air Group 6 aboard USS Hancock during World War II. In 1965, Rear Admiral Miller took the first nuclear task force in history into combat off the coast of Vietnam, and later became Chief of Naval Information CHINFO (during my Vietnam stint), and Commander, Test Center, Naval Air Station Patuxent River and China Lake. Time Magazine said of Miller during the Viet Nam conflict that he was indeed, "A Navy man's man," which is the ultimate honor for a sailor. He is survived by Lucille Dean Miller, one brother four sisters, two sons, and two grandchildren. End of the obit . . .

He was one hell of a man and, as I used to say, "MY father's a pistol and I'm a son of a gun." He was very quiet and unassuming but under that tough exterior lay the soul of a Yugoslav descendant who believed strongly in the Catholic church, in family values, and in non-material ascendancy to equanimity.

I had to put up with his temperament long before my brother, Rich, who is 12 years my junior. I had to endure the wrath of his totalitarian behavior and social norms until I hit the magic age of 18, and my departure for Auburn University. Not until I joined the Navy flight program in Pensacola, 1964, did I realize that he was truly a Navy man's man after several visits from him as I progressed through flight training; and when he was there to assist Mom with pinning the Wings of Gold on my uniform.

Mom pinning my Wings of Gold March 1966, with Dad approving.

While I served aboard the USS Oriskany in the Tonkin Gulf he came to visit me and to enjoy my squadron mates while we were on liberty in Sasebo, Japan. His motto was, "Sailors were meant to be on ships and ships were meant to be at sea." I did not share this same enthusiasm with him in that I preferred the Geisha houses to flight operations. We differed immensely in that philosophy.

He taught me to love ice skating and I'll never forget his taking me to an indoor rink while I was a sixth grader, in Bethesda, and the all night pain that ensued from sever leg cramps. Thanks Dad! Now, I take my daughter Kimberly on the ice whenever possible and she loves it albeit no leg cramps.

He drove me to my first dance at Our Lady of Lourdes School, Bethesda, and even offered to take the gal I wound up with at the end of the evening back to her house. As I remember, she wasn't very good looking, so I had nothing to brag about with my mother when we arrived home later that evening. So much for puppy love, seventh grade style.

When my Aunt Luree wrote her history about the Miller clan I discovered where his father, Grandfather Tirsc, was a real tyrant. So, it was easy for me to understand why Dad treated me the way he did on numerous occasions. He was a product of his environment but one generation for the better. In turn, I have learned to be two generations for the better towards my daughter and not to fall back on DNA excuses for my intolerant behavior.

The old man loved life. He loved smoked oysters, steamed clams, autumn leaves, old cars, swing bands, tradition, segregation, the Navy and definitely not the Army, combat, the sea, fresh vine-ripened tomatoes, Perry Como, boxing, anything to do with the Tokyo Raiders, chopping wood, and last but not least Lucybelle, my Mom.

They celebrated their fiftieth anniversary several years ago and we presented them with a restored, hand-tinted photo of them while they were on their honeymoon at Tally Glen's Dude Ranch, near San Bernardino, California, during the 1930's. They were a sight to see in their chaps, boots and tall white hats standing next to the corral.

Now, Mom was left standing alone in her own corral without her sidekick and roping pal Hank. They shared each other's love and companionship for over 50 years and now, her man is buried in Arlington along with years of cherished memories, of countless relocations to unknown military bases and substandard housing, of numerous friends mad along the way, of two sons who have managed to stay out of jail thus far, of two beautiful grandchildren, of the deaths of countless comrades in arms and family relatives, of trips to Annapolis for the colorful Fall pageantry of Homecoming, of official soirees with kings and queens while stationed in the Philippines, of fresh field peas, corn bread, fried chicken, buttermilk, butter beans, cheese grits and Mrs. Byrd's lemon cake consumed during their summer visits with Granny and Daddy Dean down in Opp, Alabama – Mom's parents, birthplace, and my home of record.

Dad's only surviving brother, Uncle Bob, flew down from Fairbanks and accompanied his sister Aunt Beanie, along with Aunt Luree and her son Scott for the services. Numerous friends including their sons and daughters from around the world and from decades of friendship were present. Ironically, Dad is buried just three rows down the hill from the father of one of my high school sweethearts in Washington. She was there during the services to pay homage to both men.

My little brother Rich and I held Mom's arm during the two days and three funeral services. She is strong for such a little woman but she finally lost it when the American flag was presented after the lone bugler sounded Taps that echoed through the peaceful hills of the countryside.

As the symbol of another lost comrade, one more silver goblet is now turned upside down in the display case representing the heroic flyers who comprised the famous raid over Tokyo fifty years ago.

We miss you Dad. We miss your laugh, your silly jokes, your fresh garden vegetables, your tales of the South Pacific, your annual cry, Beat Army", and your adoration of Mom.

Hank and Lucy on their honeymoon, Tally's Glenn Ranch, California, Circa 1939

USN SPAD DRIVER PATCH - ATTACK SQUADRON 152

USN Air Medals & Vietnam Campaign Ribbons

Table of Contents

ONE   **Pg 17**

TWO   **Pg 118**

THREE   **Pg 236**

ONE

Vacation Bible School Dropouts ©

Panky, Rego, and Butch, Opp, AL

The Author with his first dog Jerry, Norfolk, VA

"Panky, why don't you write a book someday?"

"Hey, Miller, old boy. Tell us another one of your yarns 'bout the days when you lived in the Philippines, back durin' the '50's."

"Lordy pray tell, young man, you sho' can tell a tale. Why doesn't you put some of those crazy ideas in yo' head down on paper? Folks 'round here jus' might like to read 'bout you while you was growin' up durin' the summers down here, in Opp."

"Hank we've always thought you were crazy and now, with sixty five years of proof, we are totally convinced. How anyone has been able to get away with the things you have, and lived to tell about it is, in itself, nothing short of a miracle. Please share your insanity with others vis a vis the written word."

"Panky, do you suppose it's the Dean genes or simply the fact that being raised in that Navy family, traveling around the globe and never really settling down, always looking for a party, that has provided you with countless excuses for more bullshit to expound? I'd love to know the truth, if that were even remotely possible."

I was a horrible student in the developmental quadrant - probably read a total of five books during eight years of elementary academy. Then, college preparatory school at St Johns College demanded I become prolific in the procurement and the reading of <u>Classic Comics</u> which depicted, in summary and picture form, the entire length of the boring books assigned to us as homework. Suddenly, college arrived all too quickly and I was one lost plebeian in the numerous stacks filling the halls of the Auburn University Library, Alabama.

One summer, while working in Coronado, a predominately Navy town in southern California, I developed the urge to read, read, read. Suppose the primary reason for this newfound madness was that my compatriots, mostly Navy Juniors like me, were constantly dragging me into Perkins Book Worm, the local source for everything from Aristotle to Zorach, including Voltaire, Kafka, Clemens, Michener, Faulkner, Hugo and other authors' works that became my preoccupation while I endeavored to catch up on decades of lost time. Hence, I began a trend towards self-imposed literacy that would commence around the evening campfires on Coronado's North Beach while reading books recommended by my more enlightened peers. And, a catharsis ensued which resulted in this uncanny desire to write. Trouble is that it took me over thirty years to learn how to put pen to parchment.

My cousin, Rego, said that I should seriously consider writing a book that depicts the old country churches still standing in the rural deep South, juxtaposed with the last remaining honky-tonks close by. He seriously believes that both are entering a final chapter and that it would make for a good read and photojournalistic portrayal of our region. Saturday nights when Patsy Cline, Hank Williams, Webb Pierce, and many others would sing up a storm to be followed by quiet Sundays as folks spent their day around church services and family members asking the Almighty for forgiveness. That will be my next collaborative effort.

I acknowledge, first and foremost, my maternal grandparents, Birdie and Daddy Dean, whom I love and, in return, they taught me how to love the South. Then, I want to say how proud I am to have enjoyed five years of Baptist bliss at Auburn University where certain instructors hammered home the meaning of spirit, of being southern, of being creative, and technically correct when putting pen to paper. Next, a "Wheaties, Wheaties, Wheaties" hello and thanks to my former Navy wingmen in Attack Squadron 152 aboard USS Oriskany during the Viet Nam conflict. I consider you and your families as brothers and sisters, and we need another reunion soon, and not every decade, for heaven sakes.

Last but not least, thanks to my family who is chockablock with English majors, English journalists, English minors, English honor students, and authors. The die is cast. The legacy continues. Hell, I have nowhere to go but to my Macintosh computer for solitude. This newfangled contraption has everything-MacWrite, Word finder, Spell Checker, Correct Grammar, even a talking icon when I enter a misspelled word. Still, the creative portion is left entirely up to me. So, if it's crazy stuff you're looking for…

I acknowledge sixty five years of what some courts of law in this fine land of ours would describe as temporary insanity - not unlike the infamous defense used during Dan White's trial in San Francisco, during the late '70's, - after he assassinated the city mayor and a supervisor (albeit no assassinations on this side of the family).

Dan White's counsel pleaded the "Twinkie Defense" by scientifically deducing that the sugar contained in these delicious morsels caused a chemical imbalance and was largely the cause of White's temporary insanity, thereby leading him to shoot the mayor and supervisor while he was experiencing what we call a "sugar jag."

For various preposterous and unfounded reasons entirely devoid of Aristotelian logic, this writer has pleaded what is a first in the annals of jurisprudence. On the advice of those who are guarding my completely padded and highly secure future residence up at the California Veterans Home in Yountville, I have been strongly advised to cut through the deep voodoo and plead the "Boiled Peanut Dee-fense."

Can't you hear the bailiff now?

"Order in the court! Order in the court! You, in the rear of the room, quit spittin' those shells on the floor! Everyone please stand!"

"Your honor, may it please the court to know that we rest our entire case for the defendant, one Henry Louis Miller, Jr., alias Panky, on the fact that, as a young and innocent child, he consumed countless five cent bags of those boiled peanuts sold by a crazy man named Fireball, down in Opp, Alabama. The defendant's brain has been immersed in tons of that salty peanut brine for more almost seven decades, and this is why he fell off the deep end of surrealism and wrote a so-called anthology, titled <u>Vacation Bible School Dropouts</u>."

"Amen, brothers and sisters, have a good read!"

Invitation !

If you are a dreamer, come in.

If you are a dreamer, a wisher, a liar,

A hope-er, a prayer, a magic bean buyer . .

If you're a pretender, come sit by the fire,

For we have some flax-golden tales to spin.

Come in!

Come in!

                              Sausalito, California

Daddy Dean's Drugstore, Opp, AL

The Sweet Shoppe

    I am a southerner. I am from the Deep South and I can feel it right down to the kudzu between my toes. I can feel it in the pit of my stomach as the sour buttermilk oozes down my esophagus and curdles the cornbread awaiting its arrival. Outside, lightening bugs dot the night and become my beacons that signify the arrival of summer.

    I am a southerner and my genes are saturated with the essence of those who inherit the soil and the sky and the swamps and bayous that comprise our geography and, of course, our soul. The red clay dirt permeates my skin and the sandy loam washes up from the Gulf to cover my paths. Southern oaks with the green moss clinging ever so gingerly between the scrawny branches fill my view around the lake. I know when the Magnolia are supposed to come into bloom save the harsh Winter that delays the process of Spring. The Dogwood sprinkles the rolling landscape bringing life to the otherwise homogeneously green pines. I am a southerner because I know these things and I anticipate the changes of the seasons where history records yet another passage, harvest, and the foliage expunging chlorophyll thus providing magnificent collages of leaves falling on the black asphalt byways and rutted dirt roads leading to wooden one-lane bridges, and to our farms. I am your county. I am your creeks and woods. I am your crossroads out in the middle of nowhere. I am your legacy to the town just over the ridge and down the country road past the turnoffs leading to somewhere. See those worn ruts down the sides of the mound left standing on that dirt road. The tires on my car fit perfectly as I careen towards somewhere but it seems like nowhere.

My ancestry can be traced back to President William Henry Harrison, Judge Barganier, who is Granny's adopted father, and the Dean family. Ancestral demons and demagogues and pimps and whores who roamed these places long before we descended from the north possess me. I can feel the spirit that inhabits all men of the south and invades their souls and spirits. This has been true for generations and the records are testimony of the accuracy of my hypothesis. Andrew Jackson, Thomas Jefferson, Harriet Beecher Stowe, Booker T. Washington, Robert E. Lee, Thomas Wolf, Jimmy Carter, W.T. Cash, Morris Dees, William Faulkner, Big Jim Folsom, Tennessee Williams, Flannery O'Conner, Robert Penn Warren and the list goes on and on to the point where redundancy is ostentatious and absurd. We write of desperation, corruption, anguish, prostration and abandonment. Southerners accept these characteristics and feelings as a way of life. We are able to mask the pain and exude a smile albeit a small one perhaps out of the corner of our mouth with a lip curled up indicating some sort of rancor.

I am of the same ilk and mettle of which nations are conceived. The Scottish, Irish, French and other western European civilizations dumped their bastards on our shores to purge their societies of purportedly useless illiterate peasants unworthy of assimilation into the cultured masses of Paris, Vienna, London, Stockholm and other evolving cities lying to our east. So be it. Folks back in the 1860's proposed two nations, one above and the other below the Mason-Dixon Line. Some southerners will never forget that war and the consequences resulting from abolition. Others, well it really doesn't matter because we are all slaves to this region, indentured forevermore to the unexplainable cosmos that captures and holds us to her bosom.

We are a visual people. Water towers depict where we are. I see the small dot on the horizon that signals my arrival in Opp. The bulbous gray monolith rises above the trees and low buildings and becomes the monument for high schools boys to utilize for significant rites of passage, such as hand-painted epithets. "Beat Kensington Eagles!" "Go Bobcats!" Beat those little peckerheads on the football gridiron, or my name painted here will be mud for another 365 days. Annual ritualistic misdemeanors, never enforced, surround the permanently embossed name of the town, followed by a comma, then the abbreviation of the state, like we don't really know where we are here in this county. a boldly painted OPP, AL alerts me to my pending arrival at Granny's. The juices in my body begin to flow more rapidly and my eyes widen with anxiety and anticipation of greeting family one more time. I am a southerner who cherishes friendships more than buckets of gold and ostentatious wealth. Kinfolk, fresh greens, scratch biscuits, raw buttermilk, and Mrs. Bird's lemon cake measure my pleasure. All right, I will concede and imbibe a wee bit of the 'Bama poteen, known as moonshine, when nights strikes and we meet at the Parkmore Drive In. I am a southerner.

*****

"This is one, monumentally sad, disastrous day in my life, Rue, and I'm not sure I can handle what I'm about to see. Years ago, you called and told me about it and how you felt as you drove up to the house. Now, twenty years later, I'm back to witness the biggest loss of my entire life, the reason I've been in counseling for the past five years. Ever had the wind knocked out of you? Ever had your nuts crushed on the cross bar of your bicycle? Or had some goober just plain kick the shit out of you until you wish you were dead? It's the same feeling knowing your true and blue sweetheart has been kissing some other guy, and you thought you were the first."

"Panky, you've got to get over it, boy. You'll feel the same way as I did and perhaps ever worse now that they are all gone but we have to get through this together. Butch is supposed to meet us at Delia's so we can walk the property and talk our way along and hug each other, but you kiss me and I'll knock your dick in the dirt, y'hear?"

"Rego, wait a minute. Who lived in this first house on the street? Remember we'd always stop and visit her first thing whenever I came down during the summers. She was a seamstress, the sweetest little old lady in the world. She made all of the girl's dresses for the weddings and proms. As a matter of fact I think she made Virginia's dress for your senior prom. You know what really makes me sad, fucks me up royally? The fact these folks are all long gone, dead, in the ground. Most of them I only knew slightly and I never knew when they died and were buried. The only ones I knew were Dr. Waters, Mrs. Waters, and Harriet Cummins. Even old man Cole died when I was in Vietnam. I helped to build his house that Christmas I worked in the freezing cold with those two old black men to unload all the bricks. So, here we are once again for more loss and pain. All I want to do is go on down to the Farmer's Restaurant, eat oysters, and drink some beer."

"Hush up. Here comes Butch up behind us. He knew all these folks his entire life so we have to be sensitive. This is his street just as much as it is ours."

"Hey Rego and Panky, sorry I'm late but then again I suppose you two are in no rush to get down to your granny's property. I'll pull over here and we'll walk down together."

East Ida Avenue is wide, with a landscaped boulevard strip down the center. Huge oak trees line the sidewalks on each side of the street. And, the colorful azaleas dot the center along with rhododendrons up and down the rows. Loamy sand spilling from the strip is scattered on top of the black asphalt.

There are about eight houses altogether on the entire street. Some have garage apartments in back but they aren't visible from the sidewalk. Did I say there were eight houses? Well, there are seven now. Granny and Daddy Dean's house burned to the ground sometime in the late 1980's and this is my first visit to Opp since then. Virginia Benton owned the house. She bought it from Mom and Aunt Evelyn when

Granny died. Virginia turned it into a duplex rental. That really pissed me off. She had no right to tamper with this house. Rumor has it that it was struck by Jewish lightening one night and that was the end of that. I have tried several times to purchase the land from Virginia but she holds steadfast to an unreasonable figure for one, crummy empty lot that no one wants but me. Now, we have only memories of our childhood but there is still the playhouse in the back that was left unharmed. It is totally overgrown by vines and shrubs but you can barely see the roofline. Jesus, did we have a ball sleeping out there when we were growing up.

"Hey, Rego and Butch, let's go to the back and see if the bamboo grove is still standing. That's the same spot where Mom took our picture back in the fifties, the one I had blown up into posters for you two when I came back to visit in 1973."

"What do you know? Shit, here it is! Right next to the alley just as it was forty years ago. Ever heard of d'ej a vu? I'm having it now. Feels just like Gladdy Mae is going to run out the back door to tell us dinner's on the table. No hens cackling now. Miriam Donaldson's chicken coup is long gone. It was just behind the bamboo and you could really smell the chicken poop when it was hotter than hell outside."

"I've got my camera and tripod. Let me set it up and we'll reinvent that same shot of forty years ago. Even got black and white film for the occasion. Take of your shirts, stand right here, look at me and flex those fat arms. The timer will allow me to run over and stand next to you Rue. Here goes."

At Dean's Pharmacy

Lord God Almighty. So many changes but just look at this store, which appears to have been frozen in time. The marble counter is a wee bit duller, and there appears to be several more cracked tiles in the floor, but that's about the extent of any deterioration or change. Still plenty of faded Coke signs behind the marble counter. And several Atlantic malt machines line the back mirror ready for the onslaught of kids yelling for "More malt, more malt pleeeze!" The ceiling fans swirl and swirl round over our heads just out of reach so we can't threaten our little brothers by holding them up high and pretend that we're going to stick their heads in the path of the rotary blades.

Nonetheless, the luster has faded on those blades. And, the white floor tiles have yellowed with the hairline cracks winding their way through the isles. Big deal when you consider how many revolutions the fan blades have made over the past seventy-plus years of continuous operation, and everything else has a patina that only time and use provides. I can't imagine it any other way to tell you the truth.

Aside from the drugstore, a lot of businesses here on Main Street have a permanent "Gone fishin'" sign in the front window, for one reason or another. This place is beginning to resemble a ghost town. Lord God almighty! Can't the city fathers see that their single industry mentality is killing Opp? Most of the folks around here either work at the mill, or have businesses that supported its workers. And, every time some new entrepreneur tries to pursue interests in coming to Opp, our politicians make damn sure they don't get the building and other necessary permits. All this to protect the self-serving interests of a few fat cats at Opp-Micolas Mills.

When was Opp in its heyday? I have a theory and it goes like this. I'm sure residents agree it was during the '50s. Every building in town was occupied and open for business. Opp had three drugstores, several clothing stores, hardware stores, mercantile economy stores, restaurants, jewelry stores, a thriving bus station, a hotel, a motel, two cotton gins, a theater, and a drive-in movie.

Then, a restaurant here in town suddenly closed down in the early sixties. Thus, began the decline and fall of Opp, as we know it today. Some of you may think I'm crazy, and you may be right, but my hypothesis is this:

"The rise and fall of Opp's prosperity is directly proportional to the rise and fall of The Sweet Shoppe."

Yes, brethren, I say before you that when Jim Sawyer went and killed hisself the ultimate demise of Opp's prosperity began, like that of Babylon and Rome, to crumble. And, no, I don't mean Rome, Georgia, which, by the way, had the best little whore house in the South. I surmise the correlation between the heyday of Opp, and the success of the Sweet Shoppe is when they boarded up that great little restaurant they began to board up this whole damn town! Now, if someone else has a better theory, let's hear it. Otherwise, I rest my case.

Berdie Bargarnier and Abner Dean while courting, circa 1900

About the Characters

<u>Birdie Barganier Dean, circa 1900</u>

Know what Hank Williams, Aunt Ceil, and Birdie Barganier Dean have in common?

First, I must assume that those who were either raised in the South, or simply love country and western music, are familiar with the greatest singer of all times. Hank Williams - songwriter, singer, vagabond, father, carouser, drunkard, strictly Alabama southern - has his guitar, his fancy boots with the rhinestones and various reptile skin appliqués, his oversized engraved silver belt buckles, his Stetson hats and his western-style cowboy suits, with the pointed pockets and pearly buttons, enshrined in the Alabama State Capitol Museum, for those of us who worship his music to view, forevermore.

Second, some folks are most likely asking, "Who in the hell cares what these people have in common? Never heard of the other two characters in my life." For further explanation, please continue.

Referring to a Rand McNally Road Atlas of the United States, locating the page outlining the great State of Alabama, the reader's eyes are drawn to the center of the state and the page where the capitol, Montgomery, is located. As the reader's eyes drift downwards to the southwest quadrant they will barely decipher one of the towns that does not warrant bold typeface or enlarged lettering because the population is less than fifteen to twenty thousand inhabitants. So, it becomes increasingly more difficult to locate because of the small size. Georgiana, is what one calls the roots, or the birthplace, or the childhood home, of the folks I just mentioned. When the state bureaucrats approved the funds to construct the great sprawling concrete horizontal tarmac, otherwise known as Interstate Highway 65, extending from Birmingham, down to Mobil, back in the late sixties, the engineers and planners bypassed many old hamlets, including Georgiana, so the once highly-traveled road for those driving from Montgomery, down to the Gulf coast, is now relegated to the locals, to the farmers, to the traveling salesmen who still rely on Georgiana, and other surrounding areas nearby for their livelihoods.

Used to be where travelers would see black men in the fields picking cotton, and the trucks parked outside the local cafe where the shop owners would congregate for coffee and the daily gossip. Never will forget driving through Georgiana, Monroeville, and other towns in the dead of winter, and seeing the older blacks huddled around the fifty-five gallon drums, with hot flames pouring forth, being used as makeshift fireplaces, to help take the freezing chill from the early morning air. Ain't supposed to get that in South Alabama, but it sho' nuff does.

In Georgiana, most of the townsfolk barely remember Hank Williams because he left as soon as he was old enough to sing and to earn his way while working in honkytonks around the state. However, the same is not true of one person who remained in Georgiana, for the greater part of her life. Aunt Ceil was one of the town matriarchs. And, an aunt she was not - only a title assumed by my ancestors. She is remembered as being one hundred and ten percent southern, and as being one hundred and ten percent dictatorial, territorial, and strict as hell.

Mr. and Mrs. Barganier lived and worked in Greenville, just a short piece down the road from Georgiana. Mrs. Barganier was a consummate teacher of music and she played the piano until the day she died. Mr. Barganier was a judge and a good one at that. Tough, but fair, was his reputation. Unfortunately, Mr. and Mrs. Barganier both died at early ages, leaving their daughter an orphan. But, for good fortune, a dear friend of the Barganiers, who lived down in Georgiana, assumed the responsibility of caring for and raising this young orphan.

Aunt Ceil was suddenly entrusted with the care of this baby in addition to three other small girls who resided in her household. This infant is known as Birdie, and Birdie Barganier was born in Greenville, on July Fifth, 1890. She passed away in Amory, Mississippi, in 1977 was laid to rest next to her husband of fifty-five years, Abner T. Dean, here in Opp. Between those two dates were countless episodes and memories that comprised her make-up, her personality, and her spirit that have lasting impressions on everyone she met because this is one person who, like others of her generation, had true grit. Her chemistry includes the stubbornness of the Scottish, the physical stamina of the Teutonics, the arrogance of the French, and the charisma of the Italians. This lady, Birdie Barganier, is my maternal grandmother.

For those of you who remember Birdie Bargainer Dean, otherwise known as Granny, she was a small person, in physical stature, about five feet plus an inch - basically a spit in the wind - who moved like a tornado through the streets and the dirt roads of Covington county. She followed the Baptist persuasion and she insisted that members of her family attend church services every Sunday morning. The only person who was exempt from this mandate was her husband. Lordy knows how he got away with missing services because the rest of the Dean clan, including "this Catholic", had to attend services even if it required driving twenty miles over to Andalusia in order to join the circuit priest for nine o'clock Mass.

Granny had absolutely no use for wimps. Right or wrong, she wanted you to stand tall and be heard, even if it resulted in her disagreeing with your convictions. Course, Granny'd never, and I mean never, tell you if she was dead wrong on a subject. Simply a thrust of her head in a sudden, upward manner, with a roll of her eyes, and a quick walk from the room would be the barometer of victory or defeat. And, that'd be the last you'd hear of it!

Granny's philosophy was, "Keep moving, do something worthwhile for the po' folks, and don't forget to say your prayers at bedtime." Sounds a lot like the philosophy stated in that best selling book, All You Really Need To Know You Learned in Kindergarten* Granny had simple tastes but she was very progressive for a woman raised in the deep South during her generation. I remember her introducing me to members of the only three Jewish families, in Opp. These families had suffered under the discrimination of so-called Christians, who professed brotherly love, and under the scrutiny of the Ku Klux Klan, whose members hated not only Jews but, in addition, Catholics and blacks. Granny recognized these three families, the Finkelsteins, the Muellers, and the Bukantzs, as God-fearing people who were stuck in a time and place trying to do their best just to survive in a small town. She taught me that these families and poor folks, like their more fortunate counterparts, have dignity too. Time and time again, Granny would reiterate that everyone, regardless of their color, religion, or income level, has pride, so they should be treated accordingly.

When I was home from Auburn one summer's day, she and I loaded up the old Chevy with some discarded clothes and linens, and we headed out towards the area of town near the hospital. I asked where we were going, and Granny said that we were donating these clothes and sundry items to a poor white family who lived up the road, apiece. Granny made me stay in the car as she walked up to the front door of this tar paper shack that was located across the highway from the Mizell Memorial County Hospital, on the back road to Red Hill. When the front door was opened and a figure appeared Granny merely handed the bags of clothes to the occupant, and she was back in the front seat within two or three minutes. She indicated where this was a family on the down and out, had a streak of bad luck, and needed some help for their children, but the family was too proud to ask for any assistance. Granny found out about the needs of these destitutes from Brother Hall, up at the First Baptist Church, and she set out on her task of collecting clothes and food, get the job done, and move on to the next daily activity without much dialogue.

Granny didn't stand there and dwell on the hardships of life or philosophize on the benevolence of good Christians but, instead, went on with her business fully cognizant that she wouldn't receive notoriety or compensation for her actions. Some force larger and more global would guide Granny throughout her life, and those of us who witnessed and experienced her actions, such as the donation to this poor family, never forgot them, and especially their significance. To this day, I am for the underdog, for the oppressed, for the poor, for the troubled masses, for Auburn whenever they play 'Bama."

For as long as I can remember Granny made me feel like someone special. My self-esteem soared whenever I reentered her sphere, and I'll never forget her visits with us in Bethesda, Corpus Christi, Washington, or Coronado, when, prior to her departure from Opp, Granny would load up a spare suitcase chock full with sugar cane just for me to peel, eat and suck the sugar straight from the stalk.

Soon after she arrived at our house I would ask, "Granny, let me help you with your bags. How long can you stay? Got enough luggage here for a month of Sundays. So good to see you, Granny, and I hope you never leave."

"Panky, you old, sweet thang, one of these bags is full of sugarcane, just for you. Now, don't go and eat it all the first day, or you'll be sick as a dawg!"

As far back as I can remember Granny employed black maids. I prefer to call these maids nannies because not only did they cook and clean but, in addition, they watched over Rego and me as if we were their very own chillun'. The first nanny, who I can remember, was Ro Ceil who was very large, very, very black, sweet as could be, and dressed identical to the image portrayed on the Aunt Jemima Pancake box. I can still visualize her sitting on our back porch, under the shade of that white trellis, shelling field peas and cleaning sweet corn that she was preparing for the noontime dinner. Ro Ceil was full of spirit, proud and hard working.

When we drove Ro Ceil home in the mid afternoon she would get out of the car (always from the back seat) on the Montgomery highway, and walk over to her tarpaper shack situated near the city dump. The actual dump and saw mill adjacent to it were rather neutral in my mind's eye at that early age, but today the vision rings with depression, poverty, survival, disease, and every other negative aspect of segregation and deprivation so common in the rural South. Eventually, Ro Ceil and her family moved to the big city of Detroit, so her husband could secure better wages and, hopefully, work his way out of this downward spiral.

Following Ro Ceil was another maid named Gladdy Mae, who was Rego's and my perennial favorite. She reminded me of the slave's daughter Butterfly in <u>Gone with the Wind</u>. Gladdy Mae was small in physique but possessed a very large bosom for her petite size. And, her voice was rather high and squeaky, like that of a field mouse. But, let me tell you, she had Rego's and my numbers, and she knew that, if we misbehaved, one word to our mothers was all it would take for the switching hour to commence. That was the situation where Rego and I would be told, in no uncertain terms, to go into Granny's backyard, pick the greenest and most moist and flexible willow branches, return to the house, drop our freshly-starched, stiff-as-a-board Levi's, and then our BVD's, and bend over for several extremely painful blows to our hind legs and our butts! One of the most sever penalties we received for misbehavior, which included our being banned from the Royal Theater Saturday matinee double feature starring Whip Wilson, Lash Larue, Gene Autry, or Roy Rogers, "The King of the Cowboys," was because one day Gladdy Mae ratted to my mom and Aunt Evelyn. Reason being that Rego and I had referred to her physical endowments simply as her having big "titties." I cannot begin to tell you that hardened criminals down on the Atwood Prison Farm had an easier go of it than the two of us for this most heinous of crimes. Our legs and fannies were swollen for days, and our pride was hurt for weeks. When you missed a double feature at the Royal Theater matinee the news spread like wildfire among our peers. "Wonder what happened to Rego and Panky? Must have said something about Gladdy Mae's big titties again, or maybe they got caught chewing tobacco!" As the line in a popular southern movie released many years later would state, "Rego and Panky were simply having a bad day."

Everyone has rituals. Everyone has some sort of tradition that affects the moment; that affects the spirit, at the time, whether it is something as sophisticated as religion or voodoo or something as simple as clothing it is a colloquial statement of one's individualism and freedom. Rego and I had a colloquial statement and it went like this.

We would buy the absolute tightest fitting Levis that could be buttoned around our waists. And, they had to be at least four inches too long in order to have the perfect two-inch double cuff. We're not through yet. In addition, our nanny was told, in no uncertain terms, that these Levis had to be starched so stiffly that they could literally stand up in the backyard by the tree that supported one end of the clothesline without any personal interference or assistance. When the Levis had dried Rego and I would slip into these ersatz cardboard stick figure cutouts, and a catharsis would ensue. Suddenly, we were as tough as those matinee idols we worshiped everyday, at two o'clock, right after we strapped on our two six shooters slung low around our skinny waists, with the holsters tied to our skinny legs. Watch out Roy, Dale, Trigger and Buttermilk, here we come!

Granny and Gladdy Mae never truly blended as employer-employee. I suppose that, both, possessed strong personalities that would not permit the other to get the upper hand, or to endure any criticism. Nonetheless, Gladdy Mae was a great friend, a great cook and we hope that she will have the opportunity to read this story one day.

<u>Abner T. Dean, circa 1940</u>

Where was A. T. Dean, Granny's spouse, when all of this chaos was occurring? Well, for the greater part of our childhood, he was busy running the store - Dean's Pharmacy. At one point in his career he owned every drugstore in Opp, which numbered six. During his career he eventually sold all but one and managed this store, until the late '40's, at which time he sold Dean's Pharmacy to old Charlie Williams, from down in Kinston, who ran the business for many years. Abner T. Dean became known as Daddy Dean to us.

Strange thing about southern folk and their colloquialisms and nicknames. Every boy with the Christian name of William, Stephen, Robert or Beauregard enlists an abbreviated title, such as Billy Bob, Bobbie, Bo, Stevie, Bubba, or another ridiculous macho concoction.

God only knows where his nickname originated but that was what we called Daddy Dean until he passed away in 1967 while I was in Vietnam and we still refer to him that way whenever we reminisce about those days. The only explanation for Daddy is none other than a simple abbreviation of granddaddy. Any other hypothesis would seem unlikely and unnecessary because, regardless of the reason, the South will always rely on these symbols of family traditions. Amazingly enough, one would think that, with the tremendous influx of families from northern and western states, these age-old habits would diminish. To the contrary, they seem to be self-perpetuating and a symbol of the southern heritage that will endure longer than the Appian Way leading out of ancient Rome, or the road to Sprayberry's Barbecue, up in Newnan, Georgia, just outside Atlanta.

My parents never told me about my family's roots. I suppose they didn't think I had the need know or was interested and that was a big mistake. I had to ask questions and listen to stories and facts spontaneously while attempting to accurately record items for future dissemination. One afternoon I was sitting on the bed and talking with Daddy Dean about my previous quarter at Auburn, and he began to tell me about his educational background and life prior to marrying Granny and moving down near Opp. I learned more about him during the next hour than I had during the previous twenty years. To hear Daddy Dean tell about his life was special, and I cannot even begin to convey the spirit with which he spoke in this writing. While all of the situations were either occurring or in the developmental stages, good old Daddy Dean was steadfast, hard working, and always up at his drugstore. He was the silent one, the rather intense one, who remained quiet and pensive. Daddy Dean wasn't a controversial person in that he preferred to play dominoes and to fish rather than discuss his political views. His origins were extremely southern, rural, and steeped in poverty. Born on a farm near Elba, AL he made his way over to the booming logging community, of Poley, which was situated on the outskirts of what was now his home of Opp. At that time, Poley, was the main community in this area and Opp, was in the rudimentary stages of evolving into a town. Daddy Dean found his way to the Poley store, which was referred to as the commissary, where he was given a job by the owner, a gent named Miller (no relation) who, also, owned the lumber mill. Miller soon realized that this hard working young man with great potential was virtually illiterate and, in order to retain him as an employee, he offered to provide Daddy Dean with free schooling, up in Montgomery, at the local business college. Daddy Dean accepted his kind offer and reported to school where he learned "The Three R's," and the basics of running a business.

Upon Daddy Dean's return to Poley, he was soon made the manager of the commissary and of the associated businesses at the Poley mill. Eventually, Daddy Dean had an opportunity to become an entrepreneur, thus began the start of his successful business career. He purchased the only pharmacy in the growing town of Opp, and Daddy Dean began to bring that fledgling business around to a profitable one. He hired registered pharmacists to handle the prescriptions while he took care of running the store. Soon thereafter, he purchased another pharmacy, which eventually led to his owning six pharmacies in this town of approximately six thousand denizens. Along with the acquisition of the pharmacies came the ownership of several buildings in town, which Daddy Dean leased, to other businessmen. And, then, one by one, he began to sell the pharmacies until there remained only one, Dean's Pharmacy, which still operates under the family name. As I said earlier, Charlie Williams purchased Dean's Pharmacy in the early 1950's and his widow, Charlotte, sold it to the present owner, Lloyd Sellers, in the early '70's. He recently sold it and retired n 2005.

Dean's Pharmacy is a landmark, in Opp. The store has an honest-to-god soda fountain, serving the only real Coca Colas formulated from carbonated water and patented syrup. The octagonal marble floors are original as are the porcelain-topped tables and drugstore chairs where we gather for morning and afternoon coffee breaks, and gossip. I must add that missing today are the china plates that held Delia Barganier's truly delicious homemade chicken salad sandwiches, with the white bread crust removed, wrapped in Cut-Rite wax paper - ten cents each - and the best you ever tasted!

I was told about Daddy Dean's death in a letter from my cousin, Stevie Rue, while serving aboard the USS Oriskany as a Naval Aviator, and it was worse than being shot down and taken prisoner in Hanoi. I felt like I had lost a portion of my spirit, my soul, my whole being. And I cried. I cried for hours as I slammed down a bottle of Grand Mariner, or Benedictine, or Black Jack. Can't remember the liquor label but I can remember that traumatic occasion vividly thirty years later.

I have an original photograph of Birdie and Abner while they were still courting, and my guess is that the photo was taken in 1911, one year prior to their marriage. This couple was glamorous in their Victorian attire - she in her long, white summer dress and he, wearing a suit, starched white shirt and his straw hat, typically referred to as a Boater. As a matter of fact, this may very well be the only photograph in existence portraying them in a candid pose. I personally don't believe either of them realized, at this time in their lives during the Great Depression that Abner would eventually become a very successful entrepreneur, and that Birdie would assist in the creation of two fine southern ladies, Evelyn and Lucille.

Now, there is a real duo who roamed all points of Covington county namely Opp, Kinston, Andalusia, Florala, Lake Gant, Red Level, and the dirt, two-lane ultra-narrow country back roads that are simply just too numerous to mention. Evelyn and Lucy's finest, or so we thought. Anyway, we are the oldest which seems to be very significant when people ask about members of one's family. The middle aged kids get lost in the shuffle and the youngest always seem to get along in spite of being dealt a short hand on many occasions.

The two primary characters are blonde with hazel eyes. Panky was the skinniest kid who ever walked the earth. Rego was more athletically built taking after his father. Both were full of mischief and grew up only a few inches of escaping full fledged child abuse inflicted by their parents who would have been found innocent in any court of law once the judge witnessed the boys' behavior.

Lucille and Evelyn, circa 1974

Birdie Barganier Dean bore two daughters, Evelyn and Lucille. Aunt Evelyn and my mother, Lucy, were born and raised in Opp, where they resided at 309 East Ida Avenue, the same address where those of us who would follow resided, if only for a summer's vacation or a holiday. Evelyn and Lucille Dean were two lucky dames because not only were they very attractive but they were, also, blessed with aptitudes that would eventually provide them with a first rate education after high school. Both my aunt and my mother had propensities for music and that was a preferred career or hobby for southern belles so they, both, applied and were accepted by Huntington College, up in Montgomery, to begin their studies of voice and piano. Upon graduation, the bright lights and the big city beckoned, so the Conservatory of Music's enrollment was increased by the quantity of two as these two Laura Lovelies ventured out of Dixie and into the cosmopolitan river town metropolis of Cincinnati. Abner and Birdie would determine many years later this was money well spent because Evelyn sang and taught piano and voice to many students for years; and Lucy has continued with her music for well over half a century.

Rumor has it and this will *NEVER* be corroborated by the Dean girls that one of the eligible bachelors, down in South Alabama, was and aspiring young writer, named Truman Capote. Granny shared a story with me that Truman was paying a call on Lucy. Her refusal to accept his invitation for a date was based on the fact that Truman made a crucial error in that he appeared at the Dean residence one afternoon with liquor on his breath. Yes, brethren, this vile person had the audacity to partake in the drink of the devil, but the most contemptuous action was his appearance at 309 East Ida Avenue, under the influence. Needless to day, this was Truman's first and last attempt to court a Dean, and his reputation was forever cast as that of a real dandy, in lower 'Bama. Should this episode be brought to the attention of my mother she will emphatically deny any knowledge or participation in this verbally documented event that occurred during her adolescent years.

While Evelyn and Lucy attended Huntington College, they befriended Harriet Waites, from Andalusia, who was about to wed a young man from Bryn Mawr, Pennsylvania, by the name of Bill Rue. Evelyn was in the bride's court and this is when she met Bill's brother, John R. Rue IV, who was the best man. Talk about people from opposite ends of the earth. There couldn't be a broader range of socioeconomic disparity than that of rural Opp, versus cosmopolitan Bryn Mawr, where the only poor folks were those who served as domestics to those families like the Rues. Well, the marriage of Evelyn and Johnny was the beginning of a relationship that would last well over fifty years - consummated in Pennsylvania, and nurtured down in Alabama.

After Evelyn and Johnny were married, they resided adjacent to the family estate, in Bryn Mawr, to be joined by other brothers and their families who lived in contiguous houses. Johnny, their brother Howdy, and Bill Rue began their married lives and the conception of many cousins commenced on that estate during the early 1940's. The Rue clan was comprised of Nona Michener Rue and John R. "Pierpop" Rue, who emanated from old Philadelphia aristocracy. Their business was shoe manufacturing and extreme wealth was derived from this family enterprise. The Rue house, which I shall never forget, was a sprawling stone mansion set on several acres of rolling Pennsylvania countryside. The kitchen, alone, was the size of some apartments while the remainder of the house is a blur in my memory.

Aunt Evelyn and Uncle Johnny remained in Bryn Mawr, for about five years while their children grew, and they eventually relocated to Opp, around 1948. Because of Uncle Johnny's association with shoe manufacturing, he decided to open a retail shoe store adjacent to Dean's Pharmacy, in Opp.

Lucille Dean in Pensacola, FL, circa 1936

CDR Henry L. Miller, circa 1940

Simultaneous, with this courtship and marriage between Evelyn Dean and John Rue, was the relationship between Lucille Dean and one Henry L. Miller, a Navy Lieutenant, in Pensacola, Florida. After Lucy graduated from the Cincinnati Conservatory of Music she moved down to Pensacola, to begin her illustrious career as a piano teacher. Many damsels flocked to this small city to take advantage of the proliferation of eligible men of sound breeding and education. Yes, the birthplace of Naval Aviation was the home for all Naval officers who were to earn their Wings of Gold, and this was terribly exciting to those gals who were eager to expand their not-so-worldly charms and horizons. In what other town could a relatively naive damsel meet a graduate of Annapolis, a commissioned officer, an aspiring aviator, and enter that social strata of gala festivities held at Fort Barrancas Officers Club, afternoon teas at the Admirals home, squadron family outings on the whitest beaches in the world, travel to every corner of the globe, and have a relatively secure *albeit not opulent* economic foundation for the rest of their lives? So, Lucy made a wise decision and established her piano studio smack dab right in the heart of Pensacola.

Whether the marriage was consummated in the piano studio, in the Bachelor Officers' Quarters, or in the honeymoon suite, I was born, in

Pensacola, on December 26, 1941. Don't remember the occasion and, as a matter of fact, didn't return to Pensacola, for twenty-two years until I entered Navy School, of Pre-Flight, Class of 29-64. Must be something in the genes that makes people yearn for the attainment of those abilities that break the surly bonds of earth, otherwise known as flight.

<u>Lucy on her honeymoon, 1939</u>

And, so began the lives of Rego and me and the germination of those families of Deans, Rues and Millers that would become the basis for these yarns and factual episodes; and to far corners of the globe - the Philippines, Pennsylvania, Hawaii, California, Mississippi, Yellowstone, Maryland, Bryn Mawr, Bethesda, Opp, Amory, Starkville, Norfolk, Yosemite, Panama City, Manila, Los Altos, Coronado, Auburn, San Francisco, and others.

I have this color-tinted photograph of my aunt and mother supposedly taken when they were about thirteen years old. The image is one of my prized possessions and it is the only one of its kind, in existence. In this image I see my genetic likeness and those of my cousins. More important, I see the eyes that portray innocence and purity, and I feel sad because I, too, was that age and of that serenity many years ago which, in some respects, seems like yesterday. My daughter, Kimberly, is thirty and she is so very different from my mother and aunt because of her urban culture and California ersatz sophistication, but she has that same twinkle in her eye, and is of that same maverick spirit. My regret is that she was unable to experience some of those marvelous aspects of my childhood spent, in Opp, during those years of innocence in the late '40's and '50's. Perhaps she will have the opportunity to visit Opp, some day when she feels it is important to her psychological development. Or, she may simply choose not to identify with the blacktop rural byways of my southern past, and to simply move on down that smooth California concrete urban interstate with her present life.

One of these days I'll travel to Georgiana, and research the Barganier family tree. The only recollection of ancestry from the maternal side of my family is that we are descendents of William Henry Harrison, ninth President of the United States. Other than that legacy I am not familiar with the remaining family descendants, alive or deceased, who comprise the genetics on the maternal Dean side of our family tree.

My Aunt Evelyn passed away in the early '80s and, with her, another member of a generation that will be forever lost within the next twenty years. Loosing my aunt was a severe blow not only to me but, also, to my mother because Aunt Evelyn was the only remaining link to her childhood. The two of them were real pals throughout life and they relied on each other for support whenever the going got rough. Evelyn remained in the South until her death, raising her three children who have, also, decided to remain in Dixie through their careers and marriages; Rego, in Marietta, GA and Stevie and Carol, in Richmond, VA.

<u>John Rue, circa 1975</u>

Evelyn's husband, Uncle Johnny, is, also, deceased. His last years were spent holed up in a nursing home, in Amory, but I recollect only vivid and cheerful images of my favorite uncle - not his demise in those awful convalescent homes where we place our relatives so they can die, in obscurity. We last visited in 1974, while he was in retirement, and enjoying good health. Johnny reminded me so much of Arnold Palmer, the famous golfer, in his mannerisms and his physical appearance. And coincidentally, both he and Palmer hail from Pennsylvania. But, mostly, I remember Uncle Johnny selling shoes to everyone in Covington county.

My stepson recently started part time work at a women's shoe store, in San Francisco, and he had some interesting comments after his first day on the job. His quote, "The women are beautiful and the gals couldn't wait for my assisting them while trying on new pairs of the latest shoe fashions. Wonder if it had anything to do with my soft hands, and roving eyes?" A shoe salesman's job is not unlike that of a woman's physician in that one can, perhaps, gain a different view of the world from the vantage point of being physically situated below the sitting position of the female customers. In other words, opportunities to look up a woman's dress not only become numerous but, in addition, almost a given part of the operation.

To our surprise, Uncle Johnny, our family shoe salesman, knew almost every woman in Opp, and I suspect that he could have divulged many secrets and medical theories pertaining to these damsels' lifestyles had he been the type who would spill Macy's secret plans to Gimbels. He, too, must have possessed the soft touch and the ability to view forbidden sights while maintaining lowered eyelids and neutral facial expressions.

Uncle Johnny was just one of the guys. He simply had to be especially with two sons, like Rego and Stevie. One night Rego, just starting as a high school freshman, was sitting in the kitchen while having some supper with Evelyn and Johnny. Uncle Johnny suddenly asked Rego if he could borrow a couple of dollars because he was short of cash. Rego obliged by indicating that he may have a few dollars, so he proceeded to stand up from the table and remove his wallet from the back pocket of his Levis. As Rego opened the billfold to search for the folded money a condom fell out of the folds, and landed on top of his shoe. Rego's eyes never left those of his fathers, but he knew what had just occurred. As Rego tried to keep from breaking out into a cold sweat, his eyes still glued on those of his dad's, he quickly thought of how to camouflage this embarrassing predicament. Rego quickly handed his father as dollar, or two, and then he proceeded to stiff-leg his way from the kitchen into another neutral room without lifting his foot where the condom was resting off the floor while locking his eyes with those of his dad. This was the only way that Rego could escape this situation and not have the condom fall from the top of his shoe to the floor directly in front of Uncle Johnny.

Back at 309 East Ida Avenue

"That's it, you two, let's get the film up to Virginia's for processing so we can get another poster blown up when I get back to San Francisco. I'll get us each a large black and white to frame because I seriously doubt if we'll get back here to do this again any time real soon, do you think?"

Don't suppose I want to see this place again, ever. The house is gone, my grandparents are gone, the neighbors are gone. Everyone's dead. Everything but the memories are gone. Memories of sneaking out to go down to the Sweet Shoppe. Memories of accidentally swallowing a chunk of chewing tobacco while we worked on the milk truck that one summer. The daily movie matinees and the municipal pool. All the good things we did before we were old enough to get into real trouble at the Park More Drive In with liquor and sleazy broads. Sweet, sweet memories of the families and Granny and Daddy Dean's friends whose names are now a blur.

I remember the hush, the peaceful quiet of Opp now that I stop to think about it. No blaring boom boxes and loud neighbors and obnoxious generation x types with their cellular phones, beepers, and chirpy auto alarms disturbing the natural sounds of the cats and dogs and goats and the hoofs of the horse-drawn buckboards coming down Ida Avenue occasionally. I loved the sounds of the lightening and thunderstorms during the summer. I loved the sound of Miriam Donaldson practicing her trumpet early in the afternoons.

I loved the unabated silence...

<u>**Rego and Panky in Granny's backyard, circa 1945**</u>

<u>Vacation Bible School Dropouts!</u>

"You two, Rego and Panky, have been hangin'. 'round this house for days now, and I'm beginnin' to believe that y'all is bored. Everytime I gets to sit down to shell these field peas you two are naggin' me with a thousand questions 'bout what's for dinner, or anything special for dessert, or how do I tie this bandana 'round my hair. Lordy Almighty, I can find dozens of chores for you to do like sweepin' the sidewalk and the front porch. Swimmin' pool ain't open for the season yet, and you're too young to go get jobs, so I'm recommendin' to yo mothers that you go to Vacation Bible School, up at the First Baptist. 'Sides, it'll do you good to have somethin' to occupy your time with somethin' all boys need more of, and that's old time religion."

This individual doing all the preaching was Ro Ceil who was addressing us in a very stern voice. Ro Ceil was Granny's maid, our nanny. She had been with Granny for quite a while and we have lots of respect for her. I came down from Norfolk, where my dad is stationed in the Navy. My school year ended a week before Rego's so I'm here with my grandparents waiting for the municipal pool to open and looking forward to the afternoon matinees at the Royal Theater and the Dixie Drive In.

"Aw, Ro Ceil, we'd rather play at the clay quarry or go fishing with Daddy Dean, or anything but Vacation Bible School! Please don't say anything about this to our mothers. We promise to stay out of trouble and to clean our plates at dinner if you'll let this notion slip away. Please? Please? Pretty please?"

As we beg for mercy, we realize that our pleas were truly in vain. Sometime later that day my mother approached Rego and me about this very same subject. "Rego, Panky. Evelyn and I agree that you two should attend Vacation Bible School this summer, and don't put up any argument. You're going whether you like it or not. Panky, since you're Catholic, you can say your Catholic prayers and not say the Baptist prayers, if you feel that way. Nonetheless, the school starts at nine o'clock in the morning and goes until noon. We'll get you up in plenty of time to clean up and to have some breakfast."

Mom's word appears to be gospel and our whimpering, sobbing and general complaining was useless. Aunt Evelyn's and Mom's minds are made up and that's that. Next morning we dragged ourselves out of bed, moped around with gloomy faces and report to the first floor of the First Baptist Church for our first class which is a first-class pain in the ass. Our teacher is the typical southern evangelical, even-tempered, middle-aged man whose mission is to train youngun's in the rudiments of Christianity. He is also the store manager at Moore's Economy Store, just around the corner.

This is where we learn to hum the timeless classic, "Yes, Jesus loves me. Yes, Jesus, loves me. Yes, Jesus loves me. The Bible tells me so."

Our little contemporaries appeared to love this school. Rego and I had our minds made up that we weren't going to like it, period. We tried to do the small projects assigned and to have fun, but no such luck. Our minds were at the swimming pool and at the matinees but they were not at the First Baptist Church Vacation Bible School. Eventually, I came up and whisper to Rego that we could escape through the window in the teacher's office. He can't believe his little ears because this is desertion, a crime worse than death. Never in our young lives had we done such a dastardly deed, but there was always a first. The teacher warned us on several occasions to behave, or face the consequences. Of course, our pip-squeak little classmates thought this was hysterical and giggled incessantly. I asked Rego when we were going to bolt for the window and make our heroic escape. He said that we will quietly leave the big room where we were doing the two "P's" - playing and praying - and go into our teacher's office, close the door, open the window, step out between the bushes, and run down the street. Since the class was on the first floor there wasn't going to be a problem of scaling down a wall or anything dangerous. My major problem was with the time. How were we going to explain being home early or being caught uptown at Daddy Dean's pharmacy when our folks know that we are supposed to still be in school?

The time had finally come to make our move. Rego grabbed my arm and we both walked into our teacher's private office. We slowly close the door and eaked towards the open window across the room. Our pulses raced and we were on the verge of peeing in our britches. Suddenly, Rego made his move and stepped over the sill and lowered himself onto the grass outside. I quickly grabbed the sash and yanked the top window down, and locked it so Rego coukldn't get back inside.

The last thing I heard uttered from Rego's lips was, "Panky, you little prick. I'm going to kill you when you get home. You raise this window right now, y'hear."

I reentered the main room where all the kids are working on their projects. Suddenly, one of my classmates opened the door of the private office and saw Rego running down the street. She ran back into our room and yelled at the top of her voice, "Rego's jumped out the window and is running down the streeeeeeet!" A flurry of the kids scurried for the door just in time to see Rego rounding the corner of the church. I started giggling and then laughed to the point where I was choking.

Our teacher's parting words to me were as follows, "Panky you tell Rego that my phone call to his folks will beat him home by about fifteen minutes, just enough time for his daddy to get out his leather belt and teach him a lesson that Rego and Jesus will never forget. And, by the way, tell him not to bother to return to Bible School tomorrow. We'll get along just fine without him."

Rego, for all of his eight years, was already heading down the road of truancy. He had no idea of the consequences until the door opened at his house with Uncle Johnny waiting with a disgusted look on his face and his leather strap in his hands.

For once, I made the correct decision in staying at school. Lordy knows how that belt must have felt on Rego's butt. Rumor had it that he was given the ultimatum to toe the line or else, for the remainder of that summer. In the meantime I had to find a way to keep Rego from beating the shit out of me for locking that window behind him.

A highway billboard with the large letters indicates the summer has again arrived and it's time to get those chillun into learning about the Lord. "Please call for registration information."

I think of Rego, and how terribly disappointed Roy and Dale must have been.

First Baptist Church Vacation Bible School Begins June 1st.

Rego, don't be late!

Sneaking Out

Granny's playhouse was located in her backyard at the house on Ida Avenue. Granny and Daddy Dean had this separate structure built away from the main house when Aunt Evelyn and my mother, Lucy, were still small girls in Opp, so they would have a place to play with their dolls. The playhouse consists of one small room with painted walls, a wooden floor, an overhead light, and a gas burning fake log fireplace. I'd say it was about three times as long as the bed and the ceiling was rather high, a lot higher than I was used to. The remnants from several large fig trees adorn the roof whenever that time of the season arrived and the branches dropped rotten fruit onto the shiny tin metal and gutters. There was a rather large bamboo grove with shoots growing clear up to the sky next to the playhouse so you couldn't see the chicken coup next door at the Donaldson's. The path from the back door leading from the kitchen to the playhouse was dirt, when dry, or red clay mud when wet. There was only one window in the entire building, and a crabapple bush covered the view, just outside.

Rego and I loved the playhouse because it was our playhouse now that our mothers had grown up and moved away from the main house. Granny often used it for her floral business but she would rearrange it as our guest room whenever I came down visiting during the summers. A big brass bed sat squarely in the middle of the room, leaving precious little space for anything else, such as a dresser or a vanity.

Day in and day out, Rego and I rushed to the playhouse to change into our bathing suits for the race down to the municipal pool. Or, we perform the daily ritual of afternoon naps required by our parents, just after the noon dinner. Then, we finally crashed onto the brass bed every night, but not before we stood in the doorway to pee onto the surrounding bushes rather than go all the way into the house, and to the bathroom, like civilized young boys, don't you know.

Earlier in the day we each consumed about five bags of Fireball's boiled peanuts. Suppose we should have eaten only a bag but we couldn't stop. Digestion had commenced and the flagitious event was enough to send a mushroom-shaped cloud into the stratosphere had someone dare light a match anywhere near our room. Airburst after airburst, and none more evocative or pungent than its predecessor, as the pastoral silence of the evening was interrupted by the anal cornucopia of orchestral melodies not unlike those emitted by large animals fed on unrestricted daily diets of alfalfa or barley. Rego and I released enough gaseous fumes to provide natural energy for all of the Alabama Rural Power Commission.

After the farting subsided and we are able to gather our thoughts we made a pledge that the following night we'd pretend like we were fast asleep when Granny came out to check up on us. Then, in the dead of night, we would ever so quietly slip into our jeans and sneak around the corner to the back alley and make our way by the light of that same silvery moon up town to get ourselves a hamburger at the Sweet Shoppe.

Morning was here and we asked Granny for a jar of Vaseline in order to soothe the anal chaffing that resulted from our biological ingestion, digestion, and flagitious release of those goddamned boiled peanuts that we loved so much, and the ones we simply couldn't stop eating. It was going to be a race to the toilet I could predict all day long except for when we go to the pool.

We were exhausted and Granny told us to hit the sack. I waited until the coast was clear and I shook Rego's shoulder so that he woke up. It was time to get up, get dressed, and make our way silently back to the alley. We slipped into our jeans and t-shirts and ever so slowly opened the screen door so that Granny wouldn't hear the squeaking of the rusty springs thus coming out to check up on us. Our eyes were becoming adjusted to the moonlight and we ran back by the bamboo patch and into the alley only to be greeted by the furry creatures around the neighbor's garbage cans which had been strewn up and down the one-lane dirt path as the little critters screeched and meowed in the light of the full moon. In about another hundred feet we reached the paved street, and our first real challenge to determine if we could elude the lights of the few cars to continue our trek uptown. We stood in the bushes while a lone car drove by and then we bolted across the street to another alley, and more stench and screeching cats.

By now we had this escape and evasion routine down pat, so we let our guards down and proceeded up Ida Avenue along the sidewalk as we hid behind the huge oak trees when the lights of the few oncoming cars approached us. In another two blocks we'd reach Main Street and our ultimate destination, the Sweet Shoppe.

We rounded the corner of Dean's Pharmacy and slithered along the store fronts so that the local police would not see us lurking in the shadows as we inched our way for about another hundred feet, or about four more storefronts. Whew! That was a close one past the pool hall! And, the Opp cop was heading our way in his black and white patrol car but he failed to capture us in his peripheral vision. At last, we opened the screen door to the entrance of the cafe and we were greeted by Miriam, the one and only waitress at this hour of the morning, who blurted out, "Rego. Panky. What in the dickens are y'all doing here at this time of the morning? Your mamas and Granny Dean will whip your butts if they catch you down here! Lawdy, I bet you two snuck out of your grandmother's and thought that a burger and shake in the middle of the night was just what you needed. Am I right, you two?"

Our eyes were as big as silver dollars, and we were silent, and the looks on our faces caused her and the few diners to burst out laughing. We stared in hopes that we would not be turned over to our folks. All we wanted was some food. All we wanted was cheeseburgers, French fries and chocolate malts. Silently we ate before paying the tab and retracing our steps back down Main Street and the dark alleys towards the playhouse. We were scared to death that the Opp cop would drop in, apprehend us, and take us back to Granny's in the back seat of the squad car. Just when we thought the coast was clear two patrolmen walked over to the counter, sat down, and ordered coffee. I began to tremble and Rego started to slide under the table. I grabbed him and hold him next to me so the police could see both of us if they wanted. They began to talk with Miriam and she kept their attention as we emptied our pockets of change to pay the bill. Slowly, we made our way to the door so the police wouldn't turn around to see us. We made it safely outside and scurried around to the alley and hid up against the brick wall before deciding to head on back to Granny's.

The full moon that helped guide us had gone behind a cloud, so our return was slower and more intense than coming uptown an hour earlier. My eyes were as wide open as they can possibly get and I kept an ear tuned in for sounds of night creatures lurking in the alleyways and behind the huge oak trees lining the streets. Hardly a car was on the road and it was dead silent along our path towards home.

Another musical trip as we broke wind on this, otherwise, breeze-free evening as quiet as they come with the exception of our repetitive farts and burps that echoed off the corrugated surfaces of the garbage cans, tin sheds, and into the open bedroom windows of our neighbors. But, these folks were none the wiser as they were awakened by the ear-shattering dawn alert signaled by numerous roosters signalling another hot summer morning in Opp.

<u>**Mom, Granny Dean and Me Mclean Gardens, DC circa 1946**</u>

<u>Traveling with Lucy</u>

The eastern seaboard conjures up many thoughts when it comes to lifestyles, food, weather, the seasons, mentality, diction, and clothing. I associate this region with a class system or, as they have in Hindu societies, a caste system, that delineates the haves from the have-nots. Oddly enough, this measurement isn't made just in terms of monetary wealth possessed by the famous families of this region but, also, in genealogy. Who were your grandparents? Where were they from? Where did your parents attend school? Do you have a summer place on the Cape or on the Chesapeake? Andover, Class of '39, mind you.

I have always found the region from Boston, down to North Carolina, to be special and to be as integral part of my youth while growing up in Washington, and in the suburb of nearby Bethesda. As I indicated previously, Mom's only sister, Aunt Evelyn, married a man from the North, specifically Pennsylvania. Uncle Johnny's lineage went as far back as the original Michener family, including James, the famous author. Johnny, his two brothers, and their respective spouses, all resided near the family property in Bryn Mawr, a suburb of Philadelphia.

Little did I know that the Rue family estate was literally huge, visually pleasing, and grandiose. The interior consisted of a kitchen the size of today's Levittown houses, and the rest of the house seemed to go on forever. The surrounding property consisted of acres of rolling hills, barns, and picket fences - similar to a Norman Rockwell image on canvass. The three Rue sons-Johnny, Billy and Howdy- live on a cul-de-sac on what was formerly the Buck estate. Talk about being set up with an upper crust lifestyle by one's parents. These three lads had it made in the shade. Living on the pastoral estate, rent free, in the splendor of Bryn Mawr.

My cousin, Rego, shy of my age by of nine months, Aunt Evelyn, uprooted from her native southern Alabama, and her husband, Uncle Johnny, settled in adjacent to the Rue estate and were in the process of making babies. I simply couldn't wait for the day when Rego, who was Johnny and Evelyn's first offspring, and I could visit one another, and run around those wide open fields and experience an almost surreal vacation - days larger than life itself and chock full of one adventure after the next.

My parents and I lived in McLean Gardens Apartments in Washington, D.C., in the area known as Spring Valley. This was a huge apartment complex consisting of dozens of two-story, red brick colonial-style buildings and each building housed ten apartments. These buildings looked exactly the same and we chillun constantly knocked on the wrong door, in the wrong building, in the wrong complex, forever lost. My life consisted of nursery school, then kindergarten, then first grade at the elite Miss Libby's Elementary School, over on fashionable Connecticut Avenue. Living in a complex like McLean Gardens may sound like oodles of fun for a pip-squeak, but it wasn't. Most of the denizens were transitory so we hardly had the opportunity to socialize before the pending migrations to other towns or housing complexes in the area. In other words, there weren't any kids to play with! A shitty situation, to say the least. My thoughts turned to playing hide and seek and trying to catch butterflies during the day, and fireflies during the evening.

The choo-choo train that clickety-clacked from Washington's Central Station to Philadelphia's Main Terminal was something very special in my life. Whenever my folks and I traveled up to Bryn Mawr, we took this train, usually the one scheduled to depart in the early evening, just in time for supper on board. Those were the days when the various travelers checked on board, found their seats or compartments, and asked the porter to make their reservations for a particular seating in the dining car. The porter, a black man, dressed in a meticulously starched jacket, lint-free and perfectly creased black trousers, and spit-shined shoes, would ask if we had a special time in mind for supper.

Central Station, in Washington, was god-awful big and overwhelming in scale. To any six year old, the building appeared to be the largest thing on earth. The hallways were as wide as streets, the main lobby as big as a football field and as high as the inside of a dirigible hangar. Voices echoed in the great hall and the resonance of thousands of travelers added to the drama as we located our track where the shiny stainless steel clad cars were located. Steam poured from under the various cars and engines statically parked on adjacent tracks; and the ominous patina of the tracks, the soot from the locomotives and the inadequate lighting provided quite a spectacular contrast to the gleaming sides of the Pullmans and the locomotives. Climbing up the chromed steel stepladder into the assigned car was a step into fantasy as we left reality back in McLean Gardens.

"All Abooaarrd," shouted the porter, and the steam began to pour from under the steel wheels as we slowly inched away from the station. I was so excited that we were finally leaving and heading north, towards Philadelphia, and towards my cousins who seemed light years away. But, my appetite wasn't light years away! Mom and I couldn't wait to repair to the dining car for supper because we knew the food served on board was special, and we longed for the excitement of the occasion. Most of the food prepared in those days was from scratch cooking with very little prior preparation, or use of frozen foods. The soups were especially delicious and the desserts were freshly prepared, and simply yummy. Didn't really care about the entrees, which usually consisted of a chicken dish or a roast beef plate. But, I distinctly remember those soups and desserts were well worth the trip.

"Mizz Miller, time for yo' seatin' in the dinin' car. Can I assist you with yo' son while we walk through the cars towards the dinin' car? This train is mighty rough just as we is passin' through rough parts of these tracks," said the porter.

"Please, porter, I always seem to have trouble navigating through these slamming doors between the cars. And, I seem to lose my footing on the slippery metal floors. Panky, you hold my hand tight and we'll get going towards that proverbial last car which is always that dining car. Why can't they put the dining car next to ours so we won't have to go through so many of these confounded doors?"

Why! Why! Why! Why was it that my mother always had to complain about situations that I considered to be challenging and adventurous? Hell, I thought this was fun with a capital "F." This old train moved like a hula dancer-left to right with sudden jerks, right to left with the same momentum-coupled with the screeching brakes and the steam pouring under the wheels. Passengers on the move, going all sorts of places to visit with all sorts of people, peering out the windows at the city as we made our way into the countryside heading towards Baltimore. At last, the dining car was within sight and olfactory recognition.

Have you ever experienced the mixture of food cooking and metal scraping against metal, coupled with steam emissions? It is a peculiar combination, similar to that of being aboard a ship at sea. To some travelers, it is rather nauseating while others consider this aroma to be stimulating and a sign of adventure, of travel, of something foreign to the senses. Anyway, I absolutely loved it and I still enjoy the sensation whenever I'm aboard a vessel with this concoction of odors and aromas that I consider to be a sensual aphrodisiac for this eternal adolescent.

"I'm Messus Milla, and we have reservations for 6:15. Is our table ready?" asked Mom.

The maitre'd replied, "You'll have to wait for about five minutes while the waiter clears the table, ma'am."

"Please hurry so we can sit down. This rocking and rolling has my nerves in a tizzy. Furthermore, we're hungry so we'd appreciate anything you can do."

"This way, folks, and you, young man, can sit here next to the window so you can look out at the pretty sights."

Traveling with my mother, when I was young, was probably one of the primary reasons why I am so accustomed as an adult to delays, inconveniences, and other misfortunes associated with travel logistics. She was not what I consider a mentor in this regard but, rather, an example of what not to do in order to circumvent adverse conditions. Mom had this way about her that most folks found brusque and a wee bit abrasive. Perhaps, she learned this behavior from her mother, Granny Dean, who had little if any patience with those in the travel industry.

Having said that, we enjoyed our suppers and I simply didn't want to leave that dining car because this is where I might see some other boys my age. Problem with this situation is that it usually turned out to be a very short-term friendship . . . only a few hours before we'd reach our destinations and step off the train. So, most of the times, I would go back to our car and stare out the window at the telephone poles zipping by the farms and tractors and hay stacks as the evening mist rose off the fields to form a low-flying gray haze during the sunsets.

"Next stop, Philadelphia Central Station in about fifteen minutes, ladies and gentlemen. Please gather your belongings and prepare to disembark promptly upon arrival," the porter bellowed as he walked up and down the narrow isles the length of each car, both Pullman and coach. This is the time when Mom would begin to get fidgety and start to verbalize about the problems that she would create in her mind. "What if Evelyn and Johnny have the times of our arrival mixed up? What if no one is there to meet us at the station? How long of a drive is it to the house in Bryn Mawr? Wonder how much traffic there is this time of the night?" She would slowly begin to drive me crazy with her worrywart behavior. And, she worried about nothing. Never had a problem. Everyone was always on time. The ride out to the country was effortless. For sure, I can tell you that my trait of being worried about inconsequential details stems from a formidable instructor, called Mom.

"Aunt Evelyn, Uncle Johnny, where's Rego? Didn't he come with you to the station? I want to see him so bad. How long will the ride be until we get home?" *Here I was trying to impersonate my mother with these rapid-fire questions.*

"Panky, Lucille, so good to see y'all. Let's get your bags and get on down the road. Did you have any problems on the trip or was it as smooth as I remember it last time we came down to see y'all in Washington?" was Johnny's greeting to us.

"Evelyn, that train was the roughest thing you've ever seen. We could barely walk down the isles to go to the bathroom and to the dining car. Well, I almost turned around, went back to my seat and skipped supper rather than slip and slide all over those metal floors connecting the cars."

"Shucks, Aunt Evelyn, I had a good time on the train. Should have seen what we had for supper. Boy, the soup was good, too, but I loved the pecan pie with the big pile of vanilla ice cream on top. Sure wish you could have been with us. Maybe next time we can take a trip together and I know that you will enjoy the train as much as I did."

"Panky, we'd love to do that sometime but, right now, we need to get your bags and head on up the road. Rego was pestering me to death about getting you up here," said Evelyn.

We left downtown Philadelphia, and were soon back in the country heading for Bryn Mawr. The green rolling hills with the mansion and horse barns with white fences stuck out in my mind. Lots of open space and trees and birds and everything appeared larger than life to me. You see, I lived in an apartment complex. Row after row of these three story, red brick, buildings that looked the same. Fact remains where Bryn Mawr was the antithesis of McLean Gardens, which is one reason for my vivid recollections of the magnificent beauty of the Rue property.

Now, we're talking very, very big when we refer to the Rue house. It was definitely what you would call a mansion. Stone construction, sitting on at least an acre of front yard alone, not counting the property behind and down the road. And the kitchen was immense with the huge stone fireplace, central island the size of today's condominiums, and other living areas that dwarfed not only this pip-squeak but, also, floor plans and room dimensions that we consider spacious by today's standards. Of course, when you're only four feet tall everything seemed large, overpowering, sometimes scary, and often mysterious simply because we viewed the world as if we were looking at everyone's kneecaps. Get above the knees and the waist and, wow, is this person big, or what!

When Walt Disney designed his first amusement park, Disneyland, he perceived this to be a problem for the little tykes. He didn't want to make the children afraid of large objects so his solution was a brilliant one. All of the structures in Disneyland were designed and constructed on four-fifths scale. Hence, when you view the buildings and other structures, such as the riverboats, they appear to be in scale for the smaller guests in the park. Brilliant strategy, design, and marketing.

The three houses, situated side-by-side, sat on a cul-de-sac on the Buck estate. Howdy, Billy, and Uncle Johnny, and their respective families, occupied these houses. All three of the Rue sons assumed the role of modern urban sharecroppers who left each morning for work while their wives remained home to raise the babies. All three of my cousins - Rego, Stevie, Carol - and I were inseparable. We ate together, bathed together, played together, got into trouble together, slept together, had pillow fights together.

"Panky, let's go down to the quarry where the old barn is standing, and play cowboys and Indians. What do you say?" Rego would ask over and over while we sat at breakfast.

"Let's go, Rego. Do I need my shoes or can we run barefoot?"

"Don't need no shoes, and I can beat you down there!"

Two bolts of toe-headed, four-foot, lightening shot out of the kitchen at full speed blazing through the moist green grass of the rolling meadows out of sight of the house. *Scenes from a Norman Rockwell painting are forever imprinted in my memory, and we were, most likely, two good candidates for his subjects depicting Americana in those early years.* Over the grass knoll sat the remains of a large building with the steel girders rising to the sky, rusting away from the elements. We would spend hours climbing over those beams only to discover, on one occasion, nests of green hornets just waiting to pounce. Those little buggers reminded us of the comic strip "The Green Hornet," so we expected some sort of magical drama to unfold with human characters wearing green capes and masks but, instead, we got the real McCoy, stingers and all!

The humming of these little monster produced a lasting impression; thousands, perhaps millions, of them swooping down on us, as this noise in my ears became almost intolerable.

"Boys, we're having lots of kids over late this afternoon for our Fourth of July picnic so you will be meeting boys and girls from around the area, and some from Philadelphia. They'll serve hot dogs, hamburgers, my famous potato salad, plus tons of Kool Aid. Later in the day we'll break out the horses and ponies and have an old fashioned hay ride over to the large barn on the back property." Rego's paternal gramdma Nona Rue was in charge of the day's activities and it was apparent that she was in full control of the situation. Rego and I started to meet the other boys and girls as the vast consumption of Forth of July stomach cramp food began. Certainly, our parents must have been worn out just watching their darling little children in a kinetic mode with absolutely no obvious signs of winding down.

In addition, we had the company of several teenagers who acted as babysitters and monitors for those of us too young to mount a pony or to reach the step up into the hay wagon. You could almost hear Lucy and Evelyn in the background saying, "Those two boys are certain to get hurt today with the way they're running around, jumping up on the top rails of the fences, and teasing the horses and ponies. Lordy, they're going to have such stomachaches tonight from eating everything in sight. I'm simply exhausted just from watching them. Maybe they'll begin to settle down after their digestive tracts take over, and the metamorphosis begins with the conversion of all that junk into nutrition that has to do some good, whatever it is!" These two women were in perpetual conflict with the universe. Our mothers failed to realize that children, of all ages, took chances-some more dangerous or challenging than others-but chances, nonetheless. So, our attitudes were to ignore their plebeian pleas for calm and order and, instead, we implemented what we were best at. And, my friends, that was chaos and confusion.

Our stomachs were full and the sun had set and the chill of the early evening air prompted us to ask the older members of the group if we could go into the barn for a story. Their reply was an overwhelming "Yes," because of the ease in monitoring our whereabouts and hopes that we would settle down and relax for once! After all, we had worn these grown-ups into total fatigue so they were extremely receptive to any suggestion involving rest and relaxation! One of our favorite teenagers asked if any of us had heard of <u>Rumplestiltskin</u> and we replied in unison, "No." What in the hell was a Rumplestiltskin anyway? Some sort of nut, or fruitcake, or monster? Well, we were about to find out.

Images of ancient Europe, of kings and queens, of surfs and farms, of mysteries that appeared larger than life were described as our young girl storyteller mesmerized us with her voice while reading this classic folk tale. All we could hear besides her voice was the occasional belching of the calves and the whinnies of the horses as we lay in the barn amidst the hay and the dim lighting, watching the moon rise up over the hills. Our eyes were as large as our imaginations as we stayed tuned into each and every word she spoke while the tale of the peasant weaving straw into gold was delivered precisely as if the storyteller had done this a hundred times previously, which she most likely had.

One by one, we felt as if there were magnets in the ground below acting as negative polarization in conflict with the positive ions resting on our little eyelids. In summary, we were tired as hell, so the tune "Babes in Toyland" started to hum its melody in our ears. *Can't begin to tell you the last time when I was at peace with the universe as much as I was this special evening. I suppose the child in every one of us yearns for an occasional nurturing and for a feeling that the universe is in harmony, by seizing that very special moment.*

"Evelyn, suppose we should go down to the barn, gather up the youngin's, and take them back to the house. Can you remember the last time when they played as hard as today? By the way, Johnny, this is one of the tastiest cocktails I've had in ages. What did you do to make it so special, or is it simply because I haven't experienced one of your Perfect Rob Roys before?"

"Lucy, bless you, sweet thing, for the compliment and no, this is the first time I've made this kind of drink. A Perfect Rob Roy is similar to those I concocted but with a few modifications in the ingredients. They get even better after the second or third."

"Lordy mercy, Johnny, I'll be on my knees walking back to the house if I have another one. Anyway, like I said, we should go get the boys before the evening chill sets in and they catch a death of a cold. Funny thing. It sure isn't chilly out now. Must have been close to ninety today, so we shouldn't worry too much about it getting down near freezing. Let me finish this marvelous cocktail and we'll be off."

"Panky, sure have had fun with you and I want you to come back up and see me real soon, okay? And, when you do, be sure to bring a cape and a mask so we can dress up and go back down to that old barn and play 'The Green Hornet.' Mommy was saying something about us moving down to Opp, soon."

"Mommy, where'll we live if we move down to Opp.? I mean, will we stay close to Panky?"

"Panky, we'll be staying in Silver Springs, just about half hour away from your apartment, in McLean Gardens. Uncle Johnny and the rest of us have decided to move down to Opp, because Johnny wants to open his own business down there. So, we'll get ourselves situated for a while in Silver Springs, then mosey down to Opp. I think I'm just as excited as you are because we'll be close to your mom and dad. I miss Hank and Lucy so much when I don't get to see them often. This way, we can see y'all, and you and Rego can still get into all sorts of mischief."

Unfortunately, it was time to start traveling again with Lucy. Just the thought of getting on that train and listening to my very own mother whine and complain and bitch about the noise of the train, the smell of the train, the motion of the train, the porters of the train, and the dining car's location on the train was about all this kid could take. So, like I did so many times previously, I shut out any outside interference by merely tuning out what I didn't want to hear. No, didn't have any trouble hearing. As a matter of fact I could perceive decibel ratings of a tiny little ant sleeping, but only if I wanted to. To this day, I have an uncanny ability to detect faint sounds imperceptible to most folks around me. And, at the same time, can't hear a damn thing if I don't want to. Suppose I tuned out my parents on more than one occasion. But, the humming of the wheels on the tracks was a sound that I simply didn't want to.

Funny how long that ride from the station out to Bryn Mawr appeared when Mom and I arrived just a few days ago. Now, that we had to leave my favorite family the ride seemed to take only a few minutes for us to travel the distance back into downtown Philadelphia, for that trip back to Washington. My mood always turned sour and I definitely experienced what is referred to as an attitude check, which, roughly translated, meant I was in a piss poor frame of mind. . As a child I quickly learned to suppress my emotions and not dilly-dally around with good-byes. A simple hug from my cousins, a kiss from my aunt and uncle, and a poker-faced, glaring-at-the-ground expression was my way of indicating my disapproval of the separation from those I loved.

"All Abooaarrd," cried the Southern Crescent penguin - the black man in the white coat. "Watch yo' step, madam and you, young man, help yo' mother with her bags. Time's a wastin'. We pull out of the station in about two minutes, so you can show yo' mother to her seat in car number two, seats 35A and B."

"Panky, our car is about three cars down, as usual. Every time I ask for seats near the dining car they put us up near the locomotive. I'm going to write someone when we return and express my dissatisfaction with this entire train service. Can't they ever get anything right?"

<u>The Primary reason why I am so misaligned today is because of those friggin' knickers!</u>

Bull of the Woods

Sounds of early morning, like Billy goats turning over the trash cans back in the alleys searching for last night's dinner, and Cheerios. Dogs barking way off in the distance making it nearly impossible to tell whose dog it is, so that later on in the morning you could get even by shooting that "dawg" in the butt with your Daisy BB gun. The milk truck making its rounds as it pulls up to each house, puts on the brake, and exchanges full bottles of the white stuff for empties left out the night before.

Lordy, is it that time already, or can I sleep in for just a few more minutes? Granny'll surely be up and at 'em so that she can get started on making the casket sprays and other floral arrangements for the orders that she needs to fill. Still cool in the house but it'll turn into a scorcher later when the sun gets a chance to radiate through that metal roof, down through the walls, and finally into my room. Sure does feel cool and comfortable now though. Think I'll just lay here and conjure up what Rego and I'll do today after he comes over to play.

Gladdy Mae, Granny's maid, hadn't arrived at the house and that meant breakfast was a ways off. In time, she would surely get me up to issue the ultimatum that breakfast would be served in ten minutes, and to freshen up *NOW*. I'd jump out of bed, run into the bathroom to pee, and to find my shorts or Levis, so that I could go visit with Granny for a few minutes to help her with her flowers.

I can hear rumblings in the back alley, probably some of the goats that broke loose during the night. I absolutely love goats. Goats of all colors, breeds, and coats. All sizes and shapes, with and without their little horns. Rego and I had our very own goat a couple of years earlier. One day, Granny drove us out into the country to deliver some flowers for a country funeral, and the farmer repaid her with a Billy goat. We put that goat in the back of Granny's car and headed back to town. As soon as we arrived, Gladdy Mae took us in tow and told us to take that goat into the back yard, tie it up, and get a bowl of Cheerios for food. That old goat loved Cheerios, your shoes, field peas still in the shell, and anything else it could get its little mouth around. Damn thing woke us up every morning before dawn as it deliberately crashed into cars, the sides of houses, and attempted to break down the back door into Granny's kitchen. Suppose he just wanted attention and lots of food. That Billy goat lasted about one week at the house, then back to the country, once and for all.

"Panky, you old sweet thang, how would you and Rego like to work with Mr. Presley on the milk truck every morning? He'll pay you each a dollar a day and he told me that he needs some help with the cases of milk that are getting too heavy for him to shuttle back and forth between his truck and the houses. Besides, you two could stand a little diversion from that swimming pool every day. Do you both some good to work with Mr. Presley so that you'll have some extra spending money this summer. I'll ask him exactly what time he'll arrive so you two boys will be ready."

Rego and I look at each other and say, "What do you think? Suppose it's a good idea and I'm kinda excited about working on that truck. I've never really been on too many trucks. You know, it doesn't have any doors so you hold onto a handle and stand in the doorway while he drives. Shoot, I think we'll have a hooting good time tomorrow, except for the fact we have to get up in the dark to get dressed. Means Granny'll probably have us go to bed early so we can get a good night's sleep, don't you think?"

Today would be a special day. Today would be a day of infamy for me. Today would progress into one of the worst days of my pathetic little life.

"Panky, here comes Butch now. Butch was our best friend and he lived just down the street from Grannys.

"Hey, Bracke, what do you think about Panky and me working for old man Presley on the milk truck tomorrow? He pays us a dollar each a day and it's 'bout a two week job before school starts.

"Do you each realize what time you have to get up? That's the bad news. The good news is that one of the last stops is at Zeb's Bakery, uptown, and you'll get some of their hot glazed donuts, right out of the oven, piping hot. Couple of those donuts with some cold milk and maybe I'll get up after all to meet you up there because my mouth's watering just thinking about it.

Every morning about this time Daddy Dean finished his morning constitutional and came out on the front porch to wait for his ride uptown to play dominos. "Hey, Daddy Dean, what do you think about Rego and me working on the milk truck, starting tomorrow morning? Saw you sitting out here on the glider and you look like you want some company, so here we are, your three favorite kids. By the way, can we have some change for Cokes at the drugstore?"

"Sure, boys." He reaches into his pocket and digs out a few pennies. "You'll like Mr. Presley, and working for him on the truck. Work never hurt anyone, and I started long before you on the farm, which meant we worked everyday, from sun up through sundown. While you're up at the drugstore having a Coke pick me up a box of Ha-vaTampa Jewels, will you? Just ask Charlie to put them on my account. And, don't you boys go and smoke one, y'hear? It'll stunt your growth, just like chewing tobacco, such as that Bull of the Woods I found stashed away under the back porch steps. Neither of you have any idea how it got there, now do you?"

"Shoot no, Daddy Dean."

"Helloooooo, Mr. Bird! Good morning to you and we were wondering when Mrs. Bird would be coming by again with her delicious lemon cake?

We finish supper and were now out in the yard catching lightning bugs in our Ball jars on this sweltering summer evening. The temperature surely would drop sometime, but now wasn't the time as our parents sat on the porch cooling themselves by waving the small bamboo hand fans sponsored, on one side, by the First Baptist Church, and Western Auto on the other. "You boys come on in now. It's time to hit the sack so you can get a good night's sleep for tomorrow. This is the third time I've called you, so get in here right this minute, young men!"

Before you could count to ten, we were fast asleep ready for the coming day with the milkman, the customers, and the last stop at the bakery for goodies. Only the sounds of the night could be heard, and they were generally the chorus of crickets echoing through the nocturnal silence joined by an occasional cry from some barn owl, or the screeching of bats soaring through the trees.

Morning came quickly and we were up and ready to board that milk truck as we waited on the front porch steps for Mr. Presley to round the corner and stop in front of our house. The sky was pitch black and only the front light of the Cheatam's house shone through the trees that softly illuminated the surrounding bushes and telephone poles. After a few minutes we could barely hear the sound of gears grinding as the lone motor vehicle turns down Hart Avenue and headed west on our street. We spotted Mr. Presley behind the wheel of his beat-up, not-so-shiny-new, sort of white truck. "Mornin", Mr. Presley, we're ready to go."

"Hop on board, boys, and I'm glad to have you helping out. Let's get going so I can keep on schedule." Panky, you stand here and, Rego, you stand in the door and hold onto that handle so you won't go out the door when I make a hard left turn. First stop is up here at the Williams', and they get two quarts of homogenized milk plus one carton of eggs. Rego, you grab the milk and eggs that Panky hands you, run down and deliver it, then pick up the empties and bring them back for Panky to store in back of the truck. Watch out, too, 'cause the roads are bumpy, and you're liable to bounce right off the truck before you know it, and wind up on the street face down on the concrete! I'd sure hate to have to explain that to Mrs. Dean."

'Round about 6:30 a.m. we had delivered most of the milk and sundry items as the lean, mean, milk- delivering machine approached the service entry at the rear of Zeb's Bakery. We could smell those donuts cooking and suddenly I was famished. The owner offered us as many of the hot glazed morsels as we could eat, and I could eat as many as he offers. Rego must have devoured eight and I wasn't far behind as Mr. Presley asked us to reboard for the short trip back to Granny's. We were stuffed! We were borderline sick! Another bump in the road and we would puke. Lordy, too much sugar, fat, milk, and cream for our overstretched puny little stomachs to assimilate at one time.

Rego says, "Panky, I've got some Bull of the Woods chewing tobacco for us to try today, and old man Presley won't care, do you think?"

"Shoot, I don't know but I'm willing to try some." I removed the cellophane wrapper from the dark brown rectangle and bit off one of the corners. It was gawd awful! Still, I couldn't let on to Rego and Mr. Presley that I didn't like the taste. I stuffed the plug way back in the far left corner of my mouth, next to the area where my wisdom teeth would someday appear.

Mr. Presley asked, "How is it, Panky? That Bull of the Woods is the best tobacco you can buy. Sure beats that Beach Nut loose-leaf style. Here, let me have a plug and I'll hand it right back to you."

Mr. Presley bit off a plug from the opposite corner where I had begun. Rego decided to pass and he said he wanted to think about it. The truth is he was chicken, and we knew it. Rego always had this way of goading people into something while he abstained. As we left the paved road we suddenly hit a series of ruts in the hard, clay soil as the milk truck bounced off the four wheels and landed sharply back down on the surface. I was airborne for about one second that seemed like an eternity, and the tobacco plug decided to exit my mouth and head down the old esophagus towards my tummy. Clunk! There it sat as I began to spit the remains out the door of the truck onto whatever got in the way. I began to feel real sick and woozy and my skin turned a pale shade of green.

"I can't wait for some more of those hot greasy donuts along with that rich creamy cold milk tomorrow," said Rego, and Mr. Presley agreed.

"Panky, you don't look so good, my boy. Did you go and swallow some of that tobacco that you was chewing? Lordy, that is enough to make most folks puke!"

"Can we go home now? I don't believe that I was cut out for chewing tobacco. I'm just going to lay down on the floor in the back of the truck, if you don't mind, Mr. Presley."

"Panky, go and get a big drink of water, and that'll make you feel lots better," as Mr. Presley let out this huge laugh. "Okay, boy, but you'd better not let on what happened when Mrs. Dean sees you, or she'll switch your butt for sure."

Soon after we arrived back at Ida Avenue, and Granny's house, I was glad to see that Granny had a rush flower order, so she was out in the playhouse, as I casually walked into the bathroom, puked my lungs out, and staggered to the back porch for a nap.

Rego thought the entire ordeal was a riot and he couldn'y stop telling everyone at the pool.

Soon the lifeguards began to ask, "Hey, Panky, got a plug of Beach Nut over here. Want some?"

"Panky, heard where you're an old pro with Bull of the Woods. I got plenty of it for free, so you won't have to go and buy some. Here's a plug you can enjoy."

Are you crazy? You must have mistaken me for Rego. He's the one who got sick and puked. Isn't that true, Rue?"

"Panky, you're a lying sack of sheep shit!"

Myrtle Wright, Opp Municipal Pool, circa 1955

No One Could Dive Like Myrtle

The concrete rectilinear cavity was thirty feet across by one hundred feet in length. And, the depth varied from approximately two feet to twelve down at the drain. At the twelve foot end the high-dive structure sat ominously adjacent to the low board. The Opp Municipal Swimming Pool was the center of recreation during the sweltering summer days in south Alabama, and it's no wonder that the younguns waited impatiently for the coach to open the gate at nine o'clock every morning. Hell, where else could you get a Coke and a bag of Lays Barbecue Potato Chips for sweeping out the men's and women's locker rooms, and still enjoy a full day of swimming and running 'round the concrete in total defiance of the lifeguard's whistles?

At the deep end of this man-made ersatz pond were two wooden planks mounted on sturdy iron stanchions. One board was about three feet above pool level while the other board seemed to disappear into the clouds. The high dive was reserved for budding Ester Williams or crazy dare devils like Harry Jackson, Charles Nelson, or Louie Grimes. No telling how many belly flops resulted from the last minute panics and total disorientation as the divers became airborne, only split seconds away from the rock-hard, blue-green, chlorine-saturated cold water that siphoned down from the omnipresent Opp water tower - seen for 20 miles around the county.

We southerners are a visual people. Water tanks mask where you are. The bulbous gray monolith rises above the trees and low buildings and becomes the monument for high schools boys to utilize for significant rites of passage, such as hand-painted epithets. "Beat Kensington Eagles!" "Go Bobcats!" Beat those little fuckers on the football gridiron or my name painted here will be mud for another 365 days. Annual ritualistic misdemeanors, never enforced, surround the permanently embossed name of the town, followed by a comma, then the abbreviation of the state, like we don't really know where we are here in this county. A boldly painted OPP, AL alerts me to my arrival at Granny's.

The Opp Municipal Pool was situated amidst the park which contains a tennis court, the city water tank, a seesaw, a whirl around, several sets of swings that take us up to the stratosphere, and many large trees and bushes that provide cover whenever we need to hide, for one reason or another. The pool is the main attraction and it was sacrosanct. No one would dare to vandalize the pool or its facilities. Lordy knows, all there was to do was swim and sunbathe on many summer days, so why mess with a good thing. Besides, if someone caught you trespassing or vandalizing the pool or clubhouse facilities Coach Nolen would automatically suspend your pool privileges with absolutely no recourse for appeal. This is the word that had come forth, passed down through generations, and everyone simply abided by its meaning, or woe be unto you, brother.

Most important in the daily procedures were the hours of operation because the children plan their entire schedules around this time. If you know there is going to be a western movie at the Royal Theater, at

2:00 p.m., then you swim your butt off in the morning. If the matinee consists of some second-rate comedy then take it easy in the morning and continue with your swim, and frolic in afternoon. If the movie is "Sierra Sunrise" or "Susanna Pass," then count on missing your time at the pool after dinner. Let us bow our heads in prayer, chillun.

<u>Roy Rogers Riders Club Pledge</u>

1. *Be neat and clean.*

2. *Be courteous and polite.*

3. *Always obey your parents.*

4. *Protect the weak and help them.*

5. *Be brave but never take chances.*

6. *Study hard and learn all you can.*

7. *Be kind to animals and care for them.*

8. *Eat all your food and never waste any.*

9. *Love God and go to Sunday school regularly.*

10. *Always respect our flag and our country.*

In lower Alabama, that summer sky was a dull gray as cloud cover develops shortly after sunrise. And, the temperature hovers around ninety degrees, with the humidity close behind. The smell of ozone fills the air and we nourish that sensual effervescence along with the fragrances of gardenias, dogwood, and honeysuckle.

Everyday, Rego and I run from Granny's to the pool, from the pool back to Granny's for dinner, and back to the pool after our naps. We run just to have a fountain Coke, and to shop for Levi's at Leo's Economy Store. We run everywhere. Our bodies are finely hewn machines - sinewy, lean, mean or, just plain skinny. Not one ounce of fat camps out on our puny, frames.

We lived from September until June when school was out and the pool opened for the hot, sultry summer season. We wore faded, shredded Levis with the patches sewn over holes where our knees have worn through; and we eliminated any sign of footwear. The soles of our feet were like elephant hide impenetrable by most objects, notwithstanding rusty nails and broken glass, and the ensuing tetanus shots.

Because he was the absolute leader and arbitrator of all occurrences around the pool, Coach Nolen must be discussed, and analyzed. Here was a young man, truly southern, whose mission in life was to train young boys in the fine art of a contact sport known, in Dixie, as a para-religious experience practiced in the sanctuary of a coliseum on Saturday afternoon, or Friday evenings. You guessed it - football, southern style. Coach Nolen was the supreme commander of all football activities at Opp High School. The school was located on the north side of town, comprised of one hundred percent white students and one hundred percent white faculty. It was very small school compared to those in Mobile, Birmingham, or the Division One programs, up in Montgomery.

Coach couldn't wait for the opportunity to come each summer when he could take advantage of and mock my so-called Yankee accent. He said that I call him "Coo - ach." Hell, he thought I sounded funny and I knew he was a true redneck with that Alabama drawl. This became ritualistic and I actually looked forward to arriving in Opp, and expecting this harassment from the Coach. It became part of the syntax of the summer. Coach Nolen was in charge of the pool and its facilities during the three months of operation, from June until the beginning of September. I'm certain that this task was one way of moonlighting to bolster his teaching and coaching income. In turn, all of the lifeguards reported to the Coach, and he was known as the person in charge.

Coach never suspected it but Rego and I knew how to manipulate him. Somewhere between the time the pool opened in the morning and the noon dinner we'd suffer from extreme hunger pangs as a result of all the swimming, and running, and swimming, and...you get the picture. Since we had no pocket change for snacks we conjure up ways to sucker Coach into some work for pay. Usually, he paid us the huge stipend of twenty-five cents for the menial tasks performed. That quarter, however, bought us two Cokes, and a bag of potato chips, just enough to hold us over until the noon whistle.

Coach Nolen held in his supreme command the nominations of several lifeguards during the summer months. I was never a serious contender for one of these positions because Coach perceived my physique as being similar to that of a starving refugee. How could I possibly transport someone in danger to safety while swimming in the pool? He always underestimated my strength and my ability to react in a panic situation. More importantly, he underestimates my desire to wear the lifeguard's whistle, cap, and title. That is what really hurt

"Panky, I'll race you to the pool," Rego shouted across the dining room.

"Let's go, Rego," was my reply as we blasted out the front door and I am a mere three or four feet ahead of my cousin.

We are at full speed by the time we hit our stride in front of Miriam Donaldson's house next door. Streaks of sheer light speed with the grace of two gazelles running through fields of grain, our knees pulled high as our hamstrings became fully extended, racing across the intersection in order to beat the oncoming traffic. Sometimes, it was a '50 Chevy or a senior citizen on foot, or an old black man pulling the reigns of a horse drawn buckboard. Of course, this is an illusion. In fact, we run like two Mexican jumping beans. With two blocks to go we blazed in a dead heat past the First Methodist Church, down past the empty tennis court, by the seldom occupied swing sets and now, the last seventy-five yards, it was all downhill through the trees and shrubs to the pool gate.

"Rego, last one to the gate is Harold's boyfriend."

That is all it took for Rego, the slower runner, to gain a final burst of speed held in reserve that would be crucial to the outcome of this foot race. Regardless of the adrenaline or of any supernatural ability I usually won that daily race. Reason? I run because of sheer terror because I am a small kid and, furthermore, the stakes are high. I might even have to kiss Harold, God forbid! (We consider Harold the town sissy.)

"OK Panky, you win. But, I ain't gonna kiss Harold. Wanna Dr. Pepper or a Coke?"

"Dr. Pepper'll be just fine, Rue, if I can ever catch my breath. You almost beat me this time so I'll give you less of a head start from now on, boy."

"Rego, Panky, get your butts in here, settle down and behave," said Coach Nolen, and he means it.

"Coach, how's about a couple of quarters to clean up the locker rooms and sweep 'round the pool?"

"Okay, you two, but make darn sure the women's locker room is clear before you burst in there, like you did the other day. One of these days you're going to walk in there, and Miriam Donaldson's going to come out and kick your butts!" Mirriam lived next door to Granny and Daddy Dean and she was a teenager when we were pipsqueaks.

Heck, that was the only way we can get a shot of a little tittie, and that never hurt any young boy, for Pete's sake! One of our victims was Myrtle Wright who tattled on us, and she said she would tell our parents if we ever did that to her again. Myrtle was my heartthrob, and I am very sensitive to how she feels about me. I wouldn't do a thing to upset her, and so Rego and I made sure Myrtle wasn't present when we acted up.

Boy, could Myrtle dive off that high board and she had perfect form, almost every time. I idolized her ability to do a jack knife, or a swan, or a full gainer when I could barely keep my legs and feet together for the most basic of any dive. "Hey Rue, and Butch, let's sit over here and watch Myrtle practice off the high dive. She says she's going to try a half gainer and I'll believe it when I see it."

So, the three of us placed our little frames on the bench adjacent to the life guard stand and proceeded to watch Myrtle scale the ladder clear up ten feet. Just watching her wiggle that little butt of hers as she climbed up those stairs was enough to make my day. *My hormones were racing at a tender age.* Feet together, hands down by her sides, eyes straight ahead, she began her approach down the board. She sprang up for the last jump to gain the altitude necessary to get her legs and feet up perpendicular-out in front. Then, with those feet tucked together, toes pointed, she reached for her toes, holds her position for a split second and then threw her head and upper body back to form a straight perpendicular to the waterline-line. Myrtle's hands, head, torso and legs entered the pool with nary a splash. "10, 10, 10," we shouted as she swam over to our side of the pool. "That's a perfect dive, Myrtle, how come we can't dive like you? Come in to the clubhouse and we'll buy you a Dr. Pepper and some barbecue potato chips."

About this time Harry Jackson, the senior lifeguard, came over to us as we were sitting at the deep end dangling our legs in the water, sat down beside us and said, " You boys know how to keep from getting the clap? Well, let me tell you."

I looked at Rego and he looked at me and we both wondered, "What in the heck is the clap?"

Harry said, "When you're through you pee. That's what gets rid of the bug that gives you the clap."

What in the heck does this have to do with Myrtle diving off the high board, we wondered?

"Rego, have you, Butch, and Panky been uptown to see the tinker selling all sorts of stuff?" said the Coach. "He's got pots and pans, animals and snakes that you should see. He usually rambles through these parts every summer and we like to think of him as an institution here in Opp. A little weird but he's okay."

"Rego, let's quit swimming and hightail it up there before dinner, okay?"

"All right with me, Panky, but we don't have our money from Coach yet. Coach, can you pay us in advance for sweeping out the locker rooms, plus a couple of extra quarters? We'll pay you back this afternoon."

"Here's some change, you two, and I'd better see a return of my investment or it'll come out of your hides," was Coach's reply.

Shortly before noon we changed back into our jeans and then we ran up the street towards the post office where this vagabond had his wooden wagon, sort of like the sheep wagon you'd see in the western movies, with all of his paraphernalia displayed. What a character he was - scrubby, with a beard and tattered clothes, but his sales pitch was eloquent. Here was a natural born salesman with that critical ability of creating a need within everyone within earshot and being able to negotiate the correct sales price for whatever goods or animals being considered by the townsfolk. This tinker had rabbits, foxes, squirrels, pots, pans, clothing, herbs and snakes. Snakes!

Rego, Butch and I literally went crazy when we spied the slithery creatures in their makeshift cages, and we simply had to have one. Our pulses accelerated and when the tinker opened the cage and gathered this small reptile we couldn't believe our eyes. This vine snake is about a foot long, a quarter inch in diameter, and couldn't hurt a flea. Well, maybe a flea but nothing else would fit down its measly mouth. Other that the fact that it moved the most significant characteristic of the snake was the color. On its back the color was a bright Irish green and its belly was a softer, more yellow-green. It was the cutest "thang" I'd ever seen.

"Hey boys, hold this one for a while. Won't hurt you. Get familiar and you won't be afraid. Put it around your neck and feel it move," said the tinker.

I reply, "Are you out of your mind?" I am terrified at the thought of this thing creeping 'round my body.

Rego says, "Panky, put it 'round your neck and I'll do it too."

Rego always maked me go first and, like a dummy, I did. "Say, it feels weird but not too bad. Tickles and its a strange sensation but, otherwise, I don't mind." Knowing that this was totally strange and unlike anything we'd ever done before we got a wild charge out of it, like we were getting away with something."

"Panky, bet you won't wear that snake around you neck when you go home for dinner, just to scare your folks," Butch challenges us.

"Bet I will too, Butch. I'll wear it and Rego gets to ring the doorbell. When they answer they won't know what's happening until they stare at my neck and see the snake begin to slither."

"Mister, how much do you want for the snake?," we asked.

"Gimme fifty cents and he's all yours. It eats insects and small leaves, so don't go feeding him grits, and stuff like that."

We gave the tinker everything we had, and then proceed to giggle all the way home. Butch went on down to his house and said he'd join us back at the pool later. As we approach Granny's house we stopped to regain our composure, as if we had any to begin with. I coiled the snake around my neck and then proceeded to put on my poker face. Rego and I slowly and quietly walked up the front porch steps when we heard everyone inside the house preparing for the noon dinner. Rego reached up to turn the mechanical doorbell as I stepped squarely in the middle of the front door, with our friend slithering from my shoulders up to my ears.

Our mothers, Lucy and Evelyn, opened the door and said, "What are you two doing now? You never ring the doorbell. Why are you standing in that doorway with those silly grins on your faces? You talk to us, young men. And, what is that thing around your neck, Panky? Granny, come here and look at how strange these two are acting."

At this point the two of them recognized the object around my neck, and their perfectly lipsticked mouths begin to let out screams that could pierce a steel reinforced concrete bunker. These damsels came apart at the seams. Neighbor's doors flew open, cats scurried up the trees, the hens in the backyard flew the coup, and Rego and I fell down laughing. We were choking to death and our stomachs cramped from the strain of our own laughter. It was a marathon of comedy and, by far, the liveliest event to occur on Ida Avenue since a young and well-endowed Miriam Donaldson walked out to retrieve her morning newspaper clad in a very short negligee. Rego and I'll never forget that sight. Think that was the point in our physiological development when we began to feel some serious hormonal changes.

Mom and Aunt Evelyn almost had to be taken to the Mizell Memorial Hospital, and Granny to the couch for respiration, because of our prank. Rego and I assured them that the snake was harmless and we found a glass Ball jar in the kitchen so our little buddy could have a home. Throughout our noon meal Rego and I couldn't keep straight faces. We'd take a few bites of food and then burst into laughter. This pattern was repeated about a dozen times before we were warned that one more outburst would result in a serious switching. This threat settled us down for about five seconds. There was absolutely no hesitation in my mother's and Aunt Evelyn's voices when they emphatically say, "The snake WILL be returned now to that tinker for a full refund, or else."

Do you think that Rego or I questioned the "or else" for one, single minute? We did not. Discretion dictated that we capitulate and get uptown quickly to return our newly acquired friend.

Laughing all the way up Ida Avenue across the empty lot and up to the post office we rehearse what we would say to the tinker. "Sir, our mothers said we can't keep the snake, so can we have our money back?"

"Boys, I don't want a used snake. How can I make a living if everyone returns what they bought? Tell you what. I'll take it back but it'll cost you a quarter for my troubles, so you get only a quarter back. Fair enough?"

It's all right with me, Panky," Rego said.

"Okay Rego, let's get our money back and beat feet back to the pool."

We reluctantly surrendered the snake to the tinker in return for half our investment. Obviously, he was miffed with our return but he made fifty percent on the deal so he could resell the little fella to other idiots, like us. Soon, we left the post office to headed back to the pool but not before stopping at Dean's Pharmacy for a fountain Coke. Nothing, absolutely nothing beat the taste of a fountain Coke along with one of Delia Barganier's chicken salad sandwiches, which were stocked fresh daily on a plate situated atop the fountain. These delicacies consisted of fresh chicken salad spread on Holsum bread, with the crust removed, and then wrapped in Cut Rite wax paper to preserve the flavor. Delia was Granny's sister-in-law who lived next door to us, and this was one way that Delia picks up some extra change.

Next stop was Uncle Johnny's store, right next door to the pharmacy. We loved going into his store and teasing Rego with slogans such as, "See Rue for shoes," or "Rego Rue has holes in his shoes," or "I'm Rego Rue. My dog, Buster, and I live in there too." Silly stuff, but fun. Most of all we want to use Uncle Johnny's shoe X-ray machine to view our feet under the green light, and use the pointer to measure our big and little toes. Uncle Johnny yelled over for us to curtail this activity because he had paying customers who needed to be fitted for shoes. And, our feet were filthy and probably crawling with microscopic creatures just waiting to jump off into his machine.

When we returned to the pool and told Coach Nolen and the lifeguards about our purchase, and the terror that ensued, they couldn't stop laughing. As a matter of fact, they thought it was the funniest thing they've heard in a long time, and their only regret was not being present to witness the hysteria, first hand. Coach said, "Panky and Rego, you're darn lucky that your mothers didn't break your necks after that silly stunt. Maybe your fathers will take care of that personally, knowing them. Nonetheless, it is quite a tale and you two never cease to amaze me with your antics. By the way, go ahead and keep the quarter as good luck. I'll work it out of your hides tomorrow."

So, back to Myrtle and her diving. A much more gentile way to enjoy our leisure afternoons at the pool. First, she performed a beautiful side jack knife, then another half gainer, followed by an Ester Williams type swan dive. Shoot, I couldn't follow this act so around back of the clubhouse for some smokes. Is Coach here or has he gone home for lunch?

Who's got the Pall Malls?

My All Time Hero 'sides Roy, Dale and Gene

was Straight Arrow!

Blue Ribbons I won at Camp Grist, circa 1950

The Whampus Cat and Other Chuckles

"OK boys, tomorrow, bright and early, we leave for Camp Grist. All of your clothes have been marked and tagged with your names. Do you think you'll need anymore underwear, or are there laundry facilities up there?"

"Heck, I don't know, Mom, why don't you just put a couple extra pairs in our bags anyway? Rego, can you hardly wait or what? Have you ever been to camp, or is this your first time too?"

"No, Panky, I've known some kids here in Opp, who went last summer but this'll be my first time, just like you, and I can't wait. We are going to have a whole bunch of fun up there. Some of my buddies told me about the Girl Scout camp across the lake from us and that they raided the girls late at night by stealing the canoes and paddling over in the middle of the night."

"I wonder how long we'll be there. Mom, how long does camp last?"

My mother, Lucy, replied, "Seven days total and I'm sure you two won't miss us for one single minute."

Rego and I looked at one another, grinned, chuckled, and silently left the room before we uttered a reply. Silence in this case was golden. I think I remember running out the front door and tackling Rego right into the pampas grass bush. If our moms only knew the actual degree of excitement we felt they assuredly would have canceled our plans and kept a very close eye on our activities for the remainder of the summer vacation.

We woke the following morning at the crack of dawn because of our restless night's sleep. Our duffel bags were packed. We were dressed. We said good-bye to Granny and Daddy Dean, we had reserved our seats in the back of the station wagon, and, now, we were ready to get the show on the road. This summer was a first. First, in our annals of freedom from home for seven, whole days. Seven days off with the fellows and totally new adventures, and all of it without our parents' presence so we could barely control our emotions. As a matter of fact, we couldn't. We were two, nervous wrecks - two jumping beans trying to remain still in the back of the car. This was not going to be an easy task and we knew that Selma, AL was about two hours away from Opp; and the camp was another half hour out of Selma, up on a hill.

The four of us - Mom, Aunt Evelyn, Rego, and I - packed into Evelyn's station wagon, which was a Chevy woody and painted egg shell blue as I remember, to head up the road through Brantley, stopped at Highland Home for breakfast at Jack's was a treat for us. The only way folks from out of this area ever'd know that Highland Home existed is someone either referred to the tiny hamlet, or they had stopped at Jack's during a previous trip. Highland Home isn't even included on some road maps. As a matter of fact I recently tried to locate this town in my Rand McNally's atlas, but no such luck. In addition to the public school that was set back a few hundred feet from the highway there were only a couple of other buildings, one of which was the Esso station - home of Jack's Cafe. This had been a regular stopover point for many folks between Montgomery and points down this way for the Saturday shopping exodus. That Esso station was the typical white stucco, one story, with the corner of the building constructed from art deco glass bricks and, at one end of the building, was Jack's. This "Main Street Style" of architecture was prominent durin' the fifties, and has recently come back into vogue. And, the decor inside the cafe was rather plain, with linoleum floor, several plastic laminate-topped tables, and the counter provided seats for approximately ten customers. But it was the marvelous aroma of homemade sausage and sugar-cured bacon on the grill that truly aroused the senses especially after a long drive. Those biscuits were freshly made from scratch, the grits weren't runny, the eggs practically chuckled, the milk pasteurized, but not homogenized, so the cream sat on top in your glass. And the freshly brewed coffee kept our parents asking for more servings. To the best of my recollection, Jack's Cafe still exists in the '90's, and so it should . . . simple food for a reasonable fare served up by good ol' country folk.

On the road again towards Selma, and Camp Grist as we witnessed one small wide spot in the road after another, town after town, until we reached the city limits of Selma. Needless to say, our mothers never stopped to inquire about directions, so we spent another half hour riding around in the back seat as they tried to obtain directions out of town and up the hill to the camp. At last, we found the dirt road which was your typical Alabama red clay that eventually found its way through the pine trees, up the hill, round the bend to Camp Grist. Rego and I bolted from the rear of the station wagon, raced up to the main building to meet other boys and Mr. Grist. Yes there really was individual named Grist and he was a man's man. . . tall, handsome, with a pure white head of hair cut in the flattop style. Rego and I introduced ourselves, told Mr. Grist the names of our hometowns and, last but not least, introduced our mothers as a matter of southern courtesy. Mr. Grist advised our parents to come back in seven days around dinnertime so that they could take us home. He also advised our parents that church services would be held on Sunday, and for them not to worry about the logistics of our religious persuasions. Indeed, we would go to Catholic or Protestant services under his guidance. Being a Catholic I was sorely disappointed because I thought this camp was a definite escape from the Sunday rituals observed at least fifty-two times a years, in addition to the Holy Days of Obligation. No matter how hard I tried the monkey called Catholicism made a permanent home on my back.

Our mothers then helped us to unload our duffel bags as they delivered last minute instructions as well as some spending money. Then came the flurry of hugs and kisses right in front of our peers. Yuk! I suppose this was necessary for their peace of mind but it always embarrassed Rego and me

Finally, Lucy and Evelyn hopped back into the Chevy as they probably whispered under their breaths, "Thank heavens, we're free for seven glorious days and I think we should really take advantage of it. Why don't we all go down the coast for a few days. I'm certain that Hank and Johnny will be ready in a heartbeat."

"Evelyn, I thought you'd never ask. Hank will want a few days away from Granny I can assure you. Let's get a move on as soon as we hit Opp. What is the name of that cute hotel in Ft. Walton Beach, the one with the cabins in back? You know the one I'm talking about but I can't remember the name."

"Lucy, I don't care where we stay as long as it's as far away from Granny as possible."

Rego and I gathered along with the throngs of other boys as the counselors read the cabin assignments and we were assigned the Cabin B Team. Each of these rustic wooden cabins housed eight lads, plus one counselor. "Panky, I'll flip you for the top bunk, and I call tails."

"Okay, Rue, let me get this quarter out of my jeans and we'll just see who's sleeping up or down. You called tails, and tails it is. Shucks, I lose again for the five thousandth time."

Rego beat me at almost everything in life and you will see how this trend changes as our lives evolve.

Soon, the remainder of our cabin mates filtered in and chose their bunks and began to store their belongings. We all introduced ourselves and discovered that, for the most part, we all hailed from similar small towns scattered throughout Alabama, with few exceptions such as Mobile, Birmingham, Mobile, or Huntsville. In the relative quiet a much larger and slightly older fellow jaunted through the door and introduced himself as our cabin counselor. He said he was from Phenix City, and that he was our guiding light for the next seven days. This rather young and semi-tough drill instructor type asked, "Does anyone here have cigarettes, chewin' tobacco, or liquor in their bags? I'll take it now if you do because if Mr. Grist discovers where you are holding back he will call your parents immediately, and you'll be outta here, just like that. I know you're too young to buy any beer so I assume there ain't any stored away."

Our reply, in unison, was, "No Bull of the Woods in this group, sir." And that translates into no tobacco with these troops.

In these camps described in the back pages of Boy's Life there are photographs of beautiful log cabin style buildings with forest green awnings. These buildings are surrounded by tall pine trees for as far as you can see, and the buildings are located on the shore of a magnificent, deep blue alpine lake. And, the boys in the photographs are all attired in clean, white tee shirts embossed with the camp logo on the chest, and their moccasins are worn with perfectly clean white socks pulled up over their calves. These young lads, in addition, possess ersatz Third Reich Young folk smiles glued on their freckled faces. Indeed, these images were not, repeat not, Camp Grist. Camp Grist was ever so slightly different in that our primary building resembled a fire station. The pine trees were juxtaposed with scrub oaks and laurel and the lake was down the hill out of view and resembled more of a large, slightly muddy pond. Our facilities were, indeed, that of the YMCA ilk and our brochure that was mailed to entice boys to attend was printed in black and white with a small photo or two of the amphitheater, rifle range, canoes and, of course, our gleaming Mr. Grist. No clean white tee shirts and kids with toothy smiles screwing up our image here folks! This was summer boot camp, 'Bama style. To us, however, the camp was paradise because we were away from home, the dominance of our parents and the teasing of our sisters for a whole week. What trouble could we get into now? That was the sixty-four thousand dollar question. And, we were determined to find the answer(s).

I might add that there wasn't a black child to be seen anywhere. Alabama was segregated not only in philosophies but also in facilities. Hence, no white boys at black camps and vice versa. Somehow I felt that not very many camps catered to black boys in Alabama, in the '50s. Since I had lived in northern and western towns the thought of attending school, or camp for that matter, with boys and girls of different colors and nationalities did not bother me. I never understood segregation then, and I still don't today, especially regarding children.

The supper hour approached so we walked over towards the dining hall only to pass by our community bathroom. This small building was our only facility for showering and for other obvious biological requirements. Adequate, but not very pristine. It would do, and since we had absolutely no intention of maintaining hygiene, the showers really were of little concern to most of us. You know what I liked about the whole camp? The rustic buildings, the red clay soil that inched its way right up to the bases of the pine trees, the trails that led in all directions to the places where our activities were scheduled, and the friendliness of most of the boys. If the camp were constructed today the buildings, in all probability, would be constructed from stucco, with tile roofs, and there would be a distinct addition of concrete paths, patios and other unnecessary physical plant. Instead, Camp Grist was exactly as it should be - slightly remote and rustic and warm in spirit.

"Rue, what do you suppose we'll have for supper; and I wonder how late we can stay up?" I was always interested in the next meal as if it was the biblical last supper, and what would lie ahead in the wee hours long after our counselors had retired for the evening.

"Lordy, Panky, it had better taste like Gladdy Mae's cooking or else we're in for a long week here at camp. To tell you the truth, Miller, I'm so excited that I won't be able to eat for a while anyway. I've dreamed about going away to camp so being here is almost too good to be true. You know what I want to learn while we're here? How to braid those lanyards the lifeguards use to hang their metal whistles around their necks. I don't know how to braid and the counselors teach you in classes. Trouble is what colors do I want in my lanyard? Shucks, don't matter long as it looks good."

During supper, which I remember as being palatable, we were introduced and given a short speech by the larger-than-life, gleaming Ipana-like smile, white-flat-topped Mr. Grist. This man towered above most of us pip-squeaks, and his voice rang true throughout the dining hall. The crux of his talk was about discipline and that our respective cabin counselors had control of our lives for the next seven days mainly because they had our balls in their hands. If we stepped out of line the counselors were to squeeze our family jewels as hard as they could. Mr. Grist got my immediate attention and held it for the greater part of the next seven days. I couldn't think of anything that would accomplish this objective and be more threatening to a group of pre-adolescents than his most informative speech.

Later that evening the full contingency of campers and counselors gathered down at the amphitheater, which was located a few hundred feet from the dining hall, under the tall, fragrant pines.

Lordy, the smell of the pine needles was something I'll never forget and, to this day, I consider being one of the favorite sensations of my olfactory nerve.

Now, the purpose of this gathering was to determine the daily schedules for our various cabin assignments. The counselors took to the stage and began to read aloud. "Boys assigned to Cabin A report to the rifle range at 8:30 in the morning. Cabin C, you report to the archery range at 8:30. Cabin B, you'll be meeting up next to the small shop to learn lanyard weaving, also at 8:30." And, so on. What we were all dying to hear, however, weren't these schedules but were the swimming schedule.

Swimming was the daily event that Rego and I looked forward to the most and I'm certain that our love of the liquid stuff was highly instigated by the countless hours we'd spent at the Opp Municipal Pool. Suddenly, the counselor announced when we were to be unleashed and the mayhem would begin at 10:00 in the morning until 11:30, and from 2:00 until 4:00 in the afternoon everyday, unless it rained. Could we be happier than two pigs in a poke? Twice a day we could revert back to a Darwin-like existence in the eternal quest of those dreaded maladies known as "pink eye", ear infections, stomach cramps, sunburn and physical exhaustion. I almost started shaking with excitement and I don't believe that I had ever swum in a lake before. Ever! Been to the Gulf of Mexico, Atlantic Ocean, many municipal pools but never a huge, deep mountain lake. All I could think of was Tarzan and how he swung down the vines, through the trees, to drop into that quintessential river or lake, only to discover other beings who occupied the same area - like crocodiles, hippos, piranhas, or other creatures that could kill little kids. Shit! Better think twice before running down that hill to the lake and diving into a totally unknown entity. I knew we didn't have those pending threats to our survival in this lake but I still thought that somehow I would be Tarzan, or another wild hero, who would conquer this vast body of uncharted water.

"Lights out, lights out," echoed throughout the camp. The counselors, almost in unison, issued this edict and, even though it was relatively early we were physically exhausted, and ready for sleep. Our minds traveled at 100 miles per hour, so we couldn't possibly slow down long enough for the fatigue to conquer our mental and physical state. As we prepared for our first night's sleep our counselor told us that, after lights out, we would hear a spooky story every night while we were at camp. With that in mind the group in Cabin Bravo took all of about thirty seconds to undress and to jump into our respective bunks. Door shut, lights out, and all you could hear was the rustling of the trees, an occasional whippoorwill, or an owl hooting in the sultry night air. The tension mounted as we awaited the first of many ghost stories that were guaranteed to curdle our blood!

"Tonight, lads, we will introduce y'all to The Whampus Cat, the scariest creature to come down the hill by our lake and wander up to our cabins here at Camp Grist," so said our counselor in a trembling voice designed to literally scare the living shit out of us.

I lay there totally spellbound with my eyes opened as wide as possible. The counselor literally kept us spellbound as we followed him through this tale of terror and the supernatural, and of the possibility that the Whampus Cat could stray into our cabin looking for a meal consisting of young, tender, white males. My nerves were tingling and I couldn't get to sleep for at least twenty to thirty seconds after the conclusion of the story; and I wonder if the beans and franks we ate for supper had anything to do with the recurring nightmares of a carnivorous cat that attacked little boys throughout the night?

"Hit the deck, lads, time to rise and shine. Get out of those bunks and straighten them up. Rego, sweep the floor and Harry, empty the trash can. Let's get finished so we can beat the other cabins to the showers, and still be first for breakfast. We're having flapjacks and bacon, and today I'm real hungry. Everyone be at breakfast by seven thirty."

The group in Cabin Bravo performed like a rocket shot from a canon. In all of about thirty seconds we were dressed, crew cut hair combed with the use of our hands, and chores completed. The usual race began to the showers and then to the dining hall. If one were to take an aerial photo of the ground that image would probably resemble an ant farm, scurrying in every which direction, moving in a totally irrational pattern, and getting nowhere fast. The sum total of our energies would have been sufficient to launch man to the moon. It was total madness, and all this consuming of energy made it possible for us to retire early in the evening without much hesitation or reservation.

After breakfast Rego said, "Panky, I feel sick. Boy, do I have to go dookie, so wait for me here and I'll be back shortly."

Dookie is a southern euphemism meaning human defecation. Need I say more?

Rego didn't look good. He was pale and complained of chills. Then, he made a mad dash for the community bathroom, so I knew he was in real bad shape. After a half hour I figured that it was no use waiting around, so I reported to the rifle range. This area of the camp was situated in a remote part because god only knows where the bullets would fly once those rifles were aimed by preteen, city slicker, snot-nosed brats, some of whom never fired a gun in their lives. I knew that I'd win the rifle competition because of my prowess and expertise learned while listening to the Hashknife Hartley, Straight Arrow, and Roy Rogers radio shows. My aim was keen and my hand, as steady as a rock. But, we weren't handed pearly handled, silver engraved Colts. We were given twenty-two caliber rifles! Holding a rifle was entirely different. It was placed high on your shoulder and the stock adjacent to your chin. The barrel had a sight down on the end which must be aligned with the rear sight above the chamber in order to be aimed correctly. Furthermore, the rifle shot real bullets! My adrenalin was starting to flow, like Niagara Falls, and my confidence was waning rapidly.

As I sat there on the bench waiting for my turn to fire the rifle a counselor yelled "Panky, move fast, there's a snake under your feet." I sprang up about six feet (should have won the high jump ribbon then and there) and watched this object slither in the area of the sand where my feet had just rested. The counselor took my rifle and he fired six rapid rounds into and around that snake as we all watched in horror. I mean, really! This little guy was pumped full of holes, deader than a doornail. Sure, I was scarred, but so was the little snake. The counselor indicated that this was a poisonous snake called a moccasin which was indigenous to this area. We were all previously briefed by our counselors that poisonous reptiles were omens of the devil, but not the non-poisonous species, such as the indigo or vine snakes. I ask you. How were these little buggers to know if they were good or bad?

A few minutes later after I stopped trembling we settled back down to business and then it was my turn on the rifle range. Ask me how I performed. Better yet, please don't because my ego was bruised and a city kid, from Baltimore, could have better scores than this humbled sharpshooter. Pitiful, pitiful scores at only fifty yards. A sorry excuse for a country kid. Well, I wasn't really a country kid. Even though I had lived mostly in suburban areas of large cities I was Huckleberry Finn or Tom Sawyer at heart. I always considered myself to have a dead aim with a firearm. This time, however my nerves had been rattled not by a rattler, but by a moccasin. Tomorrow was another day, however, and I still had the rest of time at camp to redeem myself. But today remained a disaster.

Rego still hadn't appeared on the scene and I never gave it a second thought. Perhaps he had decided to braid lanyards or something else that kept him close to the bathroom. After the rifle competition was completed, we walked back to check in the rifles and ammunition.

Our counselor walked up to advise me that Rego was back at the cabin with the "scoots." He was in sad shape and that it looked like the flu or something else that would ruin his stay. Later that day, we began our marathon melee down to the lake to swim, splash, wrestle, and to dive from the floating pier until our legs were virtually unable to support our meager torsos. Where was Rego? Still back up the hill saying "hello" to the commode. When the lifeguard blew the final whistle we began our run back up the hill to prepare for other camp activities, and to have supper. That run back up the hill never seemed as much fun nor did we reach lightnin' speed as the bolt down not because of the natural laws of gravity but because of the synergy caused by young boys' attraction to water molecules. I returned to our cabin to discover that Rego was one, sick kid. He had visited the camp nurse and the diagnosis was the Camp Grist flu. So much for the remainder of Rego's time at camp. While the rest of us were running, shooting, eating, swimming, braiding, weaving, reading, old Rego was performing his own four-event marathon consisting of running, sitting, crapping, and puking!

A couple of days passed by as I managed to pick up several first places in three track and field events. If my memory serves me correctly the events in which I excelled were the fifty-yard dash, the high jump (surely from previous experience at the rifle range), and the broad jump. The truth is the primary reasons for my awards were the absence of Rego, my toughest competitor. Had he been fit I might have settled for second place in one or more events. The fact remains, however, that I was the undisputed champion in the Camp Grist Olympic Games Track and Field, and the awards would be distributed during the last night's ceremonies. This was worth the trip to camp alone, because winning these events made me feel like a million dollars. I was always the runt, the skinny kid, the one who was always passed over for selection on the football or baseball team, the one who couldn't compete with his peers, or so I thought. These victories proved that not all kids were created equal, and that I actually ruled supreme in those track and field events.

I took those blue ribbons home that summer and my mother placed them in a safe spot - for about forty years. Just this past fall she returned them along with several other bits of memorabilia for my scrapbook.

Rego confined his diet to clear liquids, mostly 7 Up and soups. My oh my, this boy was sick of this restrictive intake, but then again, Rue was just plain sick. About the only time we would see him was in his bunk back in Cabin Bravo at the end of the day. The third or fourth night, as we were preparing to hit the sack, our counselor warned us of the impending horror tale that created heart attacks even among youngin's. This tale was about "Von Doom and the Blue-Gummed Niggers," the most frightening tale of all times! And, this was an understatement as he began to describe the monster in Dickensonian terms. This creature ate children, wild and domestic animals - everything in its path - after cooking them in a cauldron of boiling oil! Can you imagine Rego hearing this on top of a bad stomach? We all knew that his sleep would be interrupted with races to the bathroom, several hundred feet away from our cabin. This left plenty of opportunities for Von Doom to snatch Rego from under our noses and carry him off for the fate that none of us could comprehend.

Speaking of deep sleep, mine was suddenly interrupted by a screaming boy sitting on top of me while he was yelling, "Where's my tool box, where's my tool box?" His hands were tight around my throat and the air had been squeezed from my lungs. Couldn't scream. Couldn't breath. I was helpless and scared shitless. My eyes bulged out of their sockets and I thought this was it. By this time, the counselor jumped out of his bunk, ran over, and grabbed Rego.

"Rego, what you doing boy? Wake up. You're having a nightmare."

"I'm all right now. Must have been a nightmare. Sorry, Panky, I thought you were stealing my toolbox. The one I had in Bryn Mawr, when we were younger. Hope I didn't hurt you."

"That's okay, Rego, I'm not hurt. But you sure scared hell out of me and, soon as I stop shaking, I'm goin' back to sleep." All of our cabin mates were wide-awake and cracking up with laughter. This hysteria lasted for about an hour and I giggled throughout the night and for most of the following day. Rego never did make it through the night without bolting from our cabin and breaking land speed records to the bathroom. Served him right. This toolbox must have been something really special for him to carry its memory as his personal luggage for many years. How dare he accuse me of the perpetrator of this felonious theft? For years we have laughed about this incident, and one of these days, I'm going to buy Rego a special toolbox of his very own.

Next morning, while we were having breakfast, Mr. Grist approached our table in the great dining hall and said, "Aren't you Panky Miller, from Opp? I hear you play the piano. Is that correct?"

A lump formed in my throat as I said very softly, "Yes sir, but I don't play very well."

"That's not what I hear, young man. We're having a skit during our last night's ceremonies and you have been elected to play and dress like Al Jolsen. Please report down to the stage at the amphitheater to try out the piano and your costume. We should have a great show for the camp, and I'm personally looking forward to hearing you play that piano."

I tried to finish my supper while the knot in my stomach grew larger. Lord God almighty! This was big time entertainment and my only previous audiences had been little old ladies who attended piano recitals on Sunday afternoons out of sheer boredom. Now, I was on the block. Not only did I have to play the piano in front of hundreds of my peers but, in addition, I had to don this ridiculous costume and paint my face black. In terms of pressure and anxiety this performance was on the same level as auditioning for a movie or a musical on Broadway. How did I get roped into playing for this event? Did Rego spill the beans? Was he trying to get even with me? Was this his way of settling the score because of his illness and my blue ribbon performances?

Perhaps this is one of Rego's best-kept secrets through the years and we'll possibly learn of its outcome only moments before he is laid to rest. Nonetheless, I was going to have a most humiliating experience, one that would promote a thousand laughs from the "peanut gallery" as I attempted to complete several boogie woogie tunes - error free - and look like Al Jolsen at the same time. Suddenly, I began to sweat bullets.

Well, psychiatrists indicate that whenever asked a question and your first response is "Well", it is an excuse to buy time. They are absolutely correct. The big day finally arrived and I reported to the back stage area for the final preparation with my costume and make-up. Putting on that black oily gook was loads of fun as my hands turned the same color. The came the white mouth. Another mess and the white make-up crept into the surrounding black creating an abstract version of what would best be described as the anal area of a zebra! We're talking major butterflies and these butterflies simply refused to fly in formation in my stomach and the thought of barfing was not out of the question.

Here you have literally everyone attending camp, the counselors, the kitchen help, Mr. Grist and Rego, sitting in the audience under the pines and the moonlight screaming and shouting at every person who ventured onto the stage. Some poor boys were selected to read poems while others were asked to sing a few camp songs that they were rehearsing for the very first time on stage only to be followed by Mr. Grist taking the microphone to say, "Now, we have as our last number Panky Miller performing some Al Jolsen tunes on the piano. Panky is from Opp, and let's give him a big round of applause."

Applause? Sounded more like a few boys swatting fireflies in their hands as I walked onto the stage. My hands trembled and, thank God, I had a bench because my knees began to buckle out of sheer fright. I concentrated on the keys (which resembled my face - black/white and blurry) as my fingers blazed across the keys. Not a mistake and I was on fire! The musical notes and beat captured my audience as the boys began to clap in syncopated rhythm as my smile with the white greasy make-up grew larger and my eyes bulged out of their sockets. The final applause fell far short of deafening but the boys yelled for more. I had exhausted my repertoire so the gig was completed. I stood up, politely bowed, and repaired to back stage as I began to remove the gooey sticky black and white grease. Mr. Grist proceeded to walk onto the stage to thank those of us who performed and to make the final presentations and awards for this camp session.

Here sat Rego, probably for the first time in his life, with zero accomplishments to his credit for the week. Can you imagine his humiliation as those of us who won awards walked up to accept the first, second, and third prizes? I had won three blue ribbons in track and field.

"Panky, if I hadn't been sick you probably would not have won those blue ribbons."

My retort was, "That's just fine, Rue, but the fact remains I did and you didn't, so there. No doubt about it, though. You should have won first place blue ribbons for dookying, puking, and snoring!"

Next morning came all too quickly because this was the day when our parents arrived to retrieve us for the long drive home. We did everything possible in order to plan our getaway down the hill to escape from our parents. Car after car began to arrive from every conceivable county throughout Alabama, as the boys greeted their families in various ways - some tearful that camp was over, some happy to see their folks, some silent with the typical body language of boys, and then there were those who ran and hid - like Rego and me. Let's face it. We firmly believed our parents were simply going to drive for two hours from Opp, ask Mr. Grist our whereabouts, hear that we deserted camp, only for them to get back into the Woody and return to Opp, empty handed. Seemed like a good plan to us but, after hiding under our cabin for several minutes, we decided to capitulate and face the music.

"Rego, Panky, you get your tails out here this very minute. What do you think you're doing? Get your duffel bags, thank your counselor and Mr. Grist, say good-bye to your friends and get into this car. Now, get moving! You two look like you didn't bathe for a week. I know there are showers up here so I simply can't understand why you look like hoboes. Evelyn, do you notice a distinct odor in this car? Seems to me that we have a couple of piglets, not young men, for the long, hot ride home."

Roy Rogers Riders Club Prayer

Oh Lord, I reckon I'm not much just by myself.

I fail to do a lot of things I ought to do.

But Lord, when trails are steep and passes high,

Help me to ride it straight the whole way through.

And when in the falling dusk I get the final call,

I do not care how many flowers they send -

Above all else the happiest trail would be

For You to say to me, "Let's ride, my friend."

Amen

Roy and Trigger

D. C. To Dixie

The year was 1954 and I was in the 7th grade. My classmate, Chuck, and I had just completed our daily baseball practice out on the Bethesda Municipal Golf Course. We were very fortunate to have this monstrous open area only a few blocks from our houses, so the golf course became our playground for hours and hours everyday after school. This area backed up to the National Institute of Health, and there were zillions of new windows to break as we practiced our curve, fast, slider, knuckle and spit ball pitches until our arms were numb.

"Chuck, Panky is getting ready to have supper, so it's time for you to run along now."

"OK Mrs. Miller. I'll see you at school tomorrow, Panky."

Chuck was one of those kids you tolerated. He wasn't very nice. He didn't have many friends. He was basically a creep but a necessary creep in my life. Being a military kid moving from town to town every two or three years I needed all the instant buddies I could get. So, Chuck was a temporary friend. Chuck was about my size. . . small frame, blonde hair, sinewy, tough as nails, and insecure like me. He lived about a mile away in the typical eastern-colonial style house. Anyway, we were classmates and spent much time as a team reigning terror in the neighborhood and in school. We were always in detention hall. Always in trouble. Small insignificant trouble but still trouble as defined by the Papal archdiocese, in Washington, D.C.

To tell you what kind of a guy Chuck really was, he stole my one and only prized Rawlings baseball glove, scratched up the back, changed some of the lacing, and then had the audacity to say it was his glove that he bought it from some kid at Bethesda Chevy Chase Chase High. I never accused him to his face of stealing my glove. What kind of friend would steal his best friend's baseball glove? Only a total asshole.

After breakfast one morning my mother said, "How would you like to ride the bus down to Granny's this summer? Dad and I thought you were old enough to take the Greyhound to Opp, as long as you don't have to make too many changes enroute."

When she picked me off the floor I replied, "Are you kidding me? Shoot, I'd love to go, so when can I leave? Will Granny pick me up? What's the story?"

"I'll get the scoop from Greyhound and check with Granny to make sure you are picked up regardless of where the bus stops. You leave this Saturday, right after school lets out for the summer. I know you can't wait to see Rego, Aunt Evelyn, Uncle Johnny, Daddy Dean, and Granny. The sooner you leave the more time you'll have in Opp."

My heart was literally in my throat and I couldn't believe my own ears. For Mom and Dad to grant this much freedom had to say one of two things, or both. They trusted me enough to allow this solo journey, or they wanted to get me the hell out of Bethesda, as soon as possible. Can't for the life of me understand why they didn't just fly me down to Montgomery, except for the fact that mom was terrified of flying. I had my bags packed in about fifteen minutes after hearing this marvelous, too good to be true, proposition. I packed my suitcase, unpacked it, and repacked it, again and again. Got all of my comics ready to go. Made sure I had my Levi's, tee shirts, tennis shoes and BVD's. And, a toothbrush. Didn't need a hairbrush . . . only had a crew cut. I'd wait until I reached Opp, before buying what would become my basic wardrobe for three months - a bathing suit.

Couldn't sleep that night and I didn't put away much in the way of breakfast because my stomach was nervous. The big day wouldn't be here for another twenty-four hours, so there was still a lot of time to contemplate the adventure of my measly lifetime. The journey through the southern countryside and the small towns in Dixie that eventually lead to Opp, my favorite place in the whole world. Was I going to miss my so-called friend Chuck, and the rest of the gang from school? I began counting the hours until mom drove me down to buy the ticket. Apprehensive? Yes! Nervous? No. Excited? To the maximum! Mom made sure that I looked presentable in some new clothes she bought just for the trip because, as always, we didn't want the general public to infer Panky Miller was ill bred.

"Panky, I'll be warming up the Buick so get your bags and I'll see you in the car. Hurry it up. Jerry is in the backyard so why don't you go and say good-bye to him. He'll miss you so much this summer."

My dog, Jerry, a wire-haired fox terrier, was the apple of my eye. My parents bought him from a kennel in Virginia Beach, VA when I was in the first grade. Jerry was, undoubtedly, my very best friend, always doing his own thing, in his shy way. I was going to miss him but we were always used to going our separate ways. Unfortunately, I wasn't aware at this time that this would be our last few minutes together, because Jerry would meet his demise in the heavy traffic on Georgetown Road during the next couple of weeks. I didn't hear about his death until I returned from Opp, because my folks didn't think I could handle the news while on vacation. When I heard the news I must have cried for days because my best friend had left me, forever. I don't have a vivid recollection of Jerry the last time we were together.

"Mom, how much money will I have on the bus? And, how long is the trip? Will I be spending the night on board the Greyhound?"

"I'll give you twenty dollars for food and emergencies. Don't spend it all at your first stop or it'll be a mighty long and hungry trip for you, son. A word of advice. Try not to eat anything fishy or greasy so it won't upset your stomach, and you can call me collect on the phone it you have an emergency. Just ask the driver to help you. I'll call Granny with the route number, and the time it will arrive so you won't have to worry."

Can you imagine how I felt walking into the main Greyhound terminal, downtown Washington, D.C., in 1954? It was one scary experience. If you took every conceivable form of mankind imaginable they would eventually stroll into a bus station: Fat, thin, black, brown, white, rich, poor, well-groomed, slobs, fashionable, perfumes, body odor, sober, drunk, young and old. All walks of life from every corner of the globe. Everything I had been taught about sociology and geography was being put to the test today. Here I stood, lily white, 13 years old, innocent, very, very Catholic, the original preppie, as the ticket master asked, "Where are you headed, young man? "

I replied, "Opp, Alabama, sir, to see my grandparents and cousins for the summer."

"Here's your ticket and your mother can escort you out onto the bus ramp heading for Atlanta."

At last, the final few minutes, as we headed towards the gate where the ominous transports were parked.

"Sir, are you the driver of this bus?"

"Yes ma'am, would you like for me to keep an eye on this young man during the trip? He can sit here right behind me so we can talk, and he'll be just fine. I do this everyday and most folks seem to have a real good time on my trips. What's your name, son?"

"Panky Miller, and I'm heading for Opp, Alabama. Does this bus go that far?"

"No, we go as far as Atlanta. Then you'll have to change busses to Trailways, and maybe change again there, in Montgomery. I'll check your bag and you can put your carry-on with your magazines in the overhead rack. We'll be leaving in just a few minutes."

Ten minutes to say good-bye and to contemplate this excursion across America. What a rush I was getting from all this excitement. It was as if I had broken the tie that binds and had reached freedom at last. Let's get this bus on the road. After hugs and kisses from Mom I boarded the blue-white turkey, otherwise known as the Greyhound, and sank into my oversized, fully-adjustable, reclining, seat that was situated directly behind the driver. He looked sharp in his Greyhound uniform, was very polite, about forty years old, and from the northeast. No southern accent was detected so I assumed he was from this area. As he closed the big swinging front door I waved good-bye to mom for the last time and we rolled out of the parking lot on our journey. What a view. High up of the streets, over the tops of the cars, you could see things as never before. Nothing to block your vision. And, the air conditioning was fabulous. We didn't have the luxury of this amenity in either house or car, so this cool air was a real treat for me.

Unless you have traveled by bus you most likely have never really seen the people or the country, as you should. Can't watch all of those people and scenery if you driving - too much concentration on keeping the car on the road. And flying removes you completely from the realism of travel. The bus however provides you with the opportunity to really witness and experience travel at its best. Travel with a capital "T". Some folks say that travel by air shrinks the time when it, in fact, really shrinks the people. When you fly you do not have the opportunity to learn about the various cultures, the languages, the dialects, the smells, and the sounds. And, the changing of the clouds, the temperature, the humidity, all of those things that alert our senses to new experiences. So, flying really shrinks people rather than time because we diminish our ability to expand our horizons. Talk about the sights. Here we were passing the streetcars, the fabulous monuments and government buildings, the Little Tavern cafes that I frequented everyday after school, the beautiful tree-lined streets of Capitol Hill, and the other surrounding neighborhoods of Washington.

About this time when we were crossing into Virginia, the passengers on board began to relax and started conversations with those sitting in adjacent seats. This period in our history was during the era when black men and women were required by law to sit in the very back of the bus, and were not to fraternize with the white passengers. "To the back of the bus, boy," was heard much to often. This was, also, an era when smoking cigarettes was in vogue and almost everyone on board, save a few of the ladies, took out their Pall Malls, Camels, Picayunes, or whatever, and lit up. The smoke mixed with the air conditioning which was very unpleasant, and today it wouldn't be tolerated, but then again we're going back to the days when an individual's health was relative to other issues deemed more significant, like a good puff.

Let me tell you what you're missing if you travel by plane. All of the panoramas are opened not only to your vision but, also, to your imagination. When you travel past the various monuments, such as the one named in honor of George, or Abraham, or of the battle of Iwo Jima, your mind begins to play tricks. You begin to reenact the battles of Concord, the crossing of the Delaware, the Yankee victory at Appomattox, and the Japanese retreating from the beaches in the South Pacific. The streets whizzed by and soon we were out in the wide-open country bound for all points South, through Tyson's Corner, down towards Richmond, and Charlottesville VA; all of the names of the towns were familiar. . . Manassas, Mt. Vernon, Falls Church, Bull Run, Quantico. Counting telephone poles was another easy way to pass the time when you were tired of talking with your seatmate about school, or hobbies, or your family.

The thought of a nap was ridiculous. My nervous energy prevented such a luxury and so I was always looking out of the window just to wile away the time. Did you know that state laws require busses to stop at all railroad crossings? And, I mean every crossing, from Maine to Miami, from Norfolk to Newport Beach. Do you have any idea of how many railroad crossings exist in this land of ours? All you have to do is ride the bus cross-country to understand why the bus stops about every fifteen minutes during its journey, regardless of how long the route actually takes. For example, if your travel time is twenty-four hours you will stop at least ninety-six times **plus** the numerous times for passengers who are standing by the highway to board, **plus** the red lights, **plus** the scheduled stops. By the time you arrive at the final destination you have heard the air brakes of the bus at least a thousand times, and you will never forget for the rest of your life the smell of burning asbestos from those brakes for the rest of your life.

My excitement still was keeping the fatigue from setting in, and I wanted to stay awake for as long as possible so I wouldn't miss anything along the way. I always wondered who the folks were who waited to board, and where they were headed, whenever the bus stopped along the country roads. Some were obvious farm hands because of their odoriferous presence as they walked be me towards an empty seat. We're talking real body odor here, folks. It was as if a green cloud followed them down the isle. Whew! Our first scheduled stop was about to occur and we began to slow down in order to make the first turn-off onto the gravel in front of the country bus station.

"Folks, we're at Quantico, Virginia, and those debarking here can claim their bags inside the depot. For those continuing on to Atlanta, we'll be here for about thirty minutes."

Great, just enough time to look at the trinkets and to buy a snack because I was damn hungry by now. It was mid-afternoon and I was dying for a greasy hamburger and fries, ignoring what mom cautioned me about. I placed my order at the counter and then proceeded to wander over to the rack and eye the girlie magazines. Quickly, I came to the conclusion that it was best to move over to the comic book section to act as an ersatz cold shower. I had just enough time to gulp down my greasy cheeseburger and fries before reboarding the bus just to count what seemed like zillions of railroad crossings, and more stops. The driver began shifting through all of the gears, we were building speed, the speedometer was passing through fifty miles per hour and our high speed cruise began only to be interrupted by yet another one of those familiar circular yellow road signs with the black "X" indicating what hazard lay ahead. You guessed it. More railroad tracks, more delays, more frustration because I was in a hurry to get to Opp, so I could visit my cousins, grandparents and friends.

It was getting to the point where all of these towns, counties and states were beginning to blur, and I no longer was aware of what State line we had crossed, whether we had left Virginia for North Carolina, South Carolina, or Tennessee. The humming of the tires along the blacktop, and the humming of the telephone poles that we sped by rang in my ears constantly. The countryside was typically eastern, southern and rural with the all too familiar Kudzu vine encompassing literally everything in its path. This invasive green ivy-like plant was developed to halt erosion in the southern soil but no one ever discovered how to restrict its growth. Eventually, the vine surely would cover the continent coast to coast, strangling everything along the way. I must admit, however, that the vine was beautiful as it crept up the red clay banks alongside the roads with its huge leaves glistening in the sunlight, and in the luminescence of moonlight. The deep green color provided a perfect contrast to the red clay soil, the whitewashed fences of the farms, and the asphalt shoulders of the highways. Mother nature, again, had done the right thing in pleasing the eye and the soul, albeit not the landowners who had to cope with a species gone haywire.

One of our scheduled stops was down in Taccoa, Georgia, which was the home of the world's strongest man. I think his name may have been Paul Anderson, and all of the magazines said he could lift a truck. That's right, an entire truck shown by the photographs in the papers, *Boy's Life,* and other magazines. This was Taccoa's claim to fame and now when I hear of that town the first thing that comes to mind is Paul Anderson standing there with this truck on his back. As a 13 year old boy weighing a maximum of eighty pounds soaking wet, I was duly impressed by anyone who could lift a truck. So much for Taccoa, and it was time to move on down the road. Not too many more miles but countless telephone poles and railroad crossings until we could stretch our legs for that fifteen or twenty minutes at a whack.

"You are now entering the City of Atlanta," so read the sign as we zipped down the highway, and my pulse raced to unhealthy heights. One would have thought that this was the end of the line for me but far from it because we had several more hours until we arrived in Montgomery. Then, I suppose another bus change to Opp. Nonetheless, I was anxious to debark this thing we called home for the past twenty-four hours, and to stretch our legs. The Atlanta depot would be a welcome sight and, boy, was I looking forward to a good, hot meal, with the emphasis on good, not necessarily hot. The dining experiences over the past day and night left much to be desired and I'd rather not go into the details about how horrible most of the food tasted at those various depots stretching from Washington, down to Atlanta. Suffice it to say that the food was crummy. As we wound through the street approaching downtown Atlanta, we saw the magnificent buildings, the lovely antebellum houses, and the flowering dogwood trees. Atlanta was larger in both population and geography than Washington, and had the reputation of equal sophistication. I had relatives who lived in nearby Decatur. My paternal aunt and uncle, Uncle Bill and Aunt Jo, and my two cousins, Billy and Tommy, lived there but it never crossed my mind to inform them of my arrival so that we could possibly visit for a few hours. Heck, it was too late so I'd just look around in the shops, and take a walk down the street to Rich's Department Store, the biggest and best in the South.

Thank goodness the restaurant in the bus station had good southern food. I must have devoured five pieces of delicious fried chicken, with side orders of field peas, mashed potatoes, cornbread, tomatoes sliced with onions soaked in vinegar, and other foods that I missed for nine months of the year. I located the corner where the curios, magazines, and candy were sold. Why is it that every town has these satin pillowcases depicting local heroes, monuments or natural wonders? On top of that someone had the audacity to add gold fringe along the borders. We're talking ugly and I can't imagine anyone who would buy these souvenirs, but people do or they wouldn't still be in business. And the ceramic teepees which have Atlanta, or Stone Mountain, or the Cyclorama painted on the exterior. What in the hell does Atlanta have to do with a ceramic Indian teepee, I ask you? All across America these souvenirs were for sale and I have yet to see anyone buy a single one. A mystery of the cosmos, indeed. Of course, I could always buy a thimble for Granny which was made of some cheap metal alloy with some building, like the capitol dome, embossed on the circumference. Lordy, there wasn't one single thing left to buy for my grandmother. Only one thing left was a crummy postcard that she could keep as a memoir.

Back on the bus and on our way to Montgomery, "The Cradle of the Confederacy." Time enroute . . . four and one-half hours, estimated, as we bade farewell to Atlanta, and the magnificent countryside was, once again, our own personal panorama. Towns like Fayetteville, Newnan, Pine Mountain, La Grange, Opelika, Auburn, Tuskegee, were our scheduled stops as the topography went from flat to hilly to small mountains back to the plains of Alabama. Every small hamlet, every railroad crossing, every bus depot, every country store, every town water tank, every shanty and farmhouse had its own personal signature, albeit southern in character. And, more and more humming down that blacktop passing the endless parallel lines of telephone poles converging into a point over the horizon. Field after field of cotton waiting to be picked juxtaposed to tall yellow corn burning in the heat of the southern sun, rows of soybeans that eventually became an ingredient in almost everything we consumed or applied to our bodies. And, peanuts, my heavens, peanuts that were the staple of America. We ate them roasted, creamed into butter, boiled and ground. My favorite of all the crops grown in this region, however, was sugarcane. I can't think of a more delicious sweet than sucking the sugar right from the stalk while spitting the husks onto the ground. Messy and uncouth, but damn good.

Shortly after three o'clock we arrived at the Montgomery depot and just in time to catch the last Trailways bus heading South towards the Gulf of Mexico, and Opp, my destination. I grabbed my bags and made certain that the bus I was boarding was the right one and would eventually arrive in Opp.

"Sir, is this the bus to Opp?"

The driver said, "Sure is, sonny, and you're not a minute too soon. That bus from Atlanta almost made you late enough to miss this bus, which means you'd have to catch another one tomorrow."

Butterflies hit my stomach like you can't imagine! What would have I done if I'd missed that bus to Opp? Spend the night on a bench in the depot? Walk the streets of Montgomery, all night long and cook breakfast with the hoboes in the train yard? At this point I was extremely thankful that we were still able to make that bus. My state of panic was finally subsiding. Throughout this portion of my trip I had the luxury of sitting alone and not having to worry about making conversation with my fellow travelers for hours upon end. This situation was about to change because the bus was going to have a full contingency of passengers and the seat adjacent to mine was one of the few still vacant. One of the last passengers to board was a man, probably in his late twenties, red hair, red freckles, weathered skin, crows feet 'round his eyes, a cowboy-style plaid shirt, Levis, boots . . .and only one eye. Only one eye! Where most everyone had two eyes, he had just one eye and the other socket was missing an eyeball! Naturally, he headed straight for me and asked, "This seat taken, boy?"

I tried my damndest not to stare, to regain my composure, and to reply, unemotionally, "No sir, it's all yours."

He threw his duffel bag in the top overhead rack, sat down and, after a few minutes, asked where I was from and where I was headed. My parents always taught me it was impolite to stare at people but, in this case, I couldn't help it. "I live in Bethesda, Maryland, just outside of Washington, and I'm heading down to Opp, to spend the summer with my relatives. This is my first bus trip alone and I've been traveling since yesterday morning. Where are you from, and where are you going?"

"I'm heading down to Florida, to work in the fields. My family has a farm and it's time for the harvest, so I'm going down to help 'em. I've been through Opp, many times on my way to Kinston, where I have kinfolk. Do you know where that is?"

"Sure do, and the man who bought my granddaddy's drugstore is from Kinston. I usually get to spend the summers with my grandparents and my cousins, but sometime we get transferred too far away for me to come visit. My daddy's a Naval officer, so we travel a lot. I really look forward to the times when I come down to Opp, so I can swim everyday, go to the matinees, and eat lots of great food cooked by Gladdy Mae, my granny's maid."

This was my life's story. Didn't want to talk about school, 'cause I hated school. Didn't want to talk about my friends 'cause they weren't really my true friends. All I really wanted to talk about was my dog, Jerry, and my summers with my real friends, Uncle Johnny, Aunt Evelyn, cousins Rego, Stevie and Carol, and Granny and Daddy Dean.

Two hours into the trip we both dozed off. Upon awakening, I could tell by the towns we passed and, as we turned at the junction with about eight or ten more miles left to go, I began to get fidgety. Couldn't site still for the life of me and I began to mildly hyperventilate. After traveling through five states for over twenty-four hours I was about as excited as a boy could be. We stopped at everyone of those cotton-picking railroad crossings, all stop lights, all stop signs, until those final few hundred yards that would bring us to the Opp depot.

I almost jumped out of the bus window when my neighbor with one eye said, "Panky, don't ever forget who you are and where you're from. You're a smart kid with a good education and you've got good kinfolk to take care of you. I know that my eye scares you, but it doesn't scare me, so try to remember how other people feel about themselves. It's not how a person looks that makes 'em good or bad.

It is what's inside and in their hearts that makes them good, decent folk. You remember what I told you and you'll be all right down the road. Take care of yourself, boy."

I looked him straight in his good eye and replied, "I sure will and you do the same. Hope you can help your family down in Florida. I see my grandmother and cousins, so I'll see you later." I grabbed my bag and comics, and scurried down the steps as fast as I could into my grandmother's arms amidst the shouts from Rego that he could hardly wait to go the pool tomorrow.

Nearly thirty hours, thousand of railroad crossings, millions of telephone poles, acres of kudzu vine, countless greasy hamburgers and Cokes, incessant humming of the bus tires and the telephone poles, numerous stops in the country for passengers, two bus changes, smelly cigarette smoke mixed with the air conditioning, several very nice and professional bus drivers, and honest man with more vision from his one eye that most people have with two, I was home at last.

The End . . . almost!

TWO

Sangley Point Slumber Party Girls, 1956

High School Confidential

We were living in Bethesda, MD and my dad was stationed at the Pentegon. He received official orders to report to Naval Air Station Sangley Point, Philippine Islands, "No later that 30 June 1955." I gotta tell you that I was one, excited kid ready to depart on the adventure of a lifetime far from the basic little assholes with whom I attended Our Lady of Lourdes Elementary School, in Bethesda, Maryland. I was ready for a change because of my stereotypical existence in a white bread world known as the D.C. suburbs. Can you imagine an eighth grader having the opportunity to sever the bonds of Boy Scouts, of daily ritualistic Rosarys, of life at the local bowling alley, to enter a world of virtual unknown tribes of people who spoke a language you'd never heard of? Shit! I began to read everything I could get my hands on about the Philippines - its customs, languages, geography, climate, history and experiences during the war with the Japanese. My appetite for adventure would rival that of a young Indiana Jones, except that I did not purport to have nearly the experience and world travel as he. Still, as the days counted down until we boarded the train to San Francisco, I began to separate myself, both spiritually and physically, from my classmates. These little twits would continue on with their ever so Catholic lives while this cowboy was about to enter a world fourteen thousand miles to the West.

After spending a few weeks down in Opp, with Granny and Rego, my parents, my little brother, Richard, and I arrived in San Francisco for the fourteen day voyage across the Pacific. We were assigned passage aboard the USS Barrett, a Military Sea Transport Service vessel, which began an out-of-body experience for this entering high school freshman. The huge gray vessel was docked at the pier on Ft. Mason directly across from Alcatraz, on the northern San Francisco waterfront and she awaited our boarding just a couple day's away. We checked into the Sir Francis Drake Hotel, one block off Union Square, and my mother was in seventh heaven with all of the magnificent shops surrounding the hotel. San Francisco has always held a special place in my soul ever since living a few miles down the peninsula in Los Altos, in 1950. That was when I was in the fourth grade - San Antonio Elementary. As a special treat, Dad would pack us into the car and we would spend the day around Union Square while shopping in the City of Paris for the delicious French pastries called Napoleons, at I. Magnin's for clothes, and the Cutlery Store for Swiss Army knives. Then, we would drive over to Chinatown for lunch at a famous restaurant near St. Mary's Church, usually the Cathay House. This was, perhaps, the era when San Francisco was at her finest - men in suits and women in fancy dresses sporting gloves and hats - always. The color, the sights, the romance of San Francisco forever.

Well, the big day finally, arrived and hundreds of families proceeded down the concrete pier as the Navy band played to entertain those of us boarding and those family members who were present to bid farewell. My heart was pounding and I could tell that I was definitely second generation Navy because I coveted the idea of being at sea in something larger than a Chesapeake Bay skiff searching for oysters. The MSTS Barrett departed Ft. Mason on schedule and we sailed under the Golden Gate just in time for a magnificent sunset. Boy oh boy, did the rocking and rolling of the ship begin to take its toll on my tummy. For the next five days I walked around the decks with the proverbial brown bag sticking out of my back pocket.

After we began to meet our young peers at the dining tables some of us decided that it maybe a good idea to form a teen club on board because there were many of us entering the horny little teen years who shared the same excitement and military destinations-Guam, Okinawa, Sangley Point, Subic Bay, Clark Air Base. This eventual congregation of rock and roll cats led to several on-board romances that would endure for two years, or longer, while our fathers served out their obligation before returning to stateside.

Mine began with a lovely girl named Kay who I met in the teen club. She and her family were heading to Clark Air Force Base in the interior. Most of the places I had never heard of including Clark. She became my puppy love for almost 14 days. We would dance, attend movies, eat our meals together and take long walks around the ship. One night she asked me to come down to her stateroom where she was babysitting some infants who were fast asleep. We sat and talked and suddently I said something about kissing. Her reply was, "I wish someone would kiss me!" Did I hear her pleas of begging her to be kissed? Of course I did but I was too nervous to do anything about it. To this day I have regreted that moment.

As we approached the seas closer to the Philippines the ship announced where we were going to stop so those aboard could take a swim. We were directly over the Mariannas Trench – the deepest part of the Pacific ocean – almost 30,000 feet deep. The ship pulled to a halt and the crew lowered a ladder alongside the port so we could walk down to a small landing and dive in. I can't remember whether or not my girlfriend joined in but I certainly did. The feeling of swimming in water that is 30,000 feet deep is eery and scary. All I could think of was the giant squid from the Creatures of the Black Lagoon swimming up, grabbing me with the huge tentacles, and dragging me to the bottom. This is the time I swam back at full speed to the ship and to safety.

After nearly fourteen days at sea, we finally arrived at the various ports of call with much apprehension and a wee bit of melancholy. Some of the gang found themselves stuck on a big rock, called Guam, for two years, and those of us on board who were ordered to other Far East bases found no remorse in the fact our parents missed this tropical isle for their two-year assignment. My final destination - Manila Bay - specifically, the peninsula called Cavite.

As the Barrett passed the islands and man made structures of Corregidor, Ft. Drum, and the Bataan peninsula we skirted sunken ships that were recent relics of the war with the country to the North - Japan. Rusty old scowls with their sterns pointed up and their bows buried in the silt of Manila Bay. We could see the skyline of Manila to our port, or left, and another small colony off the starboard side of the ship. Naval Air Station Sangley Point appeared to consist of scores of small, white quonset huts juxtaposed with the beautiful fiery red Coral trees that dotted the horizon. Slowly, we inched into our berth along the piers several hundred yards south of the American Embassy and we embraced another score of farewells with our young compatriots who debarked with their parents for places, up island, called Subic Bay, Clark Air Force Base, Camp John Hay, in Baguio province, and other destinations unknown to those of use who were literally mesmerized by the entire ordeal. My shipboard girlfriend was heading up to Angeles City, better known as Clark Field. And, my best buddy, Huey Herbert, would accompany her because his father was, also, assigned to the same Air Force facility.

The captain of the Barrett was a robust man, with rosy cheeks and a large red nose. He had skippered this vessel for more than twenty years and considered himself to be a man of the sea. He was a crusty sonofabitch in appearance but, in fact, he war a real softie. One of the special treats he would provide to some of us who asked was to share some freshly baked desserts in his cabin. *And no, he was not a child molester!* Specifically, he would come around the ship and ask several of us if we'd like to have some chocolate eclairs and fresh cold milk. I literally raced up to the bridge so I could eat those little delicacies until my stomach bulged. As soon as my folks found out about this ritual they would arrive at the bridge prior to me, so I would have to wait for them to finish stuffing their faces. My father absolutely loved fresh pastries and he was the perpetrator of my craving Napoleons, eclairs, and other confectionery. The captain would continue with this ritual long after we debarked and reported to our various home bases. Whenever the Barrett returned with a fresh load of passengers we would hitch a ride our on a navy boat, walk up the outboard ship's ladder, ask to see the captain and he would, without hesitation, ask if we would like some freshly baked chocolate eclairs served up with iced cold fresh milk. My colleagues and I would be in seventh heaven for the next few minutes as we savored these rare treats, especially the fresh, ice cold milk.

The very first impression I had of the Philippines was not the climate, nor the topography, nor the people, but the smell. Yes, brethren, the odors were a blend of the various perfumes worn by more cosmopolitan denizens mixed with the food being prepared and sold in the outdoor markets along the squalor in the streets and the hair pommade worn by the locals juxtaposed with the stagnant waters of the bay and its various tributaries. Basically, the entire place stunk! These were odors that were totally unfamiliar to my olfactory nerves. These were odors that I would attempt to grow accustomed to for the next two years. These were odors that truly made one aware of his or her presence in the Philippine Islands. These were odors that were true contradictions - floral fragrances of plumeria and gardenia that were worn by the young girls and women as they walked down the muddy alleys of the barrios that were devoid of sanitation and water purification systems. Thus, one was rewarded with this smell of flowers mixed with shit! About the only time when this smell wasn't dominate was out towards the mouth of Manila Bay, or up in the mountains of Baguio, or Lake Taal away from the polluted settlements in the flatlands around Manila or other heavily populated barrios. All of these smells were relative - relative to what part of the world you were from. To those of us from America it was a rather unique and oftentimes a difficult adjustment. To those from China, Vietnam, or Thailand it was business as usual as they were reminded of home. And, most of the Filipinos thought nothing of it.

We settled into our new quarters on the navy base - a huge, white wooden building constructed in the traditional manner in the tropics one level above the ground to provide air circulation beneath and protection in case of the torrential flooding during the monsoon season. And, when I say monsoon I mean monsoon. We lived about thirty feet from the bay on approximately one secluded acre of lush foilage. My younger brother, Richard, even had his very own tree house constructed in the huge Banyan tree that dominated our backyard. The entire house was not air conditioned. The rooms consisted of wall-to-wall screen windows for ventilation with the exception of my parents' master suite that was air conditioned.

I still have vivid recollections of this house and the beautiful grounds that were dominated by Banyan, Coral, and other species of trees indigenous to the Philippines. A house unlike one that I'd lived in before and would not live in again. Sights, sounds but mostly smells that conjure up thoughts of living in a tropical paradise that would provide me with new friends, interests, and adventures for two years.

I had my own bathroom. Rich had his own bathroom. This was one, big house! And, there were living quarters for three or four domestic servants on the ground level hidden behind the shrouds of the floor to ceiling screens. This was an area that was considered off limits because those employed to work for us were young females. So, the only male allowed in this sanctuary was little Richard as he was too young to appreciate bare-breasted brown women preparing to get dressed for work. The male adolescents were, all, envious of this little tyke because we employed the most beautiful Filipinas on Naval Air Station Sangley Point, period!

Miss Lilly was a private nurse who my folks hired to be a nanny for Richard. She was from a small barrio on an small island in the southern archipelago and was very well educated besides the fact she was simply beautiful. Miss Lilly would be the only person hired to work for us who would endure the wrath of Lucy and Hank for two years. In addition, we employed a lavandera who was responsible for cleaning the house and for all clothes and linens. We also had an excellent cook who prepared three meals a day, six days a week. Most everything was prepared from scratch cooking in that we lived in the pre-microwave and TV dinner era. About the only two items that were missing from our daily food groups were fresh milk and fresh red meat. My mother never had the luxury of domestic help as a navy wife living back in the continental United States. This was entirely new to her and I'm sure that she truly enjoyed being waited on and not having the responsibilities of washing, ironing, cleaning babysitting, and cooking.

My father was the commanding officer of the base and he, also, was responsible for much of the protocol between our government and that of the Philippines. Hence, my folks were frequently going to fancy parties in Manila and dining with diplomats, dignitaries, presidents, and first ladies from around the world. Meanwhile, I was getting ready to enter my freshman year at the American School, Pasay City, Philippines. This was no easy task in that I knew only a few of my peers, and had absolutely no idea of the scholastic canyon that I was about to enter, empty-minded!

The routine for getting from the naval base over to Manila and, then, to Pasay City, and school was not what one would consider to be an easy commute. First, there was the alarm going off at 5:00 am. Then, there was the dash down to the pier to board the navy skiff that departed promptly at 6:00 for the 45 minute voyage across Manila Bay. That boat would carry about twenty of us over the rough bay, pitching and tossing, as the salt spray broke over then bow dousing us as we scurried under the canopy for protection. Upon arriving at the dock on the grounds of the American Embassy. We boarded a government school bus for the trip across town to the school.

Tropical temperatures and humidity dictated that we either repair to shady spots on the school grounds or into a well-ventilated building. After grabbing a Coke we'd stroll over to the back of the schools grounds to the newest addition to the otherwise dated campus facilities. Traditionally, the morning assembly started at the sound of the 7:00 gong with all of us seated in the open air auditorium as the headmaster stood and began to sing "The Whiffinpoof Song" and we joined in like good little lambs who had not lost their way. You see, our headmaster was a Yalie and he reminisced about his days in college, decades ago and 14,000 miles away, by asking the student body to join him in a few verses.

To this day, I can still hit the high notes in that famous tavern song, and somehow feel proud that I learned those verses as a mere high school freshman.

We became captive listeners during this daily ritual before starting classes at 7:30 on those sultry tropical mornings. One day a fellow classmate, albiet an upperclassman, from our group of navy juniors sat in assembly and plotted a scheme where we would get the attention of everyone in that building. He had decided to build a bomb. That's right, a bomb! He would place the device in the rear of the building, close to our lockers, and engineer the fuse so that the detonation would occur right in the middle of the "Baa, baa, baa" part of the song. I told him that he was crazy. Others told him if he got caught, he would get expelled. He did not heed our advice.

About a week later and much strategic planning, this industrious high school junior indicated that tomorrow, Friday, would be D Day, as he described it. And, that the device would ring throughout the hallowed halls with a sound so deafening that the professors would think the Japanese were counterstriking Manila, and the Philippine Islands. I was a nervous wreck. The thought of this illegal endeavor literally scared the shit out of me even though I had no part in the planning or execution. Simply the knowledge of the device and the time of the detonation had my nerves in jitters, and I could not foresee how I would behave after the bomb exploded. Not all of us from the navy base were cognizant of his plan, so there remained a number of fellow classmates oblivious to the havoc timed to occur shortly.

As we debarked the school bus and wound our way towards the assembly building I began to develop that crazed look of severe apprehension, and terror rang rampant throughout my entire disembodied state. Who could possibly concentrate on the daily announcements being read by upperclassmen? Who could get behind the Pledge of Allegiance to the flag? Who could tune up for the tables down at Mory's? Somehow, those of us aware of the pending holocaust managed to maintain our composure and appear to act in a typically normal manner for high school students.

Without warning a single explosion erupted behind us and the roof of the building sounded like it was going into orbit. The echo seemed to last for hours, not seconds. The assembly went silent and we were in awe of this explosion. We sat dumbfounded, apprehensive, terrified, gleeful, and literally afraid that the shit had hit the fan. Let's face it. Only for fleeting moments were we allowed the privilege of sanctuary, of asylum, of non-unanimity. Sooner or later, most likely sooner, we would be singled out as the group who contrived the holocaust, the carnage, the detonation that rocked the hallowed walls and those confounded tables down at Mory's. Reflecting back on that moment I recall possibly peeing a wee bit in my pants and attributing the minute leakage to the tropical heat. In fact, my bladder followed the physiological path that the rest of my body was taking, and that was a reaction from sheer terror.

Ever heard of sharkskin? No, I'm not talking about the epidural layer of a great white or one of the sand variety. I'm referring to that material indigenous to tropical climates and people of class. Sharkskin was euphemism for a fabric light in weight that resembled a twill weave but with a glossy surface, similar to silk. Men and women, throughout the tropics, had wardrobes consisting of sharkskin apparel tailored into trousers, jackets, dresses, shorts, and most of the fashions in these regions dictated the color to be white - bright, clean, gleaming white. Reason I mention this is because the headmaster and assistant headmaster had always worn sharkskin as their business attire. Their shoes, socks, trousers, shirts, and hats were white - bright, clean, gleeming white. Just to wear a necktie in this climate took real balls. The heat, collaborating with a freshly starched collar, would result in almost instant rash around the neck. Most of the girls wore starched cotton sleeveless blouses, starched cotton full skirts blossomed by crinoline, and not much more. On more formal occasions the gals donned white sharkskin dresses or sari silk gowns. We, in turn, took our Barong Tagalogs (Philippine native formal dress shirts) out of the closet, only to suffer from the omnipresent starched collar and cuffs.

Suddenly, an announcement was made over the loud speaker to the tune where the culprit of the mini Hiroshima detonation would be expelled as would any accomplice. These men in their sharkskin and starched cotton white attire meant business. Our behavior suddenly changed from capricious to solemn because we began to contemplate the consequences of expulsion from the American School, Pasay City, Philippines. Classes began promptly at 7:30 and we filled into our respective classrooms not with academics on our minds but, instead, the interrogations that were commencing downstairs in the headmaster's office. Who would fink? Who would chicken out? Who would drag others down the toilet with him or her? Who would make our lives miserable for the next decade as we would attempt to explain our actions to military fathers and mothers? I would rather have stood trial at Nuremberg than have to answer to my father - the captain and the base commanding officer. On the other hand, what in the hell did I have to worry about? Hell, not only was I non-participatory in the manufacturing of the device but I refused to participate in the actual placement of the bomb near our lockers in the gym. My primary concern was being able to withstand the drips of water on my forehead, and the stretching of the skin under my fingers. I was terrified of being an informant, a squealer, a fink, a tattletale, a basic asshole. Could I withstand the torture, the mind games, the brainwashing, the humiliation of breaking down and confessing to the establishment dressed in the starched white and sharkskin tropicals? Could I stand tall like John Wayne in the "Return to Bataan", Roy Rogers in "Broken Arrow", Joan of Arc at the foot of the burning stake? Without one moment's hesitation or reservation I said, "Hell no!" This ersatz cowboy would crumble like a rotten baloot.

A baloot is a Tagalog term for a half-developed embryo of a duck that one would suck directly from the egg shell. And, no. During my two years in the P.I. I never gave the thought of sucking a baloot a second thought.

We reassembled in our respective home classrooms for daily instruction in those college preparatory basics, such as languages, biology, chemistry, world literature, algebra and the remaining subjects that totally bored the hell out of us. Believe me when I say that deportment was not a problem on normal days of classes and today was extra special. We tended to be more attentive, more interested in the lectures, and our posture seemed to improve as we sat more erect in the shitty little desks provided. No air conditioning, no noise other than the usual interactive dialogue and the tension in the air could be cut with a knife. Soon, lunchtime rolled around and we congregated down in the courtyard to discuss the only topic of the day - the bomb! Rumors were flying rampant that it was one of those slovenly Sangley Point brats who placed the device. Hell no. It couldn't have been one of the student elite who lived in the Forbes Park compound with their parents who were CEO's of Coke Cola, Kodak, Ford Motor Company, Talon Zippers (*"go up and down, up and down, up and down"*)

"Maneeeela" Rum, etc. It simply had to be some uncouth navy brat from across the bay. My simple retort to these ersatz millionaires was, that if they continued to subject us to this verbal harassment, they would most likely find a similar firecracker shoved up their little assholes.

These are in all probability, the same little pricks and prickettes who eventually grew up to dominate the business and social scenes in the Philippines, and who perpetuated the rift between the haves and the have nots thus condemning the Islands to the never-ending insurgencies and revolutions that exist today, post Marcos. In other words, they evolved into quintessential Ugly Americans.

Eventually, the tension grew to the point where the students from the Manila side refused to acknowledge the existence of those from the Sangley Point side of the bay. Their little eyes were drawn to the ground as they passed us in the halls; and heaps of whispering were rampant in the restrooms and corners of the buildings. Who was the culprit? Who would come forth and divulge vital information that would lead to the apprehension, conviction, and ultimate expulsion from the hallowed halls of the American School? We were soon to find out the fink, the squealer, the dork, the shithead who would determine the fate of our batallion of hellions from the slimey dredges of navyville. Needless to say, those of us from Sangley were much more curious about the outcome than our peers because that would indicate our strength in numbers and our camaraderie had been compromised. So, woe be unto the person who would rat on his or her fellow student because we would impose fate worse than death by way of isolation, of non communications, of failing to recognize the student as a human being. As a matter of fact, the omnipresent baloot would rate higher on the evolutionary scale than this fink of finks. Not to sweat, however. No navy junior would dare do the deed because we were simply too proud of our heritage and our bonds. Or, so we thought.

The tension mounted, the day grew hotter, and more humid as we walked from one classroom to another, basically nervous as hell. Who could concentrate on Moliere, on Pythagoras, on those tables down at Mory's with all of of this pressure, I ask you? Suddenly, the calm was broken, or should I say the calm before the storm to differentiate between your typically boring school day and that of this ill-omened occasion. The headmaster and assistant headmaster marched down the first floor hall escorting one, lone student towards the main entrance of the school. All three individuals wore expressions of gloom and their eyes were drawn downward towards the ground. I was in shock. I could not speak. I stood there trembling as one of my fellow students from Sangley Point made his final exit from the American School, Pasay City, P.I. Dave Bigelow, a junior and the older brother of my closest friend on the naval base, had been briefly tried and found guilty as the manufacturer, planner, and detonator of the bomb from hell! The expulsion was immediate. There was no lag. There was no hesitation or deliberation by the administration regardin' the severity of the crime, or the ensuing punishment. Throw this sucker out, now! Get his little navy ass on a boat back to Sangley as soon as possible! Let everyone of those little navy pricks know that the same treatment will be awarded should they contemplate a counterstrike or other insurgencies against the American School, Pasay City, P.I. It was one, sad day as Dave was escorted of the campus and into an official United States Navy 1950 Chevrolet gray sedan. The feeling was similar to that of the downtrodden Irish being subjected to Protestant class oppression in Ulster. We were humiliated and saddened by the conviction and expulsion by the school administration but the scrutiny displayed by the Forbes Park pricks was almost intolerable.

The fink? The stool pigeon? The turncoat? The buttinski? The peer whose self-interests overrode fraternal bonds which resulted in the turning of state's evidence in favor of the administration thereby creating the eventual expulsion of one, Dave Bigelow? None other than Ken Flessas - a Sangley Point Navy junior who had this self-righteous air about him. Ken was one of the fellas who really didn't want to be one of the fellas. He was either a junior or a senior, and was one of those goody two-shoes, always kissing up to the senior officers on the naval base and to the teachers at school. You know the type. The one who would always polish the apple, who would hold the door open for the older women, who would be the best candidate for Mister America! God, how I hated this guy today. I wanted to thrash him, to whip his butt, to punch in that pretty face. I wanted to "de-pants" him right in front of the senior girls and hang his BVD's on the flag pole just under the Philippine pennant. I wanted to puke! My classmates wanted to kill him. Ken Flessas was officially persona non grata and he was declared a fugitive from the justice of the Sangley Point Teen Club's tribunal that would impose the ultimate penalty on him-the expulsion from our hallowed halls and pool tables. Ken would begin his shunning from the group which was determined to inflict not only bodily harm but spiritual and emotional injury as well. What a shame, too. Ken was one of those most likely to succeed types who mesmerized the gals and the professors with his good looks and goodie two-shoes personality. If there was ever a Pat Boone twin it was Ken Flessas, right down to his white buck shoes and quintessential toothy smile. The entire thought of this dork made me sick down to my shoes!

Veiled, and some not so veiled, threats against Ken's personal well-being were the order of the day and we couldn't wait for the time when someone big and mean enough took Ken behind the Gedunk (which is Navy for soda fountain) and beat the living shit out of him. Trouble was that I sure as hell wasn't about to take on the task, being around one hundred pounds of skin and bones at best and getting to enjoy my good looks as I matured into adolescence. Hell, Ken was an upperclassman and rather proficient is hand-to-hand combat, so we had to wait for the right opportunity to get even with him for committing the ultimate sin against his fellow man, and that was ratting to the headmaster about Dave's pyrotechnic prowess. We simply had to wait for the right time to get even with Ken and business so it was business usual around the American School and on the base.

My father was commanding officer of the base and he was informed of the bomb blast, and the ensuing expulsion of Dave. He immediately launched a full-scale investigation of the whole ordeal. We were about to find out what honest-to-God interrogation was really like as opposed to the way it was portrayed in the matinee movies. The officer in charge was head of the base police and security so this was about as routine as things could get in his daily chores. He probably never dreamed of mopping up after a bunch of navy brats whose sole purpose in life was simply to have a little fun exploding a homemade device during school assembly. Can't anyone take a little joke? One by one, we were asked to step forward while riding the school ferryboat enroute from Manila back to Sangley Point. Even the girls had to tell their version of what happened and if they were remotely involved or had any knowledge of the plan. My mind was racing with all sorts of stories of what the penalty would be if we were coconspirators with Dave. Expulsion? Deportation to Mindinao? Incarceration in the San Tomas leper colony? Revocation of my teen club membership? Reform school back in the states? But what the hell did I have to worry about? Not only did I have no involvement with the fabrication of the bomb but, in addition, I had no knowledge of the size or the destructive capability, so they could drill me all they want. I had nothing to add that hadn't been said before. My name was called so the time for bullshit was over. Since I was the commanding officer's son the questioning was polite, and tactful but the same underlying message was loud and clear.

"Did you or did you not participate or have prior knowledge of the detonation of the bomb?"

"No sir, it was a total surprise and shock when it went off."

"If we test any of the remains of the bomb and its ingredients for fingerprints will we find yours among those of Dave's?"

………"No, you will not since I never touched anything."

This guy was no dummy. He got right to the meat of the matter and he knew how to rope you into a corner if you had not told the truth to the previous questions. The reason I hesitated is because I paused to contemplate if, in fact, I had touched anything at Dave's house that would ultimately wind up as part of the device. In conclusion, I replied in the negative and was uncertain if I had inadvertently handled anything of a suspicious nature. The butterflies in my stomach were not flying in formation, so I felt like puking all over the deck of the boat. Eventually, all of us on board were questioned and the conclusion was forthcoming in a day or two, so we all (except Ken) convened at the teen club to discuss the raimfications of being implicated with Dave. As a matter of fact, that's all we talked about while shooting pool or doing the bop because life on the base was rather dull and we looked forward to anything for excitement. And, this was exciting to say the least as we contemplated Dave's ultimate fate and those who were found guilty as his accomplices. You'd have thought that someone had been brutally murdered, cut up, and thrown out to sea the way we and our parents talked about this rather small incident when one reflects back to what was happening in the States as we witnessed in movies like "Blackboard Jungle", "Rebel Without a Cause", and "The Wild Ones".

We were so squeaky clean compared to our counterparts who were forming gangs, carrying stiletto switchblade knives, and stealing cars back in our former whitebread neighborhoods in California, Maryland, New York, and other areas where life was true to movie mania-like form. This microcosm of military life was very regimented, strict, and full of domineering parents who treated us like raw recruits instead of beloved sons and daughters, so we greatly anticipated any activity that would raise the hairs on the back of our fathers' necks because it indicated where they had lost control for once in their fascist lives. Trouble is most of us didn't have the guts to assert our independence because of the system - the system that considered us dependents as actual members of the military establishment. We were told how to cut our hair, how to wear our peggers or Levis, how to restrict the amount of facial makeup for the gals, how to attend church services every Sunday regardless of our persuasion, how to address senior officer's wives as though they held the same rank as their husbands, and all sorts of other malarkey that ultimately would not determine our fates or how we would respect traditional values that have recently been shitcanned due to our more permissive and deregulated society.

The verdict came down two days later that Dave Bigelow acted solely in the design, procurement, construction, and detonation of the bomb from hell. We were exonerated but Dave was committed to a Philippine military agricultural and trade academy for the duration of his stay. He went to board at this school somewhere near Manila and was not considered a part of our cadre of classmates. In other words, this dude was totally humilated and separated from those other teenages who were considered to be normal high school students and denizens. Meanwhile, Ken finished his studies at the American School before heading back to the States with his family. He, too, was humiliated by us and he, by his own volition, alienated himself from and never set foot in the Sangley Point Teen Club ever agai

Philippine Jeepneys, Cavite, PI

Banana Island

How can I convey this story accurately without hesitation or exaggeration? Times have changed and so have the people, but I oftentimes believe that society in the stinking Philippines has stood still for 35 years. I say stinking because the Philippines literally stinks. It stinks not in the vernacular but in the olfactory way. Carabao shit mixed with polluted water mixed with ripening mangoes mixed with tobacco smoke mixed with barbecued corn mixed with hair pomade soon ruptured your nostrils, and left you defenseless as you went about your daily routines in Cavite, or Pasay City, or even Forbes Park, perish the thought!

And, my parents stunk too. They never let me go over to Manila for the gala parties held by the children of the corporate fat cats. My parents stunk in more ways than one. My mother had three servants all week long and she had absolutely nothing to do as a result. Think she could spend a little more time with my little brother Rich and me? Shit no! I literally can't figure out what she did all day long. She stunk.

The rich kids lived in Forbes Park. The civilian moguls, originally from Moscow to Minneapolis, residing in these huge estates hidden behind the security walls of the Forbes Park compound on the outskirts of Manila. Kodak, Coca Cola, Ford Motor Company, Unites States Steel, Credit Lionaise, Talon Zippers *Go up and down, up and down*, Banco National, and other organizations world-wide, situated their moguls in Manila for business purposes and provided them with estates and multitudes of servants in the white bread walled ghetto known as Forbes Park.

We Navy Juniors attended the American School with the rich kids from Forbes Park. Ours was a motley crew. Our student body consisted of adolescents from all over the continental United States, or CONUS, for brevity sake. Our dads were Navy Seamen-Third Class, Chief Petty Officers, Chief Warrant Officers, Lieutenants, Commanders, and Captains. The entire gammut of social breeding and strata represented our Naval Air Station Sangley Point, across the bay from

Manila. In terms of our parents' income folks determined how much each family earned because the salaries paid to each Navy grade were public record. You can rest assured that it was a mere pittance when compared to the compensation of those "Dudley Do Rights" who lived in Forbes Park. These kids were definitely bred in a white bread world and would want for naught throughout their lives. Most of the American residents were from the eastern establishments located around Bryn Mawr, Greenwich, Manhattan, Washington, Kenwood, West Paces Ferry Road in Atlanta, Lakefront in Chicago, and other pockets of the ghetto rich.

Ironically, we were also of parallel ilk in that the privileges and benefits of Naval service, and by simply being American citizens, were causes of jealousy and envy by those indigents for whom this was decidedly unattainable. For the two years I was held captive in the stinking Philippines I can vividly remember several wealthy Filipinos and Spanish dependents hounding me and my father for endorsements so they could join the United States Navy, and for sponsorship to apply for American citizenship. Some things money simply can't buy and that is the privilege of being an American, - love it or leave it, you commie pinko pig!

Nonetheless, we became friends with many of these elite kids while rubbing elbows as classmates at school, and we invited several of them to join our festivities on the base, such as our quarterly outings aboard the USS Margaret, a 100 foot yacht owned by the Navy which was used for recreational cruises to Corregidor, Subic Bay, and the Bataan peninsula. The Margaret was splendid, shiny, crewed by the Navy's finest, and free of charge for us to charter for the day. This was a perk that the kids in Frobes Park couldn't touch with ten feet of their parent's wealth. To receive an invitation to sail on the Margaret was, indeed, a true indication that we liked you! On Monday mornings, following the weekend the Margaret was chartered for the day, those who weren't invited would ensure that we heard their pitiful little cries and whining regarding their obvious exclusion from the invitation list. It became patently obvious to those students who were considered to be pains in the ass that hell or high water would come before their custom-made shoed little feet ever stepped foot onto our cherished floating trophy of the spoils of World War II. So, cliques were formed and the pay-offs were in evidence with those fellow comrades at school who reciprocated by inviting those of us from Sangley to their swinging parties in Forbes Park. I have always had the utmost respect for free trade and the free market system that propagated this type of barter for us school children without one financial pot to piss in.

And, what parties! Not just some extemporaneous get togethers in a quonset hut with tropical fruit coolers for refreshments and Filipino lumpia for hors d'ouvres. We're talking dance bands, hard liquor, swimming pools, jai lai courts, servants, dope for those so inclined, the finest looking high school girls radiating sensual plumeria blossom fragrances, and the opportunity to secure freedom from our families, and the United States Navy, if only for a few hours. Oftentimes, the wealthy parents of these young party animals would be out of town, or even the country, during the galas, so there were absolutely no restrictions placed on our behavior albeit we were expected to maintain some sort of decorum by not trashing the house, or the contents within, and even with this new found freedom there were very few nasty occurences reported during my two years in the P.I. Suppose it was mostly due to our strict up bringing and the threats imposed on us by our dictatorial parents who saw no humor in insubordination, or in our mischevious behavior. Mischevious behavior, shit! We were an intolerable group of spoiled little brats who cherished their Angeles Peggers, Hollywood flattop hairstyles, Flagg Brothers white buck loafers, Chinese mandarin-styled collar shirts, 3/8 inch wide blue suede belts, Old Spice cologne, and Latino pachuco-styled tattoos between our thumbs and index fingers above all other sanctitudes. We were hot shots! We were mean dudes! We were ersatz James Deans and Marlon Brandos and Sal Mineos, and other movietown punks whose global reputations surely preceeded ours in the realms of regional quasi-adolescence.

In summary, we dressed like we did and wore colognes like we did in order to get laid, pure and simple. No hidden agendas. No ulterior motives. Just a good, plain good fuck will do, thank you very much!

Let's cut through the bullshit and get right down to the problem regarding our hormones not flying in formation. Atoms colliding and sperms running rampant looking for a nice soft fallopian wall on which to adhere and produce a younging, if we weren't careful. Sure, we were your classic students in that we joined the various athletic teams and swam our butts off, or threw the baseball until our arms ached, or ran up and down the basketball courts until our legs felt like rubber. Or, we picked up and became masters at the game of rotation or eight ball on the various pool tables around the naval base. We discovered hobbies that, until our arrival in the Philippines, were virtual unknowns in our previously busy little Boy Scout worlds of airplane model making, leather engraving, pool shooting, sewing, and crocheting for the gals, or photography. After a fellow Navy classmate named Tom Bigelow captured my attention I became a slave to the darkroom. Decktol, hypo, and other chemicals permeated my nostrils and skin hour after hour as we processed our black and white film of subjects ranging from candid shots of our fellow students and our teachers at the American School, to aircraft operations on the base runway, to Filipino jeepneys racing up and down the main drag in Cavite, to images of our siblings playing with their little friends while the brown-skinned nannies watched under the shade of the coral trees. Countless hours lost in the black tunnels of the hobby shop darkroom where the only equipment that kept you from total disorientation was a dimly lit red light. After hours we emerged into the bright tropical sunlight, our hands looking like prune skin, and our prizes were these 3 by 5 or 5 by 7 inch shapshots for sale to any sucker who would be dumb enough to buy them, or so we thought. In essence, these dummies received one hell of a value for their 10 or 25 cents because these images were recording history of their experience in the Philippines. And, we were so diligent in the processing and printing that I feel certain these images were archival. No yellow fading or muddying over the years because of some short cuts normally taken by today's one-hour labs. We were truly professionals and we constantly strived for better ways in which to market our products.

Tom Bigelow was the Ichabod Crane of Sangley Point, and he must have weighed all of a hundred twenty pounds in his youthful, slender frame. And, to watch him walk! This boy walked as thought his feet were pointing to opposite quadrants of the compass rose. In other words, he was major league slew-footed, gangly, big eared, no muscle definition, but on top of it all, he was a nice guy

Tom possessed creative genius. One of his ideas was to photograph the girls' slumber parties with infra red film so as not to divulge the clandestine operation, and market these ersatz porn shots to our young compatriots at school. I thought the concept was brilliant! I thought Tom had literally outdone himself with this pre-Hefner-like marketing scheme. Just think. All of those little damsels with whom we rode the boat across the bay and attended classes day in and day out would have their boobs, buns, and bushes colated by photographic sizes, shapes, proportions, and, most important, desirability of those who would fantasize but dared not to tread on their physical attributes for the real thing.

Over thirty-five years later, I still have this grossly underexposed and crinkled image of a Navy lass, named Mickey, who possessed the largest nipples this side of Tonga. Tom managed to snap this image from outside the window of the girls' slumber party one night with his first roll of infra red film. Thus, we filed it as "Image Number One," for posterity. Unbeknownst to us, we never knew that any girl this young could have nipples the size of silver dollars. God, our thoughts of lust, and planting our lips on these pink mounds of love drove us literally wild!

However, the problem with our entire scheme is most boys couldn't keep their squeely little mouths shut, so leaks in our innersanctum eventually got back to the parents of these petite parsels of palpitating piscatorial pomptitude, so our long term master sceme was soon thwarted and immediately terminated. "No more nude prints will be processed in this here U.S. Navy darkroom," said the base commanding officer, who was, also, my father!

Now, the prints became rare and the laws of supply and demand dictated that the prices escalate disproportionally for reprints of Sandy and her magnificent blond triangle of love, of Barbara and her plump pear-shaped magnificent toilet *or rear end.*, of Jackie's D cup mammaries with protruding nipples pointing straight up to the sky, of Linda with her flat stomach and Irish red pubic hair obviously a symbol that her bush was on fire, screaming for relief. Tom and I begin to selectively market these priceless images only to a few prospective buyers after careful screening and obtaining written promises of silence. "Be it known to all present that I will never tell anyone where these snapshots came from, or how I bought them. This vow is under penalty of getting de-pantsed in front of all the girls on Sangley Point!" Demand was up and price gouging was assumed, so we upped the price to $1.00 for a 4 by 5 which our buyers considered to be extortion and usurious, but our attitude was, "Shut up. Next buyer, please." Eventually, we began to walk around the base or school visualizing these fully-clad cute little subjects as completely stark naked, and we visually transposed the image of their photographic nudity onto their presently fully-clothed states as they approached us in the hallways, or in the library, or in the soda fountain. Can you imaging trying to keep a straight face through this whole ordeal? I tell you it was nearly impossible for me because I was not only fantasizing but I was also mentally masturbating right there in front of them!

"Hank, what is that silly grin on your face?

"You have the look of the devil in that gleem in your eye, Hank Miller."

"Tom, what have you and Hank been up to in that darkroom for hours and hours? Rumor has it you're developing nudie pictures of girls at some party. Any truth to that?"

"Miller, if I find out it's true that you and Tom are selling snapshots of me with my pajama top soaking wet I'll tell your parents but not before my big brother beats the living shit out of you!"

A brief interlude in our adolescent development and a necessary one, I might add. Girlie magazines were not available in those days. Neither were porn flicks or "X" rated home videos, therefore we had to rely on our own ingenuity and spontaneous creativity. Tom's brilliant concept of experimenting with infra-red film was way ahead of its time, and the payoff for us was beyond words. One must remember that the dress codes in the fifties were indicative of the McCarthyism, prudish family values, strict religious piety, and that Elvis had not yet shaked rattled and rolled at this point during the decade. The girls' bathing suits were one-piece, and unrevealing as far as we were concerned. Mind you, this was not the French Riviera, where women presumably went sans tops and wore these new fangled bottoms called bikinis, named after the Bikini Atoll, down in this region of the southeastern Pacific. Hence, our imaginations had to suffice, and the advent of Tom's concept and implementation of high tech super espionage night photography was the answer to many of our prayers.

Unfortunately, we were not mature nor intelligent enough to perceive the added value of maintaining these shapshots in pristine condition for our enjoyment years down the road and decades later as we reminisced about "The Fast Times at American School!"

During my sophomore year in 1956 the folks began to finally ease up on the curfew restrictions and permit me to stay out later during the week and on the weekends, but they never permitted me to attend one of the parties in Forbes Park. Suddenly, after asking them time and time again to let me go to one of the parties my parents acquiesced, and said, "Yes. But, you have to take the last ferry back from the Embassy which means no spending the night, do you hear? We'll expect you back in this house no later than three o'clock, or you'll never go to another one of the parties, sonny."

"Yes, Mom! Yes, Dad!"

Free at last! Free at last! Thank God almighty. Free at Last!

After planning my wardrobe for over a week the big Saturday night finally came, and those of us who were invited to the party met down on the dock for the Navy ferry to take us over to Manila, and drop us at the Embassy. From that point we took a bumpy and rather expensive cab out to Forbes Park just in time to meet hundreds of other classmates from the American School, and some other students from one of the boarding schools up in the mountains of Baguio. The band was great as they blasted out the songs of the day, like "Shake Rattle and Roll," "Long Tall Sally," "Blueberry Hill," "The Great Pretender," "Heartbreak Hotel," "Blue Suede Shoes," "Smoke Gets in Your Eyes," "Moonglow," and other tunes that kept us slim and fit while aerobically tearing up the dance floor. The beer was ice cold San Miguel and there was hard liquor for those really tough guys who had supposedly graduated to manhood. The food was fantastic, with all sorts of canapes, desserts, and Filipino delicacies, such as lumpia and fried rice. And the girls looked and smelled real fine! I mean real fine, as they sashayed around in their finest silk blouses, and raw silk dresses, and pointed bras.

"Hank, A few of the guys and I plan to go to Banana Island a little later on and you can join us if you want to. Don't say anything to the girls or we'll be in big, big trouble, so we'll let you quietly know when we plan to split."

"Archie, what in the hell is Banana Island, and why are you thinking about leaving this terrific party anyway?"

"Banana Island is a section of Manila and there is a whorehouse there, so we plan to go and get laid, then come back to the party. If you're scared, then don't come. But, if you want some action, then you'll have a real good time at this place. We won't be gone all night, so don't worry about missing the boat back to Sangley. As a matter of fact we will only be away from the party for about two hours maximum."

"You guys let me think about it and I'll let you know later on during the party, okay?"

What in the hell were these guys thinking anyway? Of course I would capitulate and hop on that jeepney for the ride to Banana Island along with the other guys, just so I could be one of the guys. As the hour grew closer I grew considerably more nervous but no way was I going to remain at the party when I had this opportunity to participate in a quasi Filipino bar mitzvah, where the whores would perform their own specialized ritualistic ceremony in the metamorphose from puberty to manhood. I was certain these brown skinned little honeys would provide us with much more diversity and ecstasy than some Yiddish speaking, Mogan David drinking, gefilte fish eating, garlic smelling, neighborhood rabbi from, let's say, Brooklyn Heights, stateside. Lordy, we were about to embark on a journey from where there was no return. Banana Island. A place where ecstasy was sold for a few pesos and where the barter system was unheard of.

We were going to nn honest to heaven brothel where young girls whose families owed someone vast sums of money were literally forced into indentured servitude until the debt was paid in full, and then the whores were free to go, but then it would be too late. These girls of thirteen or fourteen would be hooked on heroine or sex or both, and many would die of syphilis or drug overdoses by the time they reached twenty.

On second thought, I was beginning to have second thoughts about this forthcoming ritual. All I would need is a good case of the clap to report to my folks back on the base. That would ensure my hasty return to the States and an immediate entry into some fashionable eastern reform school, somewhere around Baltimore. By the same token I was horny. Horny was an understatement in that my eyeballs experience what we referred to as a "Whiteout", and that resulted from excess sperm finding its way from your groin area up to your brain thereby causing blurry eyesight as your retinas attempted to focus through this excessive white fluid. The only solution was to drain that excess fluid either by your own mechanical methods, or by those of some external force, such as the services provided by the femmes fatales, at Banana Island.

"Okay, fellas, I'm seeing white, so let's head 'em up and move 'em out as the Duke would say. When do we leave and how much money will I need for some fun?"

Archie said, "Fellas, Hank is going with us, so now we have Tom, Dave, Bill, Dick, Wayne, and me. That makes a total of seven. Are we all here? If so, I'll go tell Sue that we're going out to a movie, or whatever, and that we'll be back around midnight so she can provide an alibi for us to the rest of the gang."

We departed from the main gates at Forbes Park and hailed down the first jeepney driving by. Seven of us crammed into that little jeep and instructed the driver to blast off for Banana Island and, as we did, he broke out into his typical Filipino giggle because he knew full well our ulterior motive in visiting this particular geographical spot.

These taxis are indigenous only to the Philippines. During World War II our soldiers deserted thousands of U.S. military jeeps on the various islands in the archipelago. These industrious denizens found ways to continue their usefulness by converting these four passenger olive drab colored vehicles into ones that could transport up to seven passengers in relative comfort surounded by the brightly painted colors of the rainbow that adorned the metal skins of what are now reffered to as jeepneys.

Our ride consisted of much giggling, talking, and conjecturing about what lay ahead at our destination. The heat of the night and the tropical humidity ensured that our clothes stuck to our backs as we traversed the rough and often unpaved avenues of rural Manila in search of teenage Nirvana. Sweat poured from our foreheads and the beer that we had removed from the party was beginning to loose it chill in the Luzon heat. After about a twenty minute ride we finally reached an intersection of two streets that were unfamiliar to us, and there was the typically tropical open air nightclub displaying the large rusting Coke Cola sign juxtaposed with the San Miguel neon over the corrugated metal roof. Looked like every other dump in the Philippines that we patronized for soft drinks and beer. Archie took the initiative and entered the building and walked to the rear where he met a Filipino who was most likely the owner. After a brief conversation Archie walked back out to those of us waiting in front and instructed us to come on in and to buy a beer. While the owner passed out the San Miguel, we all began to investigate how much collective cash we had in our possession, and I was asked to loan Bill two dollars.

That left me with only one buck, for a fuck!

"Archie, how much is this going to cost me, anyway? Bill took my last three dollars, leaving me with only one, so what will I do? Besides, I also gave him my one and only rubber, so what if I need a sock for my cock?"

"Hank, let's all go out this door to the courtyard in back where the girls are living. You let me negotiate with the madame to see if we can get a discount for seven girls."

My heart suddenly was in my throat and I couldn't believe my eyes! The rear courtyard consisted of several dilapidated wooden shacks forming a rectangular open area shaded by large banana trees blowing in the slight breeze and, as the the madame appeared with her girls, I couldn't help but notice that she was over six feet tall. Filipino women were usually no more than five feet tall and this meant she was an Amazon! And, when she smiled at me, I couldn't help but notice that her teeth were filed down into points! Shit! Why points? Was she also a cannibal and did she enjoy devouring little boys after they sexually devoured her little whores? My eyes were at their widest aperture during this whole ordeal because I was one, scarred and trembling little fella. The boys started to select their tricks for the hour and I was left with none. The cost for a honey was five dollars, and I had only one. The madame would not concede and negotiate bargain rates for a quantity discount, so I had to face the reality of trying to survive for the next hour out in front of the club while playing pin ball, or sitting at the bar drinking more San Miguel while the other six were releaving the pressure from their groins and their retinas, thus eliminating the "whiteouts."

"Hank, I couldn't talk the madame into giving you credit, so you come into the room with me. No way are you going to stay out here for the next hour. This is one, tough neighborhood and the madame suggested that one of us let you either share a girl or just sit in one of the rooms. If you stay out her we'd never find your body, so you come on into my room and keep quiet. At least you'll be safe," said Archie, to whom I would remain forever indebted for saving my ass.

She opened the rusty screen door with holes in the mesh as large as quarters, so mosquitoes were obviously welcomed. The room was about ten feet by eight at best and consisted of an unfinished wooden floor, painted wooden walls, one small window, a low ceiling, one small chair, and a single bed in the corner with a cubicle curtain that could be pulled for privacy. I almost forgot the crucifix and dried palm fron on the wall over the bed, and the Bible which Guidion surely left during his last visit. I took my place in the chair as Archie undressed and prepared for his five dollar's worth of fun. The young girl had already taken her place on the mattress of happiness while waiting for Archie to enter the cubicle, and her. Meanwhile, I strained to see what was happening through the curtain and to listen to the labors of love as the groans, moans, and bodily lubrication filtered throught the relative quiet of the night. I turned the pages of the Bible and skimmed over the words that were barely discernible in the ambient light of the moon entering through the small frosted window, while not retaining one, single word of Scripture.

Time did not fly by, and I somehow that this evening would never ever come to a conclusion. But then Archie came to a conclusion, or should I simply say he just came, so I knew we were making progress towards getting back to the party, and to girls whose teeth were white and unpointed, and whose skin was white, and whose names I knew, and whose morals were more in tune with mine. Slowly, Archie stood up, began to humm a tune, and began to get dressed while his labor of love remained in the prone position.

We both left her room and I said, "If you're ever over at Sangley Point please drop by our quarters and introduce yourself to my folks, and be our guest for dinner."

She didn't understand one single word, thank God!

By this time all of the remaining studs began to congregate in the courtyard while we waited for Bill to emerge. He was taking longer than the rest so our hypothesis was he had "seconds" while the rest only got served up "single servings." We began to realize that the hour was late and that we were beginning to overstay our five buck a fuck welcome in Banana Island, so we scooted for the entrance in anticipation that a jeepnee would be close by. No such luck. The crowd of locals in the club was much larger and more vocal than the hour before and they didn't like the idea of Americans in their own special place. I noticed where several of these little punks over in one corner began to give us the evil eye and to make sleezy remarks in Tagalog, the language of Luzon. Suddenly, this group headed towards us and began to pull out the traditional Filipino knives that most carried for protection, and some for show. These balisongs, or butterfly knives, were very lethal and my attention was immediately grabbed while the blades of these knives glistened in the neon light. Thank God as my pulse began to race so did this jeepnee right in front of the club, and I ran into his path in order to force the driver to stop. He came to an abrupt halt and the seven of us jumped onto the hood and into the rear seats as these young thugs ran after us, knives and all.

"Get this goddam machine going now, you Flip!" we screamed to the driver as he ground the gearshift down into first gear for the hasty exit from Banana Island. Behind us and closing in fast were members of this local gang running as fast as they could for the jeepney-knives drawn and looks of hatred on their little brown faces. We told the driver, in no uncertain terms, that he had best do whatever it took in order to evade the locals, be it running red lights, driving up over the curbs, or setting land speed records for a four cylinder, ten year old overladen and underpowered piece of Army surplus, motivating on four bare convention bias pre-Michelin tires. He was lucky. We were lucky. The group of hooligans ceased to pursue us and so we headed back to Forbes park, in relative security and peace of mind, and, for some, piece of ass. Neither applied to me, so the trip back was restitution for my inability to eliminate my extreme affliction of "white out."

Back to the party and to our hostess, Sue, who greeted us at the front door as our driver screeched to a halt. The band was still blasting away and the crowd hadn't diminished one bit and it appeared as though many more compatriots had arrived.

Archie said, "Sue, can we use your shower for a few minutes in order to get this dirt and grime off of us? It was one hell of a ride from Manila, and I need to get clean."

"Archie, who do you guys think you're fooling, anyway? Don't worry, I won't let on that you have been over to Banana Island for some poontang. And, if you think for one minute that taking a shower will keep you guys from getting the clap, you're entirely mistaken. Don't make a scene and you wait your turn in the bathroom. In other words, don't be so obvious by walking out to the poll humming some tune, or on Monday the word will spread like wildfire that the boys from Sangley were out with the whores at Banana Island over the weekend. Then, see if any of the girls at school will ever date you after that! You will be abhored like those poor lepers isolated at Santo Thomas Prison. I'll go back out and mingle so not to draw any more attention than we already have. Please, please, please hurry up and come out into the backyard by the pool, and wipe those shit-eating grins off your faces."

Was I depressed or what? My big chance and I blew it by lending the majority of my funds to the fellas. Perhaps it was destiny that I was the honored guest in the whore's room while the others were graduating from apprentice status to that of journeymen. Still, my pride was hurt and I felt as though I was definitely the odd man out, the outsider, the odd ball this evening of evenings. Take a shower? No reason to take a shower with one, major exception. I didn't want any of the Forbes Park kids to think that I had retained my virginity, so I took a shower right along with the rest of the guys in order to have this assumption that I was a participant remain intact. My machismo walked about three feet ahead as we strutted out to the pool area, looking like roosters departing the hen coop, with big cock a doodle doos!

The evening finally wound down as the hands of the clock approached one in the morning and we began to regroup to think about catching a cab back down Dewey Boulevard, and to the American Embassy for our eventual ride across the bay to Sangley. This was the latest that I'd ever been up and I must admit that my eyelids were at half mast, and drooping faster than a mid-aged woman's boobs. Of course, our group couldn't let on that fatigue was setting in or else we'd be considered pansies not worthy of late night teenie bopper extravaganzas in Forbes Park, or extraterrestrial extravaganzas at Banana Island.

The cab ride seem to take forever and all I could think of was sleep, sound sleep in my own room without any ecoutrements, such as the disheveled bed complete with a cubicle curtain, rank odors of lust, a Bible, and mosquitoes, all of which were overseen by madame Amazon with her pointed teeth.

Our ferry was waiting for us and we hopped on board just in time to catch forty minutes of shut eye as the Navy skiff rhythmically cruised the smooth moonlit waters towards our ecclesiastically safe and antiseptically clean homes on the Cavite peninsula, geographically proximate but light years away, metaphysically, from the world we just left at Banana Island.

Got to make sure I don't stink. No beer on my breath, no smoke on my clothes, no fishey smell from that dark room. Why should I give a shit if I stunk? After all, my parents were the biggest stinkers of all

The author's senior high school graduation photo.

Penne, Vicki, or Bunny

"Front Seat or the Back, Ladies?"

I often think about Jackie Lee. He was a soda jerk at the drugstore back during the '50's. I believe Jackie was originally from down in Kinston. Anyway, Jackie had the absolute fastest Ford in town which was being contested out on that Kinston highway, almost every night. We would issue Jackie the challenge that our car would beat his in the all-out, top-end race, from somewhere out on that highway back to Bob's Drive In, at the "Y". Usually, he would win literally by a country mile. Also, this was the era when the drive-in movie was in its prime, and we had three of them surrounding Opp. The closest was the Dixieland, just down the road where the Pizza Hut is now located, and we would be there with some local honey all snuggled up against us on the front seat when the ticket office opened. Our objective, once the movie started and the concession stand had been visited for refreshments, was to coax the young cute honey into the back, and onto those slippery woven nylon seat covers of our car. Evidence of this accomplishment could be verified by the fog emanating from the car interior thus coating the windows, making them opaque, and impossible for others to peer in. Waylon McKinney kept a cigar box of condoms under the front seat of his car, and it's a good thing since he was dating Jeanie Jordan at the time. I was so envious of him as we snuck into his car and counted the missing rubbers daily. Hell. I would have given my right nut to have the opportunity to use just one, single Trojan with Jeanie Jordan. What a beauty! Anyway, I thought I'd share this tale about my senior high school years, up in Washington, before I moved down to Opp, during the summer of 1959.

Penne attended Mass at the Church of the Little Flower, in Northwest Washington, and I met her at a Catholic Youth Organization dance on a Friday night, during the Fall of 1957. We were introduced by a fellow classmate of mine, at St. John's College, which was a private Catholic high school with a military curriculum, deep in the heart of the city. Tom, a member of my squad in the military segment of our daily activities, asked if I had plans one Friday afternoon, and I replied that I did not. He suggested that I attend the CYO dance where I would meet young ladies from the surrounding Catholic girl's schools, and that he would be taking his girlfriend, Virginia, so we could meet him there. Then, Tom would introduce me to the coeds who were standing around on the dance floor, just waiting for someone to ask them to dance. Since my previous summer had been a social and sexual disaster (mostly sexual) I was excited about the opportunity to meet other girls in my neighborhood. This was my junior year in high school, and I had just returned from my first two years of school in the Philippines, so any opportunity to meet new friends was a main priority.

I put on my civilian coat and tie, shined my saddle oxfords, brushed back my Hollywood hairdo, and applied plenty of Old Spice cologne in preparation for the evening ahead. I met Tom inside the Little Flower gymnasium where the latetest rock and roll music was being broadcast from a reel to reel tape recorder through the same, no fidelity speakers used to announce the school activities and basketball scores during the day. "Hank, remember when I mentioned Virginia's friend? Well, I want you to meet Penne. She goes to Immaculata High School, the same one as Virginia."

God, was she cute! My horny little heart was in my throat! God, was she cute! Penne was about five feet two inches tall, with great legs, a dark brunette, a lovely face…and big tits! Thank you, Lord. I could hardly speak! The only way I was going to make any impression on her was to simply ask her to dance…and shut up!

"How long have you been at St. John's, Hank?"

"This is my first *stutter stutter* year. My parents were transferred from the Philippines to Washington, this summer, and I *stutter stammer* wound up at St. John's, not under my own volition, thank you very much. *stammer…stammer* Are you from around here? Did you and Virginia grow up together? Sorry, but I'm full of questions, just so you don't say anything about how bad my dancing is."

And, I simply couldn't stop staring at her big tits!

"Don't worry. You're a good dancer, and I'll let you know when you step on my feet. I've known Virginia since we were in the first grade. Tom and Virginia have been together since the eighth grade. Can you believe that? Anyway, I'm glad you're here and that we have a chance to dance together."

I'll say it again. God, was she cute! God, did she have big tits! I was stepping all over my saddle oxfords in a feeble attempt to do the bop, and to impress Penne with the combination of my Arthur Murray moves and Elvis style.

We left the dance around 11:00 for the Hot Shoppes Drive In, at Four Corners in Bethesda, for a midnight snack, but primarily so the guys hanging around their cars would see me with this cutie pie and quickly determined where I had excellent taste. I simply couldn't get over how cute she was. Neither could the guys hanging around the drive-in as they began to walk by the car to gawk and to razz me with the typical cat calls and whistles, which were their indications of approval. Soon, we left for her house in time to meet the curfew imposed on most of the kids our age in this metropolitan city. I asked if she was going to be at the dance next Friday night at the Little Flower, and she replied yes, only if I was going to be there. Oh! I forgot to kiss her good night! I could only think about next Friday night, dancing breast to chest, and cheek to cheek.

I was in love. During the entire week of classes at St. John's, I was in love, and my thoughts were totally immersed with Penne. I counted the days until Friday afternoon when school let out for the opportunity to change into my widewale cords, sand-colored desert boots, and alpaca sweater, for the dance. We met in the corner of the gym and proceeded to move ever so slowly around the dance floor to "Earth Angel," "Born Too Late," "Smoke Gets in Your Eyes," "Sea of Love," and other slow songs programmed on the school's tape recorder. Penne was the prettiest girl on the dance floor. I was with the girl with the best body on the dance floor. I was with the girl with the biggest tits on the dance floor, by far. I was in heaven!

The Eastern seaboard was a far cry from the Philippine archipelago, and the stench, and the unbearable heat and rain. Our wardrobes in Manila consisted of short-sleeved shirts and cotton slacks, twelve months out of the year. Everything, from the hills to the rice patties and palm trees, was immersed in green, and the evergreen plants and trees had never experienced the metamorphosis of the changing of seasons. I liked being back where the Fall colors lead us into another cycle, and the opportunity to witness the summer solstice disappear just in time for us to prepare for advent of the autumnal equinox. In plain terms that meant glorious red and orange colors of the leaves falling by the billions, the winds picking up, the shadows getting longer, days getting shorter, the gradual temperature decline, and football games every Saturday, around Washington. Fall was, in addition, the commencement of another school year and the opportunity to discover new friends... and girlfriends, especially.

Penne and I met after school almost everyday when we would watch American Bandstand, and smooch (mostly smooch), in the basement of her house. Virginia and Tom would drop by occasionally, or Tom would drop me off at Penne's while he would take off with Virginia to some undisclosed location, possibly for some serious, long term (since the eighth grade), relationship smooching. We had smooching down to an inexact science while missing most of the Bandstand episodes. By Thanksgiving, Mr. and Mrs. Poole had become my surrogate family, and I must admit I felt closer to Frances Poole than to my own mother. She would offer me snacks in the afternoon and even a ride back to my house should I require transportation, at supper time. I thought she was a fantastic person who cherished her only daughter, so I knew that I must treat Penne with respect, or I would suffer the dire consequences of my horny little actions, on and off the dance floor. Hence, I never even thought of asking Penne into the back seat of my parents Ford Fairlane 500 sedan. We simply smooched in the front seat, and that was good enough for this cowboy whose hormones were imploding into his eyeballs causing that ever-present phenomenon called a "whiteout." Shoot! Can't have everything, I always said, and just having the privilege of escorting this young, ersatz Elizabeth Taylor was almost enough for me. I say almost, because my hormones were still in the active search and destroy mode for not only the perfect tits but, in addition, the perfect pussy. Or, should I say, any pussy at this time of my celibate life. Penne had a strict set of moral standards, God bless her little Catholic heart. I, on the other had, had no moral standards, and the only factor that kept me from participating in serial encounters was the consequence of a trial by Rome, by the Papal Archdiocese of Washington and Baltimore, resulting in castration at the stake. Otherwise, I would have been arrested as a junior transfer student, from the Philippines, well schooled in the voyeurism of Banana Island.

"Hanky, what's this girl like? The one you talk to for an hour every night after your homework is finished? You never mention her to me. Is it because you're embarrassed for me to meet her? What's her name? Penne? And, where did you meet her? Where does she live?

"Mom! Never mind! Why all the questions, I ask? Can't I have any privacy when I'm talking on the phone? Anyway, her name is Penne, and I met her at a dance at the Little Flower a few months ago. Tom, one of my classmates, introduced us at the first dance I went to last September. She goes to Immaculata where she is a freshman. *With great, big, beautiful tits!* I'm thinking about asking her to the Regimental Ball, at the Shorham Hotel next month. It's a formal dance and I think she'd like to go. Do you think I should go ahead and ask her this far in advance?"

"Hanky, you'd better not stall around or she'll accept someone else's invitation, if she's as cute as you say. *Mom, if you could only see those magnificent tits!* It's only a month away and she will probably want to have some time in order to get her dress and all the things that go with it. You asked me for my opinion and now you have it, so go ahead and call her, after you finish your homework.

Rejection. Fear of rejection was my curse throughout life: My cross to bear and I dreaded the thought of Penne saying that she wasn't interested, or that she had another date for this dance which was my first formal dance. What in the hell would I do if she said no? "Penne? Hi! This is Hank. We're having our Regimental Ball at the Shorham in three weeks and I was wondering if you'd like to go with me" *pause...pause...*

"I thought you'd never ask, Hank. I'd love to go with you. What is the exact date so I can tell my mother. She'll help me with my dress and hair and all of that stuff that we do to prepare for a big dance like this. Tommie asked Virginia several days ago so we'll see them there, or we could even double date if you have trouble getting your parent's car. Anyway, we have plenty of time to discuss the dance and I'm just excited that you asked me to go. My brother wants to use the phone, so I have to hang up. Talk to you tomorrow. Why don't you just plan on coming over to the house as usual? See you then."

My heart was in my throat! Quote, "I'm just excited that you asked me." Unquote. Three long weeks before the dance and I was already on a jag that would not subside until the Sunday morning following the big ball. I began to count the days until that Saturday night when I would pick her up, drive down Connecticut Avenue, and promenade down the isle of the Shorham Hotel's grand ballroom, arm in arm, with this magnificent girl, with the even more magnificent tits! It was easy to tell that my hormones were in full afterburner, ready for the eventual blast off that would sooner or later occur with one unsuspicious young maiden in the burbs. Might as well be Penne as anyone else as far as I was concerned. Might as well be Penne my ass! It simply had to be Penne!

My mother had washed and ironed my only white shirt, had my uniform cleaned, and I had polished my military brass and shoes to the highest luster possible in preparation for the big night. And, I made sure that I hit the Capitol Barbershop for a trim to ensure that my flattop was, indeed, flat. The family Ford looked showroom clean and I rearranged the corsage for Penne on the front seat as I approached Worthington Drive, and Penne's house. Her mother answered the door and said, "You look just like the perfect young military man, Hank. Come on it and say hello to Mr. Poole in the living room. Perhaps we could get a snapshot of you two before you leave for the dance. Penne will be down for her grand entrance shortly, and here's a Coke and some cookies."

"Thanks Mrs. Poole. Good evening Mr. Poole. How's it going?

"Fine, young man. We want you two to have a wonderful time tonight but we'd like to have Penne back to the house no later than one o'clock. Do you have a problem with that?"

"Absolutely not, sir. As a matter of fact I have to be back at my house by one, so she'll be here by twelve thirty, or twelve forty-five, at the latest."

When Penne sashayed down the stairs into that living room, and into my heart, I thought my eyes were playing tricks. She looked like a goddess wearing this lovely strapless gown of brocade silk, with matching shoes and purse. And, her hair was arranged in a style that she hadn't previously worn. She smiled and game me a peck on the cheek. I was speechless, for once. I couldn't talk, so I merely stared at her as my mouth dropped. She reminded me of Elizabeth Taylor in the movie, "National Velvet," and believe me when I say that Liz had nothing over Penne Poole at that age. She snuggled up next to me for the drive into Washington, and we arrived at the Shorham just in time for the grand promenade down the isle as the Johnnie's starred at us, and talked with envy of Penne, and of her escort. We danced briefly, very briefly. Then, we left the main ballroom for the closer confines of the hall closets so we could embrace and play Roman Catholic tongue tag until our lips hurt. Then, a little more dancing, and a drink of Coke. Then, back to the hall closet for more primeval petting and smooching. What a night! What a night! Bright lights and big city, watch out 'cause here comes Hank and Penne!

This all occurred in the year 1957. It seems like yesterday when I reminisce about those days in Washington, Somerset, Chevy Chase, Kenwood, and Bethesda. Penne and I dated for two years, almost exclusively, and we never consummated our relationship, which, by the way, was not my own personal short or long term intention. This girl with the big tits eluded me for twenty-four months but I could never bring myself to even suggest the back seat of the family four door Ford Fairlane to her. Shit! The only way I'd ever get her into the back was for her to suggest it, and she never did. So, my interest in her began to wane as I began to run out of ideas for the ultimate conquest of one, Penne Poole. Still, she was my date for our Christmas Ball at the Sheraton Palace, the Junior Prom back at the Shorham, summers at the Kenwood Country Club, (as her guest member), pizza at the Connecticut Avenue Piccolo, and many school functions, such as the football and basketball games, held around Washington, at the various public and parochial schools.

In the middle of the school year, 1959, I began to have a change of heart towards Penne. Our celibacy contract was what I considered to be null and void since it was never ratified by both parties (I, being one of the two participants), so I went on the prowl for some serious opportunities to score around the burbs of Bethesda. This is when I met Bunny.

Bunny! Now, here was a real woman in a Catholic girl's clothing. We met at some social function held at Immaculata, Penne's school, and I immediately fell in lust with Bunny. As a matter of fact, it was her name that turned me on - Bunny. If I were lucky she would demonstrate the meaning of her name, and fuck like a bunny. She had all of the right equipment for this mission - beautiful dark hair, a fantastic ass, lovely long legs, smooth olive skin, Brigitte Bardot sized boobs, and a mouth that could melt you with one, small pucker. Lordy, here was a lean mean Mediterranean screwing machine, and a young lad's dream come true. Bunny was the exact opposite of Penne. Penne was wholesome, demure, sweet and charming. Bunny was raunchy, sexy, sultry, and ornery. Penne was front seat material, while Bunny was definitely "remove the hose, loosen the garter belt, slip onto the nylon mesh seat covers in the back seat, undo the top three buttons of her blouse, and cram her tongue half way down your throat" type of date.

Decisions! Decisions! Decisions! Take Penne out for the show, or take Bunny out for show and tell. My mind was made up. I stopped dating Penne altogether in the latter part of 1958, and concentrated my energies on Bunny, and with another young lass named Vicki, who I met at a National Cathedral School event. Talk about big tits! Hardly anyone saw Vicki's eyes and I defied anyone in my class to name their color. We simply stared at her 34 D cups, and still growing, breasts in total amazement. And, she was beautiful. And, she was rich. We dated a few times on the weekends and talked occasionally over the phone during the week. Vicki was originally from Hagerstown, MD and she was boarding on the National Cathedral School for Girls campus, in Washington. Hence, ours was a weekend romance in that she had no freedom to leave the dorm during the week. *I digress ever so slightly but I digress.*

Back to Bunny. Bunny was a free spirit. Bunny's parent were never home. Bunny liked to tease as a prelude to the real thing. Bunny would love to get on top and rub her crotch until you could get trouser burn through your Levi's. Bunny preferred getting onto the back seat as opposed to sitting in the front of the family Fairlane. Her ritual consisted of getting in the back of the family Fairlane and asking that I not turn around until she said it was okay. During this time she would remove her hose and I would be focused on this sexy foreplay through the rear view mirror. After the third or forth date Bunny said it was all right to look as she hiked up her dress around her waist, and slowly unhooked each one of the four garters from her hose. Then, came the loosening of the blouse and she would ask if I had a condom in my wallet. Just for Bunny I kept a cigar box full of condoms in case she thought a marathon fuck was in order. (Never got past the first condom per night, however. Too excited, I suppose!)

Spring was finally here and it was approaching that time when graduation was rapidly becoming a reality, and so was the senior prom. What to do? Who to ask? Who do I really want to be with on this special occasion? Who really and truly deserves to go? Why, Bunny, of course. I might as well go out with a blowjob as with a bang, I always said. And, Bunny definitely gave more fuck for the buck. Penne didn't know a bang from a gang, and a blow job was totally out of the question. Vicki, on the other hand was undiscovered and uncharted territory, and, being a student of geography, I was most interested in exploring her mountainous areas, as well as her valleys.

"Hank, if I get it on with you tonight will you take me to your senior prom?," Bunny asked one night while on the back seat of the family Fairland.

"Bunny, I told you that I've already asked someone else to the prom because I thought you were going with one of my classmates. *Could I lie!* I can't change my mind now and you wouldn't appreciate if someone did that to you, now would you? Let's get on he back seat and discuss it, okay? Here, let me help you with your bra."

"My feelings are hurt now. You said once before that if I put out you would take me to the prom. Maybe you'll change your mind after I get through with you tonight. Ohhh! Does that feel ever so good! Move with me. Shit! Are you finished already? I was just getting going. *So much for apprehension, and nerves. Too excited, I suppose.*

"Hankie, Hankie, wake up, wake up. There's a Mrs. Kadel on the phone and she said that you promised to take her daughter to the prom tonight. You'd better talk to her."

Mrs. Kadel! Mrs. Kadel! Shit! I sprang from my bed like a fire was ignited under my ass! My eyes were are larges a melons, and I was trembling from fear. What did Mrs. Kadel tell Mrs. Miller? Did Mrs. Kadel tell Mrs. Miller that Mrs. Miller's son had screwed the hell out of her daughter, only several hours previously? And, then he reneged on his offer to take Mrs. Kadel's daughter to the prom, after he climaxed? Get to that phone faster than fast!

"Helloooo? What seems to be the problem, Mrs. Kadel?"

"You first class jerk! My daughter is lying on the bed in her room crying her eyes out because you told her that you'd take her to your senior prom, and then you changed your mind last night. I bought her a new dress and shoes. She has been talking about this for days. You had better reconsider your decision this morning, Hank."

"It's alright, Mom. Hank, I really don't care. And, Mom, please get off the phone now. Hank I want you to know that I'm proud of your graduating from St. John's, and that you should have a good time tonight with Vicki. Take care of yourself, okay? Bye."

Bunny had interrupted her mother's conversation to clear up this mess. Mom asked what the commotion was all about and I told her, "I never asked Bunny to the prom. She had fabricated the entire story and lied to her mother just to make me feel bad. I told her weeks ago that I was taking Vicki to the prom, and that's that!"

I immediately went to the bathroom just to wipe the cold sweat that formed and crystallized into dried salt rings on my forehead. My hands were still trembling, and I almost tossed my cookies thinking about the revelation that nearly occurred between Bunny, Mrs. Kadel, and Mrs. Miller. Indeed, I was in a shit storm. Mom just couldn't comprehend why Bunny and Mrs. Kadel would go to all of this trouble to call me at 8:00 in the morning if there weren't some truth to her accusation, and I was probably up to my old tricks again of stretching the truth, or just plain out lying to this girl about my plans for the prom.

Thank God Mom had absolutely no idea of what occurred on the back seat of her family Fairlane the preceding night while we were parked behind the Giant Grocery store hidden from view by the Dempsey dumpster and by the fog that coated the windows, as Bunny bumped and ground like a 25 year old experienced woman of the world of fuck. The thought of last night enabled me to maintain a slight shit - eating grin on my face with wonderful erotic thoughts of a repeat session with Miss Bunny Kadel in the future. After this episode with Mrs. Kadel, however, I was certain that my trysts with her daughter were fait accompli. And, if I had my head screwed on straight, instead of having screwing as a priority, I would have asked Bunny to the prom months ago, and made her sign a contract in blood on the back seat of the family Fairlane that she would not capitulate and go with someone else at the last minute. Bunny was a sure thing. Bunny was in a constant state of heat and I would have been blessed with the absolute best sex object at the prom had I surrendered and taken her on my arm down the promenade isle of the Sheraton Palace Hotel, for a few quick dances then into the well-concealed coat closet for a long slow fuck. But, noooooooo! This social retard concealed in the body of a 17 year old senior was too stupid to analyze the ultimate objective of his senior prom gala. Form was supposed to follow function, you idiot! You were moving down to Alabama within the month, so who gave a rat's ass what anyone thought about who you took to the prom? You never cared for any of your classmates anyway with few exceptions, like Tom. As for the Christian Brothers who taught you for two years, those assholes could fall of Dante's face of the earth as far as you were concerned. And, your mother and father would never meet your date anyway, so there was absolutely no reason whatsoever for not taking Bunny - strapless gown, front-hooked lace bra, black lace garter belt, black sheer nylons, and sweet smelling, to your last formal event before graduation. But nooooo! You made the worst decision of the three possibilities in asking Vicki. Granted, she was lovely and charming, and you two looked good together, and you two like being together, but as far as the ultimate objective of the senior prom was concerned, Vicki was a less than 500 percent probability of surrendering on the back seat of that Fairlane. Penne, on the other hand, could have been considered better than 500 percent odds for transitioning from maiden to woman after the prom, or in the well-concealed coat closet, down the hall from the grand ballroom. After all, we had dated for almost two years, and we both felt like it was time to continue the explorations of each other's physical attributes, but that goddamn Catholic upbringing wouldn't permit either of us to lower or pants, less our morals with each other. So, I suppressed the thought of asking Penne to the prom mainly out of spite, I suppose. Suppose, my ass! That was the only reason not to ask her.

    My friend and classmate, Joe, and I met the girls at Helen's house (who was a classmate of Vicki's) that evening, and Vicki couldn't have looked lovelier as she walked down the huge spiral staircase dressed in a cocktail length, silver colored strapless gown, with matching shoes and purse. And, those huge tits! We're talking serious tits, here boys. Her cleavage alone was larger than most of the girls' chests at Immaculata. Tonight, she was obviously proud of her tits because they were definitely the focal point of her entire aurora, and the focal point of my 20-20 vision.

    Dinner with Joe and Helen at Duke Siebert's Steak House where the customers gawked and applauded as we entered the famous eatery with our lovely escorts. Congressmen, senators, grandmothers, and nobodies walked over to our table to complement us on our appearance, and to stare at Vicki's tits. I had the best vantage point, however, as I was admiring her navel, clearly past her silver lace bustier, and down to the top of her half slip.

Now, for the grand entrance at the Sheraton Palace Hotel. My fellow classmates, or Johnnies as they were less than affectionately called, starred and whispered, "How could that dickhead Miller get a date with that? Wow!"

"Did you see who that little shithead Miller has as his date tonight?"

"What's a great looking gal with those huge tits doing with that perkerhead Hank at the prom?"

"I've never seen her before. Where in the hell did he find a woman like her?"

"Miller, old boy, why don't you introduce us to your date?"

"Fuck off, assholes! Who is that dirt bag you asked? Did your mamas give you permission to ask a Protestant to the prom? Obviously, you have the same taste as your father, 'cause you date looks like your mama. Butt ugly! And, don't even think about cutting in while we're dancing, cause you'll find yourself on the floor."

Tonight, I embraced the most attractive and well-built date for the senior prom, without a doubt. Not many of the girls offered to come over to talk with us at our table because they were out of Vicki's league. Vicki and Helen were major league ladies and the remaining girls looked as thought puberty had passed them by. We danced and danced, then snuck off to the well-concealed coat closet for Anglican tongue tag (Vicki's school was operated by the Church of England, commonly known to us commoners as the Episcopalian church). We departed the prom shortly after midnight and rendezvoused at Helen's, so the girls could change into casual attire. Meanwhile, Joe and I had changed in the car as we donned clothes that were easier to remove on the back seats of our respective family Fairlanes. Soon, the girls reappeared wearing sleeveless loose fitting cotton blouses and Bermuda shorts with their Bass Wejuns. Still, Vicki's tits were my focal point as she had opted not to wear her bra for this special post senior prom occasion. And, those beautiful tits maintained their upwardly positions because of youthful muscles that, over the years, would most likely require retightening by minor surgical techniques. Tonight, however, these magnificent mammeries were ripe for our adolescent experimentation, and we couldn't get out of the house fast enough at this point. We departed in separate cars together with Joe and Helen in their Fairlane, and Vicki and me in ours. Soon, we found the two cars parked on a dirt road between the tall pines as the moonlight radiated through the car windows, helping me to see well enough to unbutton her blouse and to caress her breasts as Vicki said, "Careful, Hank, I've never done this before, so you have to move slowly, and let me catch my breath. God, does that feel good! Can I loosen the tops of my shorts? Why don't you help me with the zipper on the side? I never had any idea that you could make me feel so wonderful. Tonight, we can go all the way if you want."

If I want? If I want? I had climaxed once already, but Vicki wasn't aware of the soaking wet stain on the front of my slacks. Concealed in my wallet was one, tightly wrapped condom, just for tonight. Suddenly, we heard a tap on our car window and Joe asked me to step outside for a moment. I opened the door as he proceeded to ask if I had a rubber with me. He needed it right away and I'd be a real pal if I let him have mine. I acquiesced and gave him my one and only protection that he was about to insert into Helen. What a smuck! What was I going to do when the big moment finally arrived and we were naked on the back seat of the Fairlane? Vicki whispered into my ear, "Did you bring a cover with you? I mean a safety, or a rubber? I think it's time for us to make love together, don't you, Hank?"

Time! It was time about half hour ago when I blew my wad in the front of my blue Hollywood peggers! "Vicki, I just gave my one and only rubber to Joe as few minutes ago. Why don't we try it without one and I'll pull out before I come. That way we won't have to worry about your getting pregnant. (Wrong thing to say at a time like this!)

"I don't think it's a good idea to take that chance, do you Hank? Let's just pet for awhile. Oh, God! I'm going to have an orgasm, my first ever!" Vicki let out a moan similar to the one a coyote or a lone wolf makes, when it howls to the light of the silvery moon. She laid there and we petted for hours, while I wondered what it would be like to recycle *always slightly ahead of my time, ecologically* a slightly used rubber as I contemplated asking Joe not to throw it into the bushes so that I could salvage it with Vicki. Forget it! Dumb idea! We spent every last ounce, and left the splendor of the tall pines around sunrise for the drive back to Kenwood, and Helen's house. We sat in the kitchen as reminisced about our evening together, as I kept starring at Helen knowing that my Trojan had been put to good use earlier that morning. We said good night and promised the girls that we'd be back over in the afternoon for a graduation picnic in Helen's backyard In the meantime, I had to air dry my clothes by the heat of the family Fairlane's radiator before going home to greet the folks at the front door.

I slept like a baby that morning, and Mom had to wake me in order to make the picnic at Helen's later that afternoon. It was a rather quiet and pensive mood that we shared because Joe and I were graduating and heading off for places far away, while Helen and Vicki entered their senior years at N.C.S., in Washington. In addition, it was the beginning of the summer vacation, and what a way to begin the summer. Vicki would be going back up to her home in Hagerstown, and Helen to their summer place, in Michigan. This meant that neither girls could attend our graduation commencement the following week at Catholic University. I asked Vicki if she could come down for the special occasion but she indicated it wasn't possible due to family commitments. She did say, however, "Hank, why don't you come visit me in Hagerstown? It's only a couple of hours away, and I want you to meet my parents. Besides, we're members of a great club, so we can play golf or go swimming if you like. I just want to see you again before you head down to Alabama, and Auburn, next Fall. Thank you for last night. I've never felt so wonderful and fulfilled as I did with you. Sorry we couldn't go all the way but maybe it is a good thing. I want to remember the prom as something really special, and it was for me. I hope it was for you, too."

My high school graduation was without fanfare. Joe and I graduated together and Helen was able to join our families since she had made other arrangements to meet her folks up in Michigan, later that week. I was without Vicki. I was without Bunny. I was without Penne as my guest for tonight....So lonely and sad.

I drove up to Hagerstown after attending Mass on Sunday to see Vicki. She lived in a magnificent house on the golf course and it was apparent that I should have dropped to my knees and asked her to marry me, so that I could have entered the lives of the rich and famous. We smooched for hours and hours before her parents arrived back at the house. Our formal introductions began and I was accepted as one of the family immediately. We left for the club and to meet others from Hagerstown who had recently returned from college or boarding schools up and down the Eastern seaboard I couldn't help but admire Vicki's fully supported and clothed tits that I had enjoyed previously with the thought that I would like to perpetuate our relationship for many years if it weren't for the fact that I was heading down South in a few days.

We took an inordinately long time in saying good-bye as we embraced and whispered sweet nothings about the night of my senior prom. Then, reality set in as she waved to me while I looked into the rear view mirror feeling about as melancholy as possible.

The Graveyard Shift

My high school graduation was bleak. Neither my sweetie pie nor my dad were present for the ceremony at Catholic University. I understand why Vicki couldn't be there, but Dad? One piss poor excuse after another provided by our navy's finest was the story of my life. Another bullshit excuse of why he had to go defend our country when there wasn't even a war. I have never been able to figure that one out. To tell you the truth I'd much rather have had Vicki there to enjoy the evening. She was up in her home town of Hagerstown babysitting her younger siblings and was unable to be with me.

The old man was off chasing another nuclear windmill for the next year so Mom, Rich and I moved down to Opp, in early June, and we rented one of those tacky, brick, low-life looking apartments up on the Elba highway. As a matter of fact, our apartment was just across the hall from one of Rego's highschool clasmates, whose name was Marshall.

We settled in this humble little apartment that was a basic dump but my thoughts were with my cousins and friends with whom I had spent many summers previously. and the thought of going off to college was exciting to say the least.

Rego was a lifeguard at the pool and one of the latest fashions, in 1959, among the guardians of the chlorine cube was a flattop of pure white hair. No, I don't mean real blonde or slightly blue. I mean pure, snow, cotton-top white. The secret of getting the hair this white was using LeRoux Purple and this was the first step in getting the color out so that a professional beautician could dye hair in another color. Well, some idiot found out about this stuff (probably from his sister) and went and put some on his head. This gooey substance would dry in a pure white powdery cake. After a few hours, you'd jump into the pool, wash it out, and repeat the step until your hair had absolutely no color whatsoever. Rego, Louie Grimes, Kenny Griffin, and several other peckerheads created this fad so I, obviously, had to join the group. Coach Nolen thought the entire bunch of us was looney tunes. And, he was right! Never will forget going home for dinner one day and seeing the expression on Mom's face when she saw me walk into Granny's house looking like a Dairy Queen. She always thought our hair styles were ridiculous anyway, so this didn't make too much difference.

After she stopped laughing and criticizing our latest hairstyles Granny changed the subject to ask if I'd found a summer job, and I indicated that I had not. She suggested that I go across the street to Ruby and Elwood's, since Elwood was a big shot out at the local cotton mill. He might be able to help me if I asked, and so I did. Elwood said I should go out to the mill, fill out an application, and he'd see if there was anything available for the summer. Later that afternoon, I went out to the mill's headquarters and gave them my life's history, and surprisingly, there was a job for an apprentice (that's me) during the graveyard shift. I said, "Heck, I don't mind any kind of work. When and where should I report?"

Thus, began one of the longest days of my life. I'd been up all day, swimming at the pool, applying for a job, having supper - all of this before 7:00 that evening. My work shift began at 10:00 that night and lasted until 6:00 the following morning. In other words, the phrase "Graveyard shift" didn't really sink in until it was too late. So, about 9:00 that night I dropped by to join my cronies at the Parkmore for a Coke before signing in. All of my buddies were dancing, drinking beer, and getting ready to go to the drive-in movie. About fifteen minutes before ten, I drove up to the ominous mill building, walked into the foreman's office to face the music. Much to my surprise, my boss was Wade Ness' father, and Wade was one of Rego's and my best friends. Mr. Ness told me that I got a five minute break every hour, and a thirty minute break at 2:00. He further stated that I would be working with another fellow who was a sweeper and who I would rely on to learn the ropes. My pay was $1.06 an hour, which was one cent above the minimum wage. There was absolutely no drinking on the job; and no smoking except in the designated hourly break rooms located around the mill. Chewing tobacco was okay and I could spit into the piles of cotton on the floor if there wasn't a spittoon handy. A few minutes after my briefing a fellow walked into the office and introduced himself as Tom. Tom, then, took me over to where the brooms were stored, showed me how to place a push broom in each hand, and began to sweep the cotton down the isles into areas for pickup. The learning curve for this task was approximately 45 seconds.

Christ! What in the hell was I doing here! This was the toughest work I'd ever seen, for the worst money I'd ever seen, and working for the dumbest man I'd ever seen - old Tom! This vagrant was about ten or fifteen years older than I was and sweeping floors was as high as he would go up the corporate ladder of Opp-Micolas Cotton Mills. Shit! There was no air conditioning, no ventilation, no cute women, no beer, no music, no friendly faces, no sunlight, but there was plenty of cotton. Tons of cotton. Airballs of cotton. Cotton webs hanging from the rafters. Cotton lint up you nose. Cotton in your mouth. *"Tote that barge...lift that bale...get a little drunk... and land in... "*

There goes that humming again! This time, it was a different type of humm. It was loud, and syncopated; and the vibrations were quite strong as the cotton looms hummed their way long into the long, hot, and dry Alabama nights.

Lots of folks have never seen the movie, "Norma Ray," so a description of the innards of a cotton mill is essential to my telling this tale. Folks, we ain't talking rooms full of Vanderbilt MBA types working at the mill. Most of the employees working at the mill lived in the mill village surrounding the factory. Little cottages, all painted white, with screened front porches and a single car detached garage in back. Laundry lines full of clothes stretched all the way from the house out to the pecan tree in back. Out of the kindness of their little hearts the philanthropists, who sat on the board of directors at the mill, provided subsidized housing for the already borderline poverty-level workers, some second and third generation, so they became what we referred to as indentured servants that we studied in the early history of our beloved United States. Hell, these poor bastards were stuck forever in a system that thwarted higher education, unionization, celebration, or emancipation but strongly urged masturbation in the form of a collective minimal subsistence jack-off, every payday. To quote the muckymucks in the board room, "Here's your measly little paycheck, and we deducted what we consider to be fair rent for your house in the village, so no need to worry about paying that rent every month. And . . . have a nice day!"

Boy, could Tom move down those rows of looms pushing two brooms faster than most people could walk. Here was your consummate worker with a sixth grade education, at best, but he had a big heart, and even bigger forearms!. First thing Tom asked me after I had become fully indoctrinated in the intricacies of broom-pushing was "Panky, wher'd you get that white hair? Never seen anything quite like it before and I hope we don't mistake you fer a pile a cotton and sweep you right out that door!" Naturally, this was the night when I became officially known as "Cotton top" - a title I would hold until the very last minute of employment at the mill. At midnight straight up and break time we repaired to one of the small rooms for a smoke or a chew. These rooms were not only small but totally void of any amenities such as windows, pictures, flowers, chairs, or carpeting. A room about ten by ten square, pine lath walls, a built-in wooden bench, and the omnipresent ash cans and spittoons. This hourly break was the only time the male workers actually fraternized with the female workers for a few minutes. Of course, this was, also, the only occasion to meet socially if the women smoked or pulled a plug of Bull of the Woods for a chew, and the ultimate spit over into the cotton residue that Tom and I would sweep, pile, bag, and discard. Now, you can also imagine how cute most of these women turned out to be. Any resemblance or one ounce of ersatz sex appeal earned them one point. If they had a full set of teeth, we would count it as two points. If they didn't reek of extreme body odor, that would count as three points. After three or four weeks on the job, if they started looking good, they considered you as four points! There goes the whistle. Time to get back to those looms, spools, brooms, and sweat. The temperature hovered around a hundred degrees inside, at night. Hell no! OSHA didn't exist in those days. So, the noise level and the air quality and the temperature tested the true mettle of both the men and women. We could still feel the vibration and hear the humming of those looms, even in this small room. There was no discrimination. If a man could do the task, so could a woman. Shit. Gloria Steinham would have been proud of the way in which the mill corporate treated the gals. No job too tough, or too hot, or too loud, for these broads!

What an exciting place to work! The culture, the climate, the working conditions, the networking potential, the attention to active ergonomics all added up to the main reason why I was so envious of Rego and the gang who lifeguarded for the summer at the pool. My only ray of hope came at the 6:00 quitting time whistle when the push brooms were stored in the executive sanitation engineers' lockers, the '57 black Ford Fairlane was started, the humming stopped, and, by no later than 6:14, cotton top would arrive at the Sweet Shoppe for his morning respite, and breakfast. I'd pull up a chair and order the usual - three or four country scrambled eggs, several slices of hickory smoked bacon, a pile of grits, four pieces of Holsum white toast, a large glass of milk, and leave me alone, please. No time for idle chatter, no time for gossip with the waitresses, no time for eavesdropping with the local "po-leese," just down-home, lip-smacking gluttony at the Sweet Shoppe. I kept a running tab so there was no wasted energy in trying to calculate a tip. Hell, this boy was tired after the mind-wrenching work at Opp Micolas Mills, so home was the next stop for a comatose, much needed sleep. And, thank God, for no more humming.

"Panky, Jackie Lee has Thursday off, and so do I. We're driving down to Panama City for the day, and we want you to come along. We'll pick you up at six and I'll have your bathing suit in the car. Should be back in Opp, around six or seven that evening."

"Rego, you're out of your cotton-picking *(excuse the expression)* mind! I work eight hours Wednesday night and the same shit begins at ten, Thursday night. When do you guys expect me to sleep?"

"Jackie and I'll drive so you can crawl in the back seat and sleep on the way down. Ain't been down to the coast this summer and this is the only time when all three of us can go. What do you say?"

"Let's go for it. Only thing I ask is that we stop at the Sweet Shoppe first so I can eat breakfast. Okay? Then, just let me catch a nap and I'll be all right."

Thursday morning arrived and I hopped into the car. Next stop was my morning ritual at the Sweet Shoppe. Then, into the back seat for some shut eye. I might add that the temperature at 7:00 in the morning would reach 80 or 90 degrees, and no one had air conditioning in his car. So, Cotton Top climbed onto the vinyl-covered back seat of Jackie's Ford and proceeded to enter the twilight zone in the span of about twenty seconds. Light's out for the next two hours, or so I thought. Suddenly, my deep sleep was interrupted by the sound of motors and loud voices. I woke up to find myself in the same backseat only this time we were about ten feet in the air, on a lift in some gas station garage in rural northern Florida. Seems as though we had a flat tire that needed changing so after he identified the problem my solution was to go back to sleep. Another couple of hours later we had the sound of fine, white Florida panhandle sand under the tires of our car. Finally, the beach, the girls, the foot long chili dogs, the sunburn, the thought of having to work that night. Hell, who could get serious about some little beach honey knowing you might never see her again. Anyway, I met some real cute gals, so we traded names and addresses hoping that we'd meet again real soon on the beach in Panama City. So, push-ups, chin-ups, and wind sprints down the sand became our agenda as we competed with the muscular lifeguards for the girls' attention. Here we were on the whitest sand beaches in the world with the whitest heads of hair in the world. Boy, we were a sight to behold! Most of the kids our age hung out around the lifeguard stand trying to impress the chicks, but we were a sad lot compared to the muscular lifeguards who routinely had a covey of quail from whom to choose.

Back on the road again, tires humming down the blacktop through Florala as our day began to wind down. My stomach was chock full of chili dogs, Dr. Pepper, and Dairy Queens. Our ride back to Opp, consisted of multitudes of "Air bursts" that polluted our olfactory senses in that hot, sultry sun. Jackie and Rego had the remainder of the evening to contemplate whether to go to the drive in or to the Parkmore for more socializing. I, on the other hand, barely made the 10:00 whistle at the mill. This evening found me barely able to make it hour to hour. Those push brooms felt like two ton weights in each hand and my feet shuffled along the isles barely able to navigate between the loud humming of the looms. At one point around 3:00 Tom found me standing there, arms resting on the tops of the handles, eyes fully closed, and falling directly into the path of a loom. Doom at the loom, I called it. Had Tom not been there to save my little ass I would have wound up on the ass of someone else because my white hair would have blended in perfectly with the cotton yarn being warped and wefted into denim. Would have just been my luck to have had the misfortune of being woven into a pair of womens' jeans, so that I could have been accused of being literally "In womens' pants" for the rest of eternity.

A ritual began just after a few days of this working at the mill. Mind you, while I was tending to the responsibility of ensuring lint free air at the mill, my compatriots were exercising their hormonal bill of rights out in that field behind the mill, or parked in the last row of the Dixie Drive In. So, it didn't take too terribly long to figure out some way to conjure up a date, go to a movie, or to the Parkmore for a few dances and Cokes, then drive out to the same empty lot behind the mill, and change into my work clothes before signing in for the graveyard shift at 10:00. Being eighteen my sexual drive was in full afterburner, so every effort was made and no resource was spared trying to snare one of Opp's fair maidens for a ride in the '57 black Ford Fairlane for a brief encounter behind the mill, and have her assist me with the changing of my wardrobe. Or, should I say, whatever clothes swapping that was accomplished was my ultimate objective, if you know what I mean. Because of my nightly ritual I made several mad dashes back to the damsels' houses in order to make that 10:00 whistle, which was so loud it could be heard for ten miles in all directions. Okay, okay so we'd get carried away sometimes, and forget the time.

And, to make the situation even more adventurous, we'd tell the tale of the stranger who would sneak up on the cars parked in the empty lot behind the mill, listen for sounds and cries of lust as the stranger would sneak up, open the car door, kill the men, and rape the women. The stranger had a hook for one hand. The stranger would gouge out the eyes of the men and slash the women from their crotch up to their throats. One night, as the parked cars began to leave the empty lot behind the mill, only one car remained. Sounds of lust, passion, and glee could be heard from the partially cracked window in that '55 Chevy pick-up truck. Suddenly, the door was thrown open, but the driver in the truck reacted just in the nick of time as he started the engine, grabbed the door, and sped off into the night with his lady friend sitting there, half dressed and in hysterics. The po-leese report indicated where the suspect had not been found but there were the remains of a prosthetic hand gripping the door handle of that truck!

No need to tell you that the moral of the story was "Girls, let's get in the back seat, roll up the windows almost all the way, lock the doors, turn the radio down low, so you can humm me a tune. Then, we can smooch!"

Even with the Opp gals the humming wouldn't go away. Something in my genes must have dictated that I was to perceive a humming sound all of my life. What could it be? What in the hell was this humming in my ears?

Suppose the highlight of the summer was the time when "Old Cotton Top" outran the Opp po-leese. Just so happens where I had the hottest stock four door sedan in town. This fact was proved over and over again on the Kinston highway as I left the formidable opposition in the dust while driving my parents' 1957 black Ford Fairlane 500 with automatic transmission and screaming down the blacktop consistently breaking a hundred miles per hour. About the only cars in town that were my nemesis were Jackie Lee's souped-up '55 Ford with the supercharged engine, so he didn't really count; and some redneck who ran moonshine for a living. Anyway, the word was out about Panky in his parent's Ford and his racing antics out there on the Kinston highway. One night, before going to work at the mill, I was parked out front of the Parkmore talking to Rego, Wade, and some of the other fellows. When we were finished, I put the Ford in neutral, revved up the engine, popped the gear shift lever into Low, and sped off into the night, laying rubber for a city block. Boy, did I think I was hot shit. Suddenly, I looked into my rear view mirror and that sight I will never forget. Unknown to me, a po-leese car was parked directly behind my '57 black Ford Fairlane at the Parkmore. I had a block head start as the Opp cops were trying to nab me for the first and last time, ready to throw away the key on old Panky Miller. I wasn't about to let that happen so I continued to accelerate and keep about a block's distance between us. I sped across the Andalusia highway, without looking in either direction, at speeds in excess of eighty. Suddenly, I was approaching my place of employment-the Opp Micolas Mill- and without one second's hesitation, I spun the family wheels into a parking space several rows off the street as my pulse raced faster than the car engine.

During this pursuit my buddies at the Parkmore had second guessed my strategic plan, because they taken a short cut to arrive at the mill just seconds before me. The po-leese never could locate that '57 black Fairlane 500 because it was blocked by several cars that had just been seen occupying the parking lot of the Parkmore seconds previously. Meanwhile, I was signed in, pushing those brooms with Tom, and peeking out the window every five seconds as the Opp cops walked around the lot trying to figure out how that '57 black Ford Fairlane 500 was able to travel at Bonneville speeds, come to a screeching halt, park, and appear to have never left that spot in the mill lot. The Opp cops never had conclusive evidence that Cotton Top was the culprit, but the Chief Opp cop paid a visit to one, Mrs. Henry Miller, alias Lucille Dean, the following day to express his disgust with my vehicular behavior. The real truth of the story was and remains: No stock auto could outrun the '57 black Ford Fairlane 500, including the black and white autos with their hot shot po-leese drivers.

Time sure does fly by when you're having fun. September was rapidly approaching which meant time to trade in the push brooms for a slide rule, drafting kit, books, and head on up to Auburn for my first college quarter. Strange thoughts entered my mind as I contemplated leaving this palace of fun and those workers who would never aspire to fraternity parties, college degrees, Southeastern Conference football, or intercollegiate debating teams. No, these folks took one day at a time in hopes that their children would have a better quality of life. So, they reported to the mill every evening, manned or womaned their respective stations, tried their best to tune out the humming, spat tobacco into the piles of fluffy cotton, and looked forward to those five minute breaks where they could meet and possibly line up a hot date with a "One" or possibly even a "Three" for a Saturday night.

Tom and I didn't do much talking during the past three months but he did make one statement that has remained with me for over thirty years. "Panky, heard you're going up to Auburn. That true? Never graduated from high school myself but know some folks who think mighty highly of Auburn. You picked a fine school and you now have your work cut out. Don't let you momma and daddy down and, most of all, don't ever forget your roots, where you came from. If you do that you'll be okay. We're simple folk here at the mill and we believe in family. You take care and I'll miss working with you, Cotton Top. You push a mean broom, boy."

The Magnificent Seven

Better Known as "Those Little Shitheads"

Noel Leon was a Yankee but we still had to admit him into our fraternity chapter. He was the product of some university up North and had decided to transfer down to Auburn to continue his quest for higher knowledge. That didn't mean we had to like him. Simply, we had to assimilate him into our brotherhood since he was already a Delta Tau Delta. Nonetheless, life changed on the Auburn campus that Winter quarter because this ersatz Ichabod Crane, pock marked weirdo was a man of destiny, of power, of focus, whereas we were men of pleasure and leisure who could give a rat's ass about global concerns and sophisticated behavior up North at some Ivy League school.

Noel Leon had a journalism background and he was employed as a stringer by the major newspaper, over in Montgomery. So, if he could uncover a story then he would get on the phone or telegraph a message to the editor's desk, day or night. In turn, he would earn enough to keep him in school and in our fraternity. He was older than the rest of us and he considered himself to be even more knowledgeable and mature than the remainder of the entirestudent body of 8000 souls. Eventually, this attitude got Leon into a whole bunch of trouble down here "deep in the heart of Dixie."

As a member of the Auburn student newspaper staff Noel would strive to get the scoop, the really big news in order to justify his existence and his income for the purported scholarship he was awarded. While the rest of our fraternity indulged in football, southern style, basketball, and winter dances he was running around trying to become another Edward R. Murrow.

He was a gawky looking character, about six foot two, a hundred fifty pounds maximum, pale white skin full of moon craters, deep set dark eyes, and devoid of a southern accent, which really pissed everyone off. The only students who could get away without a southern drawl were the professors and the few great looking coeds (girls to you non achievers of higher education) from up North. He reminded me of all the engineer majors who walked across the campus with stooped shoulders, plaid shirts, striped trousers, white socks, black shoes, and the omnipresent slide rule suspended in the leather case from their belt. Noel was minus the slide rule and the plaid shirt and, in their place, was a suitcoat and a notepad. Noel drove a Renault Dauphin which was like trying to fit a tall straw into a matchbox. His head scraped the headliner inside the tiny car and his long legs were shoved up under the dash so when he worked the brake and clutch it resembled the act of a grasshopper trying to mate with a stink bug. Gawd, it was a sight to behold!

On occasion, Noel would show up at the fraternity house with a fairly attractive woman that was to our utter amazement considering his rather homely appearance. We began to surmise that he was either a cocksman or he promised these lovelies a byline in the Montgomery paper just so he could get a date. Before long, we began to notice a pattern of the same type of date he would ask over for supper on Thursday evenings, or to the dances Saturday nights. Usually, they were borderline cute, stupid, and definitely hard up to agree to a date with this zombie rumored to have a ten inch penis. Noel would strut through the front door, with this shit - eating grin on his face, and proceed to introduce his date to each and everyone sitting in the living room. From that point he would disappear into our housemother's quarters for a brief chat with Mirrum, and then reappear with his date on one arm and Mirrum on the other as the promenade of Delts and dates began into the dining room for supper.

Auburn, in 1961, was a casual campus with few dress codes for the men. We were expected to wear coats and ties to the football games while our dates were required to wear dresses. Obviously, we dressed appropriately for the ever so few formal events held during the school year. One exception to the dress code was that Thursday nights were traditionally date nights at the fraternity houses around town. The co-eds (or broads to you macho types) who were invited over for supper were expected to wear dresses and heels. The men were required to wear coats and ties, which really pissed us off. I must stipulate pissed most of us off, not all of us. Noel loved wearing a coat. Noel loved wearing a tie. Noel loved wearing a coat and tie. We concluded that Noel probably slept in a coat and tie from his generally disheveled appearance.

Out of the blue Noel began this campaign, a personal crusade in The Plainsmen, the weekly student newspaper. Noel thought that mature men and women should adhere to a dress code while attending college. Noel believed that Auburn was way too lax in its tolerance of the way southern men dressed for class. Auburn had already enforced rigid dress codes for the coeds so Noel's concentration was towards the male student body. One day an editorial appeared on the front page of The Plainsmen with verbiage that all men be required to wear ties to class at Auburn University. You'll never guess who wrote this blasphemous article. The editor who was none other than Noel Leon and he had begun his campaign to change what was considered a sacrosanct tradition on the Plains. Men wore pretty much what they damn well pleased to class. But, as far as Noel was concerned, the die was cast and the battle had begun to bring couth, class, sophistication, and Yankee bullshit to rural Alabama.

"Leon, are you out of your goddamned mind trying to get us to wear ties to class? Shit, boy, you'd best get this thing straightened out, and we mean now, before we turn you into a steer, right fast! We ain't never heard of anything as absurd as this in our lives and, tell you what, we ain't going to start now. We could care less what you wore to class up there in New York. Down here we wear what our fathers and our fathers before them wore to class, and that doesn't include a goddamned tie!"

My blood pressure was boiling! The hairs on my neck were standing at attention! Here I had escaped years and years of Catholic and military schools where uniforms were the order of the day just to find myself back in the same predicament years later and having to fight the intolerance of one, Yankee named Noel Leon. Time for a meeting. Time for some serious strategies. Time for a little vigilante work. So, I gathered up a few of my brothers who had the same feelings as I for a clandestine meeting in order to thwart the aggression of the neo Ivy Leaguers whose idea it was to slicken up the southern retards and instill some couth in these parts vise a vie the wearing of neckties.

We met at Jack's house. There were seven of us who had assumed the responsibility of sabotaging Noel's campaign. Jack Andrade, Larry Coe, Norm Bundy, Hutson Finke, Tom McCormick, Ronnie Shaw, and I comprised "The Magnificent Seven." As a pledge to remain secret I even typed these wallet sized cards to use as our identification in the days to come. These cards would soon become status symbols and would discreetly identify us as the group whose sole mission was to sabotage the necktie campaign, and then get Noel thrown the hell out of Auburn.

"Jack, you have always been able to conjure up schemes that work while I go and screw things up and get caught. Got any good ideas of how we can get into Noel's apartment, steal his ties, and escape with none the wiser?

Jack Andrade. The poor man's Anthony Quinn I always said. Jack was a year ahead of us in class and he should have been two full years ahead except for one small detail. Towards the end of his freshman year he knocked the shit out of one of the professors and this earned him a full two year's suspension from the hallowed agricultural acreage called Auburn University. One might say that Jack stepped into one hell of a road apple on his way from the agricultural side of campus to the liberal arts classes. Anyway, we were glad to have Jack back, or, as we used to scream down the hall, "Jack's back. Or, Jack, let's see your back, Jack!"

"Listen, you guys. This is illegal entry 101. No sweat in getting into Noel's pad and doing our job. We'll strike when he leaves for

Montgomery. Word has it that he'll have to report to the newspaper day after tomorrow so let's get our plan so that we can agree on the time and who'll actually participate. No need for seven of us to hit the joint. Perhaps one should stay at the house, another over at the Copper Kettle, and one to accompany Noel to Montgomery to take the heat off our group. He knows that we all think he's a piece of Yankee shit so maybe this will convince him that others on the campus think he should pay the price as much as we do." Jack had an obvious flair for the obvious.

"Not a bad plan, said Norm. Let's determine the time for the rest of us to meet and to agree on who'll hit hid pad and who will stay at the other locations. Hank, why don't you stay outside at the corner of the apartment and signal if anyone heads our way. Tom, you go down the block to Main Street and keep a sharp eye out for his car. Ronnie, position youself at the corner so Hank can see you. The rest of us will break into Noel's pad, find his ties, and do our job in all of thirty seconds."

Winters around Auburn were anything but cheerful because the landscape was bleak and the trees mostly bare except for the few pines left standing. All of the oaks, bays, and other deciduous flora left their leaves to compost in the gutters and streets, and the grass had long since turned brown. Gray skies and temperatures down in the thirties weren't conducive to hanging around outside unless you were an athlete, a football player, or cross country runner. So, the sheer excitement of our scheme was just what we all needed to break the doldrums of campus life during this quiet time of year.

This was getting to be a big deal at times when I became nervous as hell about the whole scheme. Talk is cheap and I was perhaps the poorest man on earth because my gums kept flapping in the breeze about bravery, courage, guts, the American way, and other hyperbole. What if we got caught by the local fuzz? Or, if the president of the school found out, and threw us out on our respective asses?

We took our stations, checked our pulse rates, made certain that we had eye contact with all seven of the group in case a signal was necessary to indicate where Noel's arrival was imminent, and waited for

Jack to give the word. I placed myself outside Noel's front door at the corner of the apartment near a large bush of camouflage. Jack and Hutson jimmied the door and quickly entered Noel's pad. I watched the front door and made sure that I could see Larry at the end of the block. Everything was going smoothly and quickly as Jack and Hutson ran back out of the apartment with these shit eating grins on their faces, signaling victory or mission accomplished. I joined them as we made our way towards Larry, and down the street to Ronnie's and Norm's positions.

"Okay, Jack, did you do your thing? How many ties did he have that are now double in number, but not in function?"

"Let's put it this way. Noel will have to go down to Olin L. Hill's Mercantile in order to continue with his "tie to class" campaign. We cut everyone of them in half, and I have the bottoms in my pocket. Here's a couple as proof." We all broke out in hysterical laughter. Houtson was rolling around on the ground like a mad dog in heat. Ronnie fell over into the bushes and we had to grab him around the ankles to haul him out of the brambles. I started to cry I was laughing so hard. Tears were streaming from my eyes. As we approached the Copper Kettle our giggles would progress into full-blown chortles. Those college students who entered the cafe for a snack were greeted by a band of hysterical underclassmen behaving like ten year olds out on their first overnight camping trip. Would we tell them the reason for our behavior? Shit no!

This occurred on a Thursday afternoon. That evening Noel failed to show up at the fraternity house with his date. I surmise it was because he failed to make it to the store in time to purchase a new necktie for that evening. Not only did Noel fail to make that date night supper but he rather abruptly halted his campaign to require the male student body to don ties for class at Auburn University. At the end of the Winter quarter Noel thought it best to pursue other interests outside Auburn University. We never saw him again.

As a postscript I am certain that Noel is a born-again hippie who probably shed his hoity toity attire and attitude, for Birkenstocks, tie-dyed shirts, dreadlocks, petchulie oil fragrances, and traded in his

Renault for a VW bus as he made tracks for San Francisco, during the summer of love, 1967.

"A Hope-er, A Pray-er, A Magic Bean Buyer"

The melting pot towards the bottom of the Delta where the silt from the alluvial plains joins the salt of the Gulf and splits into a million fragmented isthmuses, islands, and peninsulas at lands end; an environment for harvesting the absolute best tasting oysters because of the union of brine and water temperature; where the language is Cajun and urban accents are not southern. At the crescent of the river lies New Orleans, and most associate the dialect of The Big Easy with the colloquial blend of Irish and Germanic colloquialisms, and you think you have just stepped off the bus in midtown Manhattan, but you're in the Garden District enjoying turtle soup on the porch at Delmonico's, or down in the Quarter sipping a Bloody Mary on the patio at Brennan's. You're not in a southern city as we define the South today, much like Baton Rouge or Nashville or Atlanta or Mobile or Charleston, but in an eclectic community of gypsies, chicory vendors, magic bean buyers, troubadours, artists, liars, merchant seamen, fortune tellers, voodoo practitioners, transvestites, cotton merchants, pretenders, river barge captains, perfume peddlers, wishers, pimps, stevedores, antique collectors, antebellum lawyers, dreamers, musicians, sailors, and what have you, all meandering around the streets day and night and day into the early morning hours before the bars and clubs close for the ritualistic daily cleansing and garbage dumping; And before some of these indigenous folks are up and going to work; the iridescent river fog inhibits visibility as you strut down Rue Royal listening to faint sounds of jazz players winding down their sets.

*****

"Panky, heard where you're going down to N'awlins towards the end of this summer. Well, my friend, have I got a deal for you and you'll be owing me for the rest of your life. You see, I'm good friends with this lady named Linda Constance, and she lives right down in the Quarter where Hutson, Jack, and you spend lots of time drinking and carousing. Quit wasting your time drinking those Hurricanes at Pat O'Briens and staggering around like a couple of idiots at Preservation Hall. When's the last time you were able to pick up a couple of chicks at The Attic, Cafe du Monde, or at Lafitte's Blacksmith Shop anyway? Think about getting serious and you'll get seriously laid, my boy. All you're going to accomplish is either a first class hangover or picking up a couple of coeds who'll leave you high and dry. Linda will take care of you after I call her to let her know that you'll be in town sometime in early September, and she'll be expecting a call from you. By the way she treats young college studs with her southern hospitality. She and her girls can really hum a tune, don't you know. Her place of business is 360 Rue Bastain and the phone is OL 4-5560 which is unlisted, by the way, so don't go and lose it or you'll be screwed. Had the time of my life with her and her lady friends last summer and you will too if you pay strict attention to what I'm about to say. She's a madam but not your typical whore running some sluts in and out of cheap hotels in the Quarter. Her operation is a class act and she's in charge of the best looking covey of quail you'll ever see. Linda provides escorts as far away as Vegas and New York to some of the most powerful and rich businessmen around. The police, the mayor, and even the governor leave her alone because all of the government officials are solicitors of Linda's services, and she would screw them to the wall by publishing their names if they ever get cocky. Face it. All of these fat cats, from the top on down to the wannabes, have occasion to need some friendly companionship, and Linda is dedicated to ensure they have nice big smiles on their pudgy little faces when her girls get through with sucking the chrome off their Peterbilt."

God, how I envied this Dick Roll. He wasn't not the typical fraternity man or ladies man on campus. Rather, Dick was in perpetual motion, doing something like writing for the college newspaper, editing the yearbook, or reporting on some campus event. Never saw him with many different coeds because he was selective and I can definitely count on the one who shares his front seat in the car to be a raving beauty. Dick never hung around the house much and he didn't live in, so I treated him as sort of an outsider even though he was a brother Delt. Nonetheless, I filed away the information he gave about Linda and friends so that I could retrieve it towards the end of the summer, down in New Orleans, when I would eventually rendezvous with Hutson and Jack.

Earlier that summer I worked for a subsidiary of Dillingham Corporation called Valley of the Temples Memorial Cemetery where I am employed as the only "haole" on an all non-white construction crew over on the Kaneohe side of Oahu, Hawaii, for three long and grueling months. Maryann Ball, from way down in Claiborne, Texas, occupies most of my non-working moments during the summer, in Honolulu. I met her at a Howard Tour mixer for the coeds over to go to the university summer school. So, I always look forward to my evenings with soft and sensuous Maryann dancing cheek to cheek down at the Garden Bar in the Hilton Hawaiian Village, or parking behind the Queen's Surf down by Diamond Head. Maryann is your quintessential Texan. She looks like she was God's perfect little creation - all legs, thin, well proportioned in the bosom, with perfect, I mean perfect hair. Her coiffure is never out of place and it appears to have just been removed from a store mannequin and placed on her lovely Lone Star State head. Her teeth are perfect with that Ipana-like smile and nary a lead filling in those perfect ivories detract from perfection. Trouble with most women from Texas, however, is that most of those cowlassies consider the fact that wanton sex will mess up that perfect hairdo or makeup or, heaven forbid, those perfect teeth, and all of the western charm school training that mom and dad scrimp and save for would go right out the Miss Texas window.

Thus, my summer is quite a celibate one, unfortunately, but I can boast about having the absolute best looking little filly this side of the Brazos River as we stroll up and down Waikiki. Lordy, once again I am the victim of form rather than function.

Summer for me in Hawaii is fait accompli, so after about a week of waiting for a space-available flight from Hickham Field to Travis Air Force Base, in California, I finally arrive at Moissant International in New Orleans, where Jack and Hutson greet me with jaundiced eyes. I have this incredible tan and wavy blond hair - exemplary of the stereotyped West coast surfer and I let them know that my free time was spent riding my surfboard on the Pipeline on the North Shore. In fact, I am terrified of the Pipeline because the surf was more than this cowboy could handle, and the ocean bottom, only feet away from terminal bliss, is lined with coral. Still, Jack and Hutson don't have to know the truth.

After departing Honolulu on a marathon flight to first Travis Air Force Base, California, then down to New Orleans, I arrived to have Janck and Hutson greet me "Miller, you look like a commercial from a Beachboys album. Have a good time over there in Hawaii?" asks Jack.

"Hell, what do you think boys? All the wahinis and the surfing is almost more than I could take. Trouble is I spent all of the money I earned on booze and broads so I need to figure a way to earn some bucks since we're going to be here for a couple of weeks before heading back up to Auburn to register. Do you guys have any ideas or am I committed to a life of abstinence while you two raise hell down in the Quarter? Shit Hutson. You have it made since you're staying with your folks here in New Orleans. And, Jack, you can always head back to Mobile when you don't have two nickels to rub together. In my case, I'm screwed. Looking into my wallet I see where there are real slim pickings for the next couple weeks. Oh well, just have to cut down on the Hurricanes at Pat's, and the Delta oysters over at Acme's."

Henry Hutson Finke. The only grandson of the maternal Hutsons, who lived next door to the Finkes, who were truly second, or possibly even third generation New Orleaneans. Hutson was and remains a truly spoiled brat. Hell, he couldn't help it. He is simply caught up in this over-adoration by his grandparents and his folks who relished in the thought that proper etiquette for a boy and family here on Hillary Street, adjacent to the Garden District, consisted of meal planning two weeks in advance of the anticipated event. Teal duck, barbecued bayou oysters, cornmeal stuffed artichokes, gumbo, pepper steak, cheese grits, beignets, chicory flavored full octane and leaded coffee, along with a Sazarac cocktail were the gastronomic delicacies on which

Hutson was weaned. While the rest of us either walked, or hitchhiked, or dated gals with cars, or drive jalopies, Hutson sported around in his continental Austin Healey 3000 two-seater roadster, knock-off wire wheels and all. To say that Hutson was born with a silver spoon between his lips would belittle the spoon. Hell, Hutson was born with a platinum spoon between his gums and a sterling silver thermometer up his rectum, God love him.

Later that evening the three of us meandered on down to the Quarter for some action. Even though it was towards the end of summer there were still a plethora of coeds and tourists hanging around the hot spots. One place in particular was called the Bayou Room, right on Bourbon Street, and a group of folk singers were booked to perform. This was the era of Bob Dylan, the Kingston Trio, Peter Paul and Mary, the Rooftop Singers, the Chad Mitchell Trio, Odetta, Pete Seeger and the Weavers, Leon Bibb, Ian and Sylvia, Joan Baez, Judy Collins, and Hank Miller. Hank Miller? Yes, as I traveled the globe one of my pieces of luggage consisted of a guitar case, sheet music and the burning desire to ring out with protest song after protest song. I possessed every folk album released - good or bad. I even owned the only copy of "Dave Guard and the Whiskeyhill Singers" long playing album in the State of Alabama. Alan Lomax's book on folklore and folk music always occupies one rather large corner of my suitcase. We're talking dedication here folks. So, I was enthralled with sitting in the Bayou Room and listening to this group of these three lads belt out those songs I had memorized, sung in the shower, practiced in the attic, and played frequently on my guitar. Jack and Hutson accompanyied me to the Bayou Room but not just to hear the folk music. No. They hd an ulterior motive which was in the adjacent building. Her name was Linda Bridgette and she performed nightly in the Gunga Den. Linda Bridgette was a "coon ass," otherwise known as a Cajun, who could literally make your hormones stand on end and send them reeling while she stripped and gyrated into these orgasmic positions atop a love seat on the dimly lit stage. What was truly remarkable was that she has a perfect figure after bearing five chilluns while cavorting around with this mobster named Larry Lamarca, the owner of both the Gunga Den and Bayou Room.

If a man or a woman could dream of a complete sexual fantasy for one night it would begin and end with Linda Bridgette. And, I feel confident in saying that Linda Bridgette was most likely an Olympic hummer One just knew that, by being employed in the entertainment field, Linda could really hum a tune.

After listening to several sets of folk music at the Bayou Room we meandered next door to the Gunga Den for some real action. Got to be where some of the coeds we got to know while drinking down at Pat's will even join us to watch Linda do her thing, and these gals will critique her performance, as if they are even in the same league with this professionally sensual goddess of Bourbon Street.

Linda performed every hour for about fifteen minutes and the lines formed outside on Bourbon Street as those who anticipated this award winning performance want to ensure they get front row tables at the Gunga Den-"Two drink minimum, please."

After a couple of nights hanging around Pat O'Briens, the Attic, the Absinthe House and other haunts, like La Casa, I was beginning to run out of money so there were two choices to make. One was to catch a bus to Opp, in the next day or two so that I could get my grandparents to drive me up to Auburn. The other was to gain employment for the next week in order to pick up some more pick-up money. That evening while we were down at the Bayou Room I noticed that the folk trio performed for thirty minutes and then was off stage for thirty minutes. Finally, I said to Jack and Hutson, "What do you guys think about my asking if I can sing during the thirty minute breaks? I'm getting desperate for some bread."

"Hank, get your ass up there and talk to the host, the one over there with the black patch over his eye. Hell, boy, worst thing he can say is no."

I get up from the table and nervously stroll over to this fellow about my height, blond hair, sharply dressed and he does in fact have a black eye patch covering one eye. "Excuse me, but I've been noticing where this folk group has thirty minutes on and then thirty minutes off stage. Who performs during that void?"

"No one right now. My name's Dana and I'm the manager here. Do you play folk music? If so, go get your guitar, come back and see me so we can listen to you perform. I need someone to fill in during that slot and so far I haven't been able to get another act."

'Okay, I'll go uptown and get my ax and see you shortly."

We drove uptown, got my guitar from the house, and beat it back to the Quarter. I approach Dana with much trepidation and told him I was ready. He instructed me that as soon as the trio breaks I was to go behind the bar, get up on the stage, adjust the mike and have at it. Now, the sweat glands were rapidly in gear and I was beginning to get nervous as hell. We started to look around the room and take note of any hostile members in the audience. None as far as I am concerned. I ask Hutson and Jack, "What songs shall I sing and which one shall I start with, you guys. Come on and hurry up. I have to get ready within the next few minutes. And, by the way, do you want to join me and we can become a trio?"

"You're out of your mind, Hank. We ain't going to join you but we'll clap like hell. Get up there and strut your stuff. Start with 'Blowin' in the Wind' and then follow with 'If I had a Hammer,' then onto 'Five Hundred Miles.' You look at us and we'll give you thumbs up or down if you're off key or if the mike isn't loud enough and we'll also try to get the gals in the audience all riled up so they applaud like mad. Don't sweat any mistakes and you'll do just fine. If it gets real bad we'll split and see you down at Pat's during your break, okay?"

My lack of confidence could be traced back two decades as I reflected on why I was literally scared to death at this moment. Up until college my self-esteem was down around my ankles as I peed into the toilet of life while urine sprayed onto my feet. My parents have seldom found anything to boast about regarding my grades or athletic achievements and I was under constant scrutiny regarding behavior, catechism classes, table manners, clothing styles, haircuts, piano lessons, where' the belt on my jeans, and so forth. Not much to cheer about around the old Miller homestead but things were different up at Auburn, and in the Delt house. I was the unequivocal leader in the knowledge of and performing of folk music made popular first by the

Weavers and then the Kingston Trio's hit, "Tom Dooley." My self-esteem began to improve but there was still this nagging that prohibited me from letting it all hang out and just being myself. Too much Catholic schooling, I suppose.

Here I was about to embark on a semi-professional gig and my head was in a cloud regarding lighting, acoustics, makeup and all of the various sundry accouterments necessary for stardom. "By the way, Dana, how much is the pay and the hours I work?"

"I pay six dollars a night and you perform every half hour until two o'clock."

"Six dollars? Shit! Are you serious? Hell, this is hard work and long hours. How much do you pay the trio? Certainly, they each get more than six dollars."

So much for the make-up, lighting, acoustics and accouterments.

"When you get to be as good as they are and you can draw a crowd like they can I'll up your pay to equal theirs. Fair enough? Now, let's hear you sing for the next thirty minutes. I'll introduce you and then you're on your very own. Want a drink before or while you're singing just ask the bartender. The drinks are on the house for you and anyone who works for the owner Larry Lamarca."

"Ladies and gentlemen, we have a young fellow from Opp, Alabama, visiting with us down here in New Orleans, and he has just finished a gig in Honolulu, at Humbums, down on Waikiki. Who knows, he might be the next Dylan. Let's give a nice round of applause for this young troubadour Hank Miller!"

I gotta tell you that I am about to puke in the sound hole of my Framus classic guitfiddle. Oh, there were a few kind folks who don't know any better so they gave me a few rounds of applause. Then the silence was deafening! As I begin the lyrics all I could think of was the hook coming out from behind the curtain (but there was no curtain) and throngs of irate customers demanding their money back (but they haven't paid any money) and myriads of other self-induced terrors. I begin to settle down, catch my breath, and belt out Dylan at his best. First song completed. Nice applause and a few cheers from Jack and Hutson. Dana walks up, leans over the bar and says, "Not bad for your first song. Now, keep it up and the thirty minutes will fly by. Sing anything you want but try asking' for some requests. That'll keep the crowd happy and asking for more," as I stared right into his black eye patch. Shit! Why can't I pick his one good eye instead of the obvious? At this point I ask the bartender for a gin and tonic, and he obliges right away. No air conditioning and it was the typical humid, sultry summer evening with barely a whisper of breeze out on Bourbon Street. Inside, the beads of perspiration are evident on everyone's foreheads, and on the ladies cleavages. This cowboy is sweating from head to toe but I suppose it adds to the color, the drama, the acting portion of this equation and this is what the folks are there for-cheap entertainment.

Later the following evening Hutson and Jack ask me to join them next door for a voyeuristic experience watching Linda Bridgette soak a sofa. Of course I replied in the affirmative, so we walked into the Gunga Den, and I told the bouncer that I worked next door for Larry Lamarca. He ushered us right up to the bar and instructed the bartender that all drinks were on the house. Nervously, I sat there anticipating this goddess, tall and blonde, to come out and wave her "thirty eight double D's" in our faces, and take our dollar bills and place them in her crotchless panties. Not the case one slight bit! As the lights dimmed and the recorded music became louder a petite brunette parted the curtain and walked onto stage not ten feet away from us. She appeared to be about five feet tall and a hundred pounds at most and her body was no less than perfect. She began to lay down on the couch-the gold gilded crushed velour couch, and move her hips and breasts in this manner similar to belly dancers except Linda is horizontal. Not one pair of eyes in the joint is focused anywhere except on Linda Bridgette, and the audience was silent. Concentration at its highest form was in evidence tonight and I memorized every single freckle and mole on her magnificent frame. Fifteen minutes later Linda phlegmatically slithered behind the curtain and the show was over, except most of the men in the audience are unable to leave their seats and stand up because another portion of their anatomy was already erect and obviously cumbersome.

Was this a summer, or what? First, almost three wonderful months on Oahu and dating the most beautiful gal on the island, living in huge quarters in Makalapa, above Pearl Harbor, which was reserved for only the top military brass, and now this. Of course, my fantasy with Linda began and ended in my libido and not even my id was informed for fear that Larry Lamarca would discover my lusty dream at which time I meet the fate all too often recognized as one philistine who winds up at the bottom of Lake Pontchartrain, with his Alabama feet permanently embedded in Louisiana oyster shell concrete.

I proceeded to walk back to the Bayou Room as I contemplated suicide because of the wanton lust that developed from my close encounter of the horny kind with Linda. Lord God almighty, could this woman speak body language as thought she had a doctoral degree in linguistics from the College of Love!

As my next set closes I noticed that Linda and her husband, and my boss, were seated in the audience watching the show. As God is my witness my eyes never crossed those of Linda Bridgette's. But, they did cross those of Larry Lamarca's. I stepped down from the stage as Mr. Lamarca invited me to join them for a drink. I sat to Mr. Lamarca's left, one seat over from Mrs. Bridgette. The three of us looked straight ahead towards the stage least our eyes wander, meet, and suggest extra-curricular activities that would eventually lead to my speedy demise. Mr. Lamarca did say, "Nice show, Miller. Hear where you go to Auburn, that true? Well, we won't hold that against you down here in Bengal Tiger Country. Been along time since the War Eagles met L.S.U. for a showdown."

My reply was directed to Mr. Lamarca while my eyes stared at some object far across the room for fear that he will somehow conjure up the idea that I was looking at his beautiful wife. "Mr. Lamarca, thanks for the job and especially for the house prices whenever I go out for drinks and food. Everyone here in the Quarter knows you, and the proprietors extend house prices to me and my friends whenever we ask." I might add that not one single itsie bitsie word was said about Linda's sterling performance only minutes before my set. Lordy, my mama didn't raise any dumb kids and I know that any mention of Linda's magnificence would shorten my life span by about ninety percent. Think what you will but utter a word about Linda Bridgette to her old man would be certain suicide, or genocide, depending on the circumstances and details of the fatality. And, the obituary column in the *Times Picayune* would be printed in small type in an obscure corner of the page preceding the Neptune Society discount coupon classified. Nonetheless, I hd this burning sensation in my groin that yearned for relief only a talent like that provided by Linda for my partner, whomever that might be at the time. Mind over matter. Mind over matter. I must repeat this over and over again in the cold shower of my psyche. So, I think of a tune to hum and I kept humming that same tune, over and over.

One evening as I was performing on stage Dana - the host, bouncer, agent, manager, and payroll clerk - approached me and said, "Hank, see that fellow sitting way back in the corner, the one in the dark suit with the shades? Well, he's a doctor of philosophy conducting this study of entertainers and he wants to do a study of you. He asked me if I would inquire about your coming up to his hotel room so he could do a sketch of you while he interviewed you."

"Dana, why in the hell would this guy want to sketch me? Is he an artist or what? Where is he a professor and what does he teach?"

"Hank, all I know is he wants you to take off your shirt, sit there while he sketches you, and asked you some questions he has in his survey. In return, he'll pay you fifty dollars for your time and trouble. What do you want me to tell him?"

'Let me think it over. I'll discuss it with my friends and let you know my answer after the next set. Okay?"

Jesus Christ! What in the hell was this guy thinking? Take off my shirt and pose for him while he asks me questions! Shit! How do I get myself into these situations, anyway? "Jack, Hutson, you overheard the story. What do you think I should do. My first inclination is to go along with his request because I need the fifty bucks and he wouldn' t dare hurt me, do you think?"

Jack's reply is, "Go ahead and go up to his room and proceed with his plan and, as soon as you give us the word, Hutson and I'll break into the room and roll the sonofabitch."

"Are you guys out of your minds? Roll him! And, you want to use me a queer bait so we can steal his money. I think you're both out of your fucking minds and I see absolutely no humor in this sick scenario. And, what if you two fail to show up at the room, and there I am sitting in this hotel room, half naked, and answering questions for a total stranger. It would be just like you two bastards to leave me high and dry with this guy who just want to cornhole me and record his conquest in his little journal of love. No dice, assholes!"

I finished the next set and watched this pervert sitting way back in the rear of the room trying to determine if he was really on the up and up. "Dana, thank this guy anyway but tell him I'm still a virgin and I intend to remain that way for the rest of my heterosexual life. Tell him I'm going into the seminary and that the good Jesuits will want to know that my rectal hymen is intact. Furthermore, why doesn't he come up and talk to me without using you as the spokesperson? Tell him that he can sketch the three of us-my two buddies and me-and we will pose for him for one hundred and fifty dollars. See how he feels about that."

"I'll go ask him but he was interested in you, Hank. Not sure he wants to talk with your friends. Hell, he is an okay guy and I simply don't understand why you won't take him up on his offer."

"Dana, I have a good idea. Why don't you take him up and tell us all about it tomorrow.? Shit, I'll bet you that this pervert has ulterior motives and that you will be "AC-DC" come tomorrow night. How's about betting me a hundred bucks on the subject?"

During all of this chatter, Hutson and Jack had meandered down to Pat's to meet a group from Tulane and I was stuck with Dana and this debate, so finally, I said to Dana, "Ix nay on the entire subject. No deal. No dice. Not interested. End of discussion. Just let me sing and pay me my six bucks at the end of the evening and we're square. The only copulation that I'll even consider is with Linda Bridgette without hesitating for one minute. "

Was I nervous? Of course. This lily whitebread kind of guy has his limits and sitting in some hotel room with a pervert is not my cup of tea. As midnight approached I beet feet down to Pat's for some action more in line with what I had in mind in the first place-cute college coeds, or nurses, or airline stews. Pat's was packed as usual for a summer's evening and I saw Hutson, Jack and other Delts from Tulane crowded by the bar. As I walk up Hutson asked, "Well, we take it you turned down the offer. Right? Can't say that I blame you, and if I were in your shoes or, should I say, BVD's, I would have refused that tryst. Say, Jack, maybe you're interested in taking Hank's place up there with the professor. Shit. You've had lots of experience over at Dixie's and out at the My Oh My Club, by Lake Ponchartrain, with those transvestites hanging all over you."

"Stick it, fellas. This cowboy is doing just fine right here at Pat's. I want you to meet this sweet young thing from Sophie Newcombe and her name is Laurie Prados. Laurie, who are your friends over there because my buddies Hank and Hutson need all the help they can get with dates. Your see, Hank has this thing with queers who want to sketch him naked, and Hutson just has this thing with getting a date, period!"

"Hi guys. That shouldn't be a problem that I can foresee and if you'll excuse me for just a minute I'll go over and ask my friends if they'll join us. You boys don't look like queers to me so I'm sure the girls will enjoy having a Hurricane or a mint julep with you and we can figure out where to go from here. There should be a party somewhere up town near St. Charles."

That evening turned out to be a total disaster in that we eventually find this party but the problem is the party is full of students from southern schools. Too many vestal virgins. Too many sweet young Catholic or Baptist things with perfect hairdos and porcelain makeup and morals worn on their faces like placards hanging around their necks, like emergency bracelets. "In case of aroused sexual appetite, break the glass, pull the alarm releasing cool water on the victim while intravenously injecting salt peter in the assailant's pecker!"

"Hutson, Jack, guess what I'm doing tomorrow? You're ever so correct! After tonight's disaster with more southern girls I intend to use this phone number of a madam down here in the Quarter that Dick Roll gave me during Spring quarter. He knows this madam real well and she is expecting a call from me this week. Dick has told her that I would be coming down to New Orleans before heading back to Auburn and that she will take care of me, in no uncertain terms. Let me see if I can find it here in my wallet crumpled up with all of the other emergency numbers I carry while traveling coast to coast. Thank God I didn't loose it this summer. Her name is Linda Constance, residing at 360 Rue Bastain. Hutson, know where that street is? I sure don't. Anyway, Dick said that she loves young studs from Auburn and that she will take care of our every needs including you-know-what."

Next morning we arose about noon due to the fact that we'd been up carousing around the Quarter until three o'clock, then up to the Magnolia Grill for a snack around four. "Hutson, wait 'till your mama leaves for the store and we'll get on the two phones, and call Linda. I'm nervous as hell so I need to calm down before I talk to her. Hell, it's just a phone call so I don't know why get this way. Suppose it's that damn upbringing screwing up my libido again."

Mrs. Finke left the house for her regularly scheduled morning grocery shop so we got on the two phones and I dial up the number that Dick gave me.

A male voice answers, "Three six-two-four-four-five-six."

"Is this Linda Constance's number? May I speak with her?"

"May I inquire as to who is calling?"

"Hank Miller, and my friend from Auburn University, Dick Roll, referred me."

"Hank, just one minute please."

"Hank Milluh, I've been expecting yo call, young man. My good friend Dick Roll couldn't speak highly enough of you and I have been waiting to roll out the red carpet for you and your friends. Tell me, do you you need a place to stay? I've got a beautiful room overlooking the courtyard, with your name on the door".

"Mizz Constance, thank you so much but I'm staying with one of my roommates who lives uptown on Hillary Street."

"Listen, Hank, you're more than welcome to come down and stay with me. And, my name is Linda, so don't be so formal. I appreciate your southern manners but I feel like we've known one another for some time just by the tone of your voice. By the way, do you need any spending money while you're here? And, how long do you intend to visit with us here in The Big Easy? We'd love to have you as a guest, and the girls hear you're a nice young man who likes to have a real good time. We heard where you love to sing folk music. That true? Well, our ladies would love to hum along, and you would truly enjoy their harmonizin' along with you. These young ladies take real good care of Dick whenever he comes through town, and I'm certain they would love to do the same for you. Do you know where I live? Well, 360 Rue Bastain is the street address and it's in a courtyard, so you can't see the front door from the street. You just have to walk in, announce yourself to my doorman, and he'll usher you right up to my office."

"Mizz Constance, since I have a place to stay why don't you let me think about coming over to your place. Let me discuss it with my friends and I'll call if I need your kind hospitality. And, thank you very much for your kindness. I really appreciate your offers and maybe I'll be in touch in a day or two."

"You go ahead and do what you think is right and my offer still stands not only for you but for your friends from Auburn. Tell you what though. You're passing up the opportunity of a lifetime by not coming by to enjoy my house. Just remember, a house is not a home, and what I have to offer is beyond whatever you could possibly afford to pay if I were to give you an invoice for my services. I'm doing this out of my love of young college men. Enough of my preaching for now. You boys have a real good time down here, and just call if I can help in any way."

"We sure will and I'll be sure to tell Dick that we talked and that you send him best wishes."

As I hung up the phone I suddenly realized that I had really screwed up. An opportunity of a lifetime has just slipped right through my fingers and I was too dumb to realize it. Just think of it. A covey of quail waiting for us to come down and snuggle with them, bath with them, and screw them to death . . . and I had a place to stay! What an idiot. Hutson and Jack suggested that we get in the car and drive down to the Quarter to Linda's address just so we could see where she live. By doing that maybe we would change our minds and call her to take her up on the offer. I could understand my reluctance to bed down with her girls, but Hutson and Jack? That didn't make any sense at all because these two urban studs had seen the insides of a multitude of whorehouse during their lifetimes. As for me, well, I was basically a coward when it comes to women. I was what you would call a social retard in the ways of young wanton lust and in my own perverted way I believe that function always follows form. Give me a good looking clean cut gal any day. Don't make no never mind that she intends to remain the vestal virgin for forty years least we forget that her hair would remain the paradigm for all the up and coming southern belles to ape.

"Hutson, I can't stand it any longer. What do you say about getting into the car and driving down to the Quarter just to see where Linda lives? Hell, can't do us any harm and it will really put my mind at ease once and for all. The curiosity of this whole ordeal is killing me, so I'd really appreciate a drive-by."

Hutson said, "Let's get going and then we can decide whether or not we proceed to step number two, and that is to go and visit Linda, first-hand."

We jammed into Hutson's Austin Healey and proceeded to race down St. Charles towards Canal and then into the bowels of the Quarter where tourists dare not tread since the cops did not patrol it regularly and it was full of stevedores and Cajuns looking for a fight.

We're talking way off Canal, like dozens of streets south of the main thoroughfare that is know for Mardis Gras and Sugar Bowl parades on New Year's day. Rue Bastain. That's the name. The street to the left, Hutson. He didn't need my silent coaching because Hutson knows the Quarter like it is part of his soul. The street numbers grow arithmetically with the increase of my pulse. 100 Rue Bastain . . .150 Rue Bastain . . 210. . .280. . .300. . .320. . . 360. . . "Slow down, Hutson, we're here and I want to get a real good look into the courtyard. Go down to the corner and turn around slowly so we can get a better look at what we're missing by driving around in this goddamned little sportscar. My butt is falling asleep from sitting on the gear shift console while you proceed to set land speed records on these horrible bumpy streets. Just think. We could be inside Linda's hacienda getting a nice massage from a blonde, a brunette or a redhead, or from all three!"

There was nothing from this vantage point that we couldn't have seen just walking down the street. No surprises and no mysteries as expected. So, we drive down to the Morning Call for some dark chicory coffee and tasty beignets to discuss the situation and our next plan of attack. Neither Jack nor Hutson are very interested in pursuing this potential tryst. The opportunity of my lifetime was slipping right through my lascivious little hands. Another great idea down the tubes, so they say. I just couldn't bring myself to walk into that mysterious courtyard and announce my arrival; and to inquire about the offer Linda presented to me and to dozens of other college lads, I'm sure. "Hutson, let's head back up to the Bayou Room so I can give notice to Dan. I've been there for two nights and I'll give him my week's notice. These hours are killing me and your mama doesn't appreciate my sleeping in until noon everyday. Can't say that I blame her, so the best move is to stop this whole thing and head on back up to Opp, soon. You guys, we'll never know what we'll miss behind those old brick walls. Visions of romping from bedroom to bedroom with all of these naked women gets my juices flowing real good. Perhaps we should try to contact Dick Roll to see if it's worth all this effort on our part. Hell, Dick would probably chastise us for our ignorance, and he'd hop a plane just to be here on a moment's notice. Here we are cavorting around with these cute little college honeys and getting nowhere while Dick provided us with a free ticket to ride. To ride the entire herd. To rope and round up all the fillies. To saddle up, strap on the spurs, tighten the cinch, and open the chute to fantasy, fun, fornication, and other various sundry fellatio."

This preoccupation with sex was my back seat companion as we departed the city limits to cross Lake Ponchartrain on our way to Mandeville, then up through Hattiesburg, Laurel, and eventually into the Cradle of the Confederacy. Auburn was only about two hours away as I reflected back on two weeks of our picayunish behavior.

Later that Fall quarter, during one particular dreary rain-soaked weekend, I was sitting alone in the fraternity house thinking about a cup of that delicious chicory coffee served up with some tasty sugar-coated beignets, wondering what was happening in those rooms at 360 Rue Bastain, French Quarter, New Orleans, Louisiana, and then I sink into an even greater state of depression. Eventually, I walked over to the corner of the room, open the case, and remove my guitar for one, last college boys lament and proceeded to hum a tune suitably titled, "You Really Pick Me Up When You Lay Me Down."

*****

The mystique of the Crescent city has captivated millions throughout the years and I presume it has nothing to do with voodoo. "You do. . . what you do. . . with voodoo. . . so well." White boys don't know nothing about voodoo. White boys don't know nothing about anything spiritual, mystical, or esoteric. Shit, boy. Let's face it. Whether you're a Jew or a Catholic or a Baptist you most likely weren't bred on ritualistic hocus pocus or secret pagan rituals that would curdle your blood, or would involve drinking your blood, or someone else's blood. After all, one of the biggest challenges to us who fell off that white bread truck at birth was what clothes to wear to mass or to synagogue or to the Southern Christian Conference First Baptist Church for some medieval procession that shouted of starched white clothes, shiny patent leather shoes, squeaky clean skin, and styled hairdos.

Our suburban white ghettoes restrict us from the cultures and traditions of those who our parents feared and tried for generations to oust from the Anglo-Saxon culture. I add that our folks failed. Not only are these Afro-Caribbean rituals alive and well but flourishing in southern Louisiana today. Long live the dreamers, the wishers, the liars, the prayers, the dreamers, the magic bean buyers who congregate to spin flax-golden tales, and who elevate many of us to a cosmic level that otherwise would have been permanently catalogued in that ever popular anal retentive tome known as Martha Stewart's Americana.

Auburn U. Delta Tau Delta Pledge Class 1960

Joanne's Chevy Convertible Troy State Respite or, "Ladies, We're Delts from Auburn. Wanna Danz?"

Picture this. Friday night at the fraternity house after five crunching days of classes stretching anywhere from seven o'clock in the morning until nine at night. I gotta tell you that we're ready for some serious partying, albeit some more so than others. After Jake, our black houseboy and sous chef, announced, "Supper is now bein' served," Mirriam Carroll, our housemother, left her private quarters situated off the living room, entered the main social area of the house when\\\\and one of us would escort her into the dining room, then to the head table. The remaining Delts then entered and seated because this is a traditional ritual at all meals with the exception of breakfast, because, as we all know, chilvary abounds in the South.

Our dining table was always the rowdiest and was usually situated as far away from Mirriam and the head table as possible. The definition of "our table" means that those of us who were nonconformists, and irreverent, picked a table where we could speak of things plain out right dirty without fear of offending Mirriam. These plastic laminate-topped, metal-edged, folding tables accommodated 10 students. This particular Friday evening found Norm Bundy at one end of the utilitarian slab with his back to the dining room wall. Norm was your quiet type but who really was a latent hell raiser, your clean cut variety and engineering major who wore white socks and his slide rule hanging from his belt. The college women loved Norm for his style and because he possesses that special quality called class. Most likely, the gals liked Norm because he had a car with a large back seat.

Three years later, Norm received his Navy Wings of Gold and we rendezvoused in Pensacola, when I entered the Navy Flight School to pursue the same objective.

Jack Andrade was sitting at the opposite end of the table. Jack was not your clean cut type and, no, Jack does not pursue engineering. Instead, Jack pursued beer, jazz, and women - not necessarily in that order. And, he was yet another rowdy originally from Mobile. Jack was what we refer to as your poor man's Anthony Quinn, because of the physical similarities of the two. The other Delts and I found the remaining six seats so we made ourselves at home, ready for some good southern grub.

I might add that, prior to supper, we had been up in our room playing rock and roll as we had formed a rock band during the school year. We played mostly benefits - benefits for beer, for food, for anything that benefited our survival. Along with performing, we consumed vast quantities of beer, namely Bush Bavarian because it was cheap, and so were we!

One could sense that this was no ordinary Friday night supper, or one could, at least, sense that we were in this strange full-moon mood. . . known as crazy. In walked Monty Peyton, a Phi Delt from the house up the street, and a good friend of mine. He had been drinking and as he pulled up a chair next to me, he proceeded to reach over, pick up a peach floating in its own syrup and slaps it in my right ear. Without missing a stroke, I returned the assault by implanting a handful of mashed potatoes in his left ear. Ronnie Shaw proceeded to throw several ballistics towards Mirriam at the head table. By now, the food fight has officially begun and Norm Bundy asked Jack, "Please, to be passing the peas." Jack accommodated Norm by lifting up his end of the table so that all of the bowls containing food begin to slide downhill towards Norm, and eventually wound up in his lap, causing his chair to collapse from the weight. Norm landed on the floor, covered in mashed potatoes, peaches, turnip greens, rice pudding, and numerous other members of your four basic food groups. The rest of us wound up in hysterics! Did we really care that Mirriam insist that we cease this behavior and hysterical laughter and leave the dining room immediately. Hell no!

We invited Monty to stay over and join us for a shower so that we could clean up, sober up and continue to party until the wee hours. "Hell, I didn't start the fight. Hank slapped me with the mashed potatoes first. Besides, I am a guest so you can't nail me with this accusation."

"Peyton, we'll nail you nuts to the banister if Mirriam penalizes us, so don't get any ideas about passing the buck."

"Listen up, you guys, we're having a rush dance down at Troy State tomorrow night so we need to get a couple of you down early tomorrow to check on the logistics, such as the place where the dance will be held, the band, and, last but not least, the girls." Tom McCormick and Fred Martin were in charge of this special program and we're all looking forward to going down to Troy State to recruit more pledges who would eventually transfer up to Auburn and establish themselves as potential pledges for the Delt House.

"Hey Peyton, let's you and I go down to check on things. Got any plans for the weekend? I'm free until Monday and then the rest of the week is screwed with exams."

"Sure, Miller, but you don't have a car. On second thought I have access to your old galfriend Joanne's Impala. She's kinda interested in me but I could care less about her. Nonetheless, I told her that I had military reserves over in Montgomery. This weekend, and she offered to loan me her car. So we have wheels, my friend."

"Joanne'll cut your balls off is she finds out that you and I used her car to hustle chicks down at Troy, but then again, who cares what Joanne thinks? Let's get up early and head out. As a matter of fact, I would like to go to my music store in Montgomery, and look for another guitar. How does that sound if you have to go over to Maxwell Air Force Base for a few minutes?"

"Perfect, so I'll pick you up at eight o'clock and we'll blast of for Montgomery, and Troy. Is this dance coat and tie or casual, Fred?"

"Casual, you guys, so I take it you are our two ambassadors until the rest of us arrive tomorrow evening."

"Right, Fred, we'll take care of the details, so please give us the people to contact and we'll ensure that everything is ready to go at eight o'clock for the dance. By the way, whose playing?"

"Larry Coe and his group, 'The Webs,' so we are damn lucky in getting them for free."

Larry was one of my roommates and one hell of a guitarist, His band was formerly led by Bobby Goldsborough, who had since left to back Roy Orbinson.

I dated Joanne the previous year but now the relationship was on the skids. She felt very strongly about the fact that our bonds remain intact during my summer in Hawaii. Joanne was what I refer to as a lightweight in the dating circles and there were dozens of local wahaini's, in Hawaii, who had much more to offer me.

Joanne was from Birmingham, and an only child of the home spun, southern Baptist ilk. However, this cowboy yearned for something more and he found it in Lynn Everett, a Navy Junior from Welleslley, who was a fellow worker at the Pearl Harbor Submarine Base Navy Exchange. Blonde, blue-eyed, small waist, nicely developed breasts, clear complexion, great attitude, loved folk music and beer, and she possessed a modern moral standard. I mean, this gal was the answer to my spiritual, physical, hormonal, and emotional prayers. Lordy mercy, I had been dating retards in Alabama, and now I had rediscovered Yankee women. Glory hallelujah; praise the Ivy League!

Monty Peyton, another service brat, was one of my best friends and he would remain so for over thirty years as we took separate paths down the narrow alley of life. He was your quintessential "Jarhead," with that tough, clean-cut, almost cartoon-like square jaw and muscular sinewy frame. Monty was second generation Marine and his home was Tucson, where his father had retired several years ago. A little whacko? Yes, but then so are the rest of my friends. Must say something about my character but then I have always considered myself to be a tad bit left of normal.

Next morning Monty rolled up to the Delt house at eight o'clock sharp and tooted the horn. I went to the window and there he is in Joanne's Impala with the top down waving for me to come on down so we could blast off for Montgomery. "Miller, get your ass in gear so we can blow this joint. I'll be across the street at the Copper Kettle for some eggs and grits, so hurry it up."

A quick shower, clothes in my overnight bag, my ukelele and off onto Highway 29 towards Tuskegee, then on to Montgomery. Bright, sunny warm day, top down in Joanne's Impala convertible with nothing but good times ahead. "Peyton, did Joanne ask if I were going with you to Montgomery?"

"Yep. I told her no, and that I had to run some errands after reserves. She has no idea that you're here or she'd literally turn me into a steer. Besides, do you really care, anyway, what she thinks?"

"Hell no, but I thought I'd ask. By the way, what is this cannon doing on the back seat? Christ, it looks like a blunderbuss from the Revolutionary War. Is this thing legal? God almighty, if a state trooper sees that gun we'll go to jail. Do not stop. Do not collect two hundred dollars. I can hear that trooper now. "Shut yo ass up, boy, and get in the back of this po-leese car now!" Can't you just see us in the lineup trying to explain what we were doing with a piece of light artillery in the back of a rag top cruising down South Alabama blacktop?"

"Relax, this is my Ruger forty-four magnum, sixteen inch, buntline special revolver. Brought if from my home in Tucson, and we'll get some ammo in Montgomery. Have you ever fired one of these? It's like holding onto the butt of a kicking mule. I mean we're talking firing with two hands on the grip with your arms stretched out straight out in front, elbows locked. The sound is deafening and the recoil is deadly. It'll tear down a road sign at fifty yards and I mean it will self-destruct from the impact of the slug. Won't see many like this, in Alabama."

"For Christsake, put that thing in the trunk so noone will see it. What do you plan to do with that cannon on our trip down to Troy, anyway? Shoot a coed? I can see you out in the desert with a magnum but not down here because everything is so close together. All of the farms and houses butt up right next to each other with not a hell of alot of room for a weapon like yours to be used for target practice. Besides, you'll be able to hear it in the next county!"

Monty's sheepish grin always giave me a chuckle. "Don't worry, Miller, we'll find a way to get off a few rounds between here and Troy. Let's stop at Pop Raines Shack for some suds, Okay? Nothing like a couple of Bush Bavarians on an early morning ride through the country, moving on down the road. Don't think I'm ready for any Slim Jims with my beer this early. You may be able to handle them, but not me. Where is it you want to go in Montgomery? We'll probably go there first, then out to Maxwell for my reserve information and for some last minute business. Also, there's one other stop I want to make, just on the outskirts of Montgomery. I'll explain after we go by the house to see an old friend."

As we left the outskirts of Auburn heading towards Tuskegee, I said, "Peyton, I'll buy lunch at Morrison's Cafeteria, in Montgomery. Always loved that place ever since Granny Dean took us there when we were little squirts. Just about all you can eat for a dollar. Hell, I think I can spring for two bucks since you're doing most of the driving, so dessert is included. Morrison's is on our way downtown, heading towards my music store. Can't miss it."

Been down this road so many times already. Got most of the side roads, shantys, and local stops memorized, and often wonder if things will ever change in Alabama. Seems like everything stays the same as it was many years earlier, when the cars were vintage, the tall, slender gas pumps with the transparent bowls so you could see the gold colored liquid right up to the top of the tank. R. C. Cola and Moon Pies advertised almost everywhere, bill boards, neon signs in cafe windows asking us to eat Holsum Bread juxtaposed with the Burma Shave slogans peppering the countryside just behind the fences that contained domestic animals on the small farms scattered across the Bible Belt.

We detoured off the main highway, just on the outskirts of Montgomery, and eventually arrived at this country estate, with the main house, horse barn, stables, and guest house. As we approached the house a woman walked out of the horse barn and came up to our car. Blonde, about forty, of medium height and wearing jodhpurs and riding pants. She yelled, "Monty, what a surprise to see you. Get over here to the house. So good to see you but I'm sorry to say that Anne is off at school for another several weeks. What's your friend's name?"

"Mrs. Ford, this is my buddy, Hank, from Auburn, and we thought we'd just stop by to say hello. Heck, it's been probably a year and a half since I was last here. How the time flies these days when you're having as much fun as we do at Auburn. Sorry I'll miss seeing Anne. How is she doing up at Vanderbilt, anyway?"

"Monty, she absolutely loves Nashville, and all of the activities associated with the university, but she's having a tough time with the academics. It is one hell of a difficult school and she thought she was going to have some difficulty, but not this much. Anyway, what can I get you two fellas? Want a tall glass of my homemade lemonade from lemons right off the tree?"

"Sounds great to me, Mrs. Ford. You sure have a lovely spread here. Do you ride much or are the horses for Anne?"

"Hank, we both ride and have done so since we were young kids. And, that goes back a long way for me. That is one thing Anne really misses up at school. She wishes that she could take at least one of her horses with her."

I wandered around the stables and scoped out the property while Mrs. Ford and Monty continued with their conversation. I was really impressed with this spread. I could have live there.

"Mrs. Ford, many thanks for the delicious lemonade, but Hank and I have to move on to Montgomery, then down to Troy. Give my best to Anne when you talk to her, and I hope to see you soon."

"Thanks, again, Mrs., Ford, and let me know if Anne has any sisters or girlfriends, so I can come back over with Monty."

"You, two, behave yourselves. See ya later."

Back into the convertible and we were only minutes from Morrisons, and my stomach was growling for a taste of their great food.

"Hank, what did you think of Mrs. Ford? Not bad for an older woman, do you think? Reason I ask is because I nailed her one night about two years ago. Came over to see Anne, but she hadn't returned from a trip she'd taken. Mrs. Ford told me that I could stay over until Anne arrived the following day. Hell, I didn't think anything about the situation until later that evening after supper when she took me riding across her property. When we returned and tied up the horses she invited me into the main house for a cocktail. Shit, who was I to refuse a free drink. She came onto me like a dog in heat. One thing about this married woman is she was a journeyman, and not an apprentice. She knew exactly what she wanted and she knew exactly how to go about getting it. Anne doesn't know about this and I hope she never does. And you'd best keep your mouth shut or I'll use that Ruger on your crotch."

"Peyton, if Anne found out that your screwed her mother she'd use that Ruger as a rectal thermometer, and pull the trigger. You are the one who had better keep your mouth shut regarding this situation. I must admit that she is enticing, and that I would probably have taken her up on the offer had I been in your pants or, better yet, out of your pants! If Anne is anything like her mother she must be a bombshell."

"You said it, but her mother has the experience and maturity where

Anne is naive and cautious. Wonder if I could take them both on at once?"

Here I was a junior in college dating these southern Baptists girls when Peyton was shacked up with a very attractive married woman. There is no justice in this world which is why I would have lowered my standards immediately if a lass lowered her pants. Boys will be boys and I was tired of celibacy imposed by the fair maidens of Auburn University. This was one of big reasons why I was looking forward to this weekend in Troy, because these ladies who attended smaller colleges admired upperclassmen at Auburn, in a lusty way. In other words, my potential for getting some poontang increased exponentially.

Dinner at Morrison's was fantastic, and just as I remember it whenever I'd go there with Granny. All we could eat going down that cafeteria line for a ridiculously small sum, and then head on down to my music store. Found a guitar I liked after testing several dozen, so I filled out my credit application, put ten dollars as a down payment, and walked out of the store with my brand new Framus six-string classical "gitfiddle." This is one big day in my life because I have been playing this pissant little ukelele that I bought the previous summer in Hawaii. Then, I moved up to a Martin four-string tenor guitar but it wasn't exactly what I wanted. I was tired of playing this shrunken-up, four-string excuse of a guitar, so I made my mind up that I was going to make a major investment in a fully grown, major league serious instrument And I did.

After Monty checked in with his reserve unit over at Maxwell Air Force Base we were back on the road for Troy, in about an hour. Once we left the outskirts of Montgomery, we are heading southeast back into the all too familiar country, and I know that we would soon enter that gray area known as felony assault of the countryside with a lethal Ruger forty- four magnum pistol.

Hell, I wasn't about to let Peyton know that I was scared as hell. Done alot of foolish stunts in my life, but this was going to get out of hand if I let it. Rather than blow my cover as Mr. Cool I would suggest the inherent dangers of firing this thing in a direction that could *prove fatal.*

"Miller, why don't you drive and I'll load the Ruger so that I can fire going down the road. Look at these metal sheds located about every mile or two. Bet this can flatten one in two shots."

"Monty, you idiot. Those are school bus stops for the kiddies. Shit. If someone is inside you'll blow them into the next county. And, my friend, I ain't going to have any part of that. Got an idea. Let's stop down here on the right so we can go over the fence into that field and shoot the Ruger to our heart's content. That is, unless the owner of the property shows up, or the state trooper comes driving by."

"Good idea, Panky, so what do you say about over here, on the right?"

"Go for it. By the way. How loud it this when you fire it? Christ! Is it going to scare the living shit out of me?"

"You ever fire a twelve gauge shotgun? Sounds louder than that so be prepared for one hell of a bang. I'm going to hold it with both hand, elbows locked and I'll aim for that fence post about twenty-five yards away. See that one over there?"

The noise this pistol made was, indeed, impressive and one could literally hear the concussion at least a mile away. And, the hole left in the fence post wasn't a hole at all. The fence post, which at one point was constructed out of one piece of wood, was now in two distinct pieces - both of which were shattered into a million matchsticks. I knew my turn was coming up and I want to get this over with fast, so I aimed the Ruger at a tree about fifty yards away, and fire. The cavity that ensued soon after the round penetrated the bark is about the size of a basketball, and just as deep. I'd never seen anything like it, and indicated to Monty that we should proceed to hit the road fast which we did. PDQ!

"Peyton, what a gun. I mean this thing is lethal and you don't even have to be a good shot to dismember your victim. Hit him in the little toe and he implosion will reach up to and include his head. Only torn fragments of his clothing would remain as they lay smoking on the ground. My suggestion is that you get rid of this gun and buy something practical, like a guitar or whatever."

What an experience and what a way to start the weekend. First, a world-class olympic food fight and, then, a firing session that would have made Teddy Roosevelt proud and, now, on to Troy State University, down in Troy, AL, and women, lots of women. The campus at Troy State was serene, southern, and small, especially when compared to the vast acreage at Auburn. This was a school that, also, had one tenth the student body of Auburn. We drove up the quadrangle to the girls' dorm and the time was approaching three o'clock. As we entered the public reception area we announced that we were the representatives from Auburn and the Delt house coming in early to set up the dance for later that evening. The coed, whose assignment it was to monitor guests and to announce our arrival, indicated that many of the girls who were scheduled to go home for the weekend elected to remain on campus just for this dance. A group of Laura Lovelies iwascoming down from their rooms to greet us and to walk us over to the gym where the dance would be held. I looked at Monty. Monty looked at me. We, both, smiled and suppressed our laughter and giggles as best we could. In other words, we thought we had died and gone to heaven!

Auburn's ratio of women to men was simply pitiful because there were about eight men for every woman, and then you had to factor in the number of Baptists who you had a hard time just getting into a car, let alone the back seat. Could this have been more opportunistic?

As the ladies approached our area in the reception room all I could think of was "Enie, meanie, miney moe. Catch a wanton one by the toe." Those were some cute gals and there were several who appear to be impressed with our major campus status. "Good afternoon, ladies. I'm Hank and this is Monty. We hail from the Delt house at Auburn and we're really looking forward to the dance tonight. Y'all coming, I hope."

"You bet we are. At least some of us will be there and I will for sure," said one of the first coeds who strolled down the stairs, and right into my heart. She was brunette, petit, cute and aggressive. Auburn women weren't aggressive, and I was duly impressed with this one, so my sights are set on her, while Monty introduced himself to another beauty in this covey of quail.

"Let's take you guys over to the gym so you can check on the decorations and whatever else. Then, let's go and get pizza and some beer before we have to come back and change for the dance. It is informal, isn't it? We'd love to just change into some bermudas and loose tops because the gym can get stiffling hot with all those bodies and the dancing."

"You bet, ladies, and we don't care what you wear as long as the dorm mother doesn't get pissed and put you on restriction. How far away is the gym? Should we walk over, or drive?"

"See that building at the end of the street? Well, that's it, so we can strolled over check it out and be back here in about half an hour, okay?"

Larry Coe had come down from the Delt house to set up the stage for the band, and to check the acoustics. The decorations had been organized by several of the coeds and we literally had nothing to do until the dance, so it was off for pizza and beer with the bevy of beauties.

Now, six o'clock and the dance begins at eight. Our frat brothers were arriving from the relatively long haul down from Auburn. We began to introduce them to the coeds who had befriended us upon our arrival. These folks at Troy rolled out the red carpet for us and we would eventually let them know just how much we appreciated their efforts. Some would receive the gratuity in the form of a great band, decorations and a spontaneous evening of fun. Others would receive whatever we could offer in the back seats of the cars parked outside the gym, or back in the dorm rooms that were surreptitiously entered by the fire escapes late in the night. Regardless of the circumstances, everyone would go away happy because we had come down from the almighty Village of the Plains, just to show these plebeians how to party! In reality, they were the true party animals, and we are greatful.

Extremely greatful would have been an understatement.

Ever notice the result of when the relative humidity meets the ambient air temperature? Well, the result is fog. This rather warm spring evening was classic for this occurrence because the humidity was high, as was the outside air temperature, thus producing fog. But, not fog as we know it. Fog, as the inability to peer into the various car windows parked outside the gym during the dance. In other words, these vehicles parked alongside the curb contained occupants whose physical activities produced enhanced breathing, resulting in steam, or fog, which eventually caused the condensation to appear on the interior of the windows of said parked autos. Nary a one vehicle was exempt from this phenomenon, so one could deduce that the male-female match making choreographed earlier in the evening resulting in eventual copulation, was an outstanding success. Along with the man/woman produced fog, an eerie sort of mystique imbued the night along with the heavy breathing, and that sound was the almost syncopated humming that was heard originating from the parked cars. Must have resulted from the music majors at the college trying to impress my fraternity brothers with their ability to hold a note for extended periods of time.

On Sunday morning, the sun well above the horizon, the party was over, a mitigating migraine headache was setting in from all the beer consumed, and now, waking up in a strange bedroom decorated with varying sizes and colors of lacy underwear, nylon hose strewn from the doors, my trousers draped over the door knob, and the sensual aroma of perfumes mingled with the flora in bloom just outside the dorm windows. Ever so slowly I got up from the strange bed and tiptoed over to get my clothes and make a quiet hasty retreat before the dorm mother made her rounds to the floors above the lobby. We say good-bye to our lovely hostesses as we shoved off for Auburn, with smiles from ear to ear. Needless to say, these coeds had valid invitations to visit us anytime their little hearts desired, and some took us up on the offers during the months to come. We're back on the road for the hour and a half drive only to greet piles of homework and term papers waiting for our arrival. The reality set back in as we reminisced about the great dance and the cute gals of Troy State who captured our horny little hearts this one particular weekend in Spring.

Later that day . . .

"Monty Peyton, you son of a bitch. You took my car, drove off to Montgomery and, then, down to that Delt party at Troy State. But, the real reason I could castrate you is because you had Hank Miller with you, in my car!" This was Joanne's opening volley early Monday morning as she stormed into Monty's room, situated atop the town dry cleaners. To say that she was irritated would compare the sound the Ruger made to that of a cap gun. This woman was about ready to launch into Monty with all fours and claw his eyes out.

"Joanne, settle down. I took your car down to Troy, but Hank rode down with Fred or Larry. Hell, you don't think for one minute that I'd let him ride in your car without your permission, knowing the way you feel about him, do you? Besides, I left a full tank of gas and the car is spotless. Thanks, sweet pea."

"Don't you swee pea me and If I ever find out that Miller's ass touched the seats of my Impala this weekend I'm going to have a piece of yours. Get it, Peyton? That's the last time you'll have permission to use my car unless I'm in it. Have you seen Hank today? I'm going up to the Delt house just to check out your story, so don't bullshit me, fella."

****

Oh well, just another quiet college weekend, deep in the heart of Dixie. A triangular junket, beginning in Auburn, with a stopover in Montgomery, and then down to Troy provided us with numerous occasions to frolic. Monty Peyton, your quintessential fraternity man with a wee bit of madness he inherited, most likely, from his military environment, little league Joanne, with oxymoronic moral values from mighty Auburn, and major league Sara, my date, with clearly defined qualities of lust, from tiny, third-rate Troy State.

Ironic ... I feel warm down to the cockles of my heart ... A truly great weekend, all the way around.

<u>Gladiolus</u>

(glad' ë o' les), n. 1. any iridaceous plant of the genus Gladiolus native esp. to Africa, having erect, gladiate leaves and spikes of variously colored flowers.

It was my senior year at Auburn. The year was 1963 and I was in Opp to visit my grandparents. I checked my watch. The Trailways bus should be rolling in around four thirty and I had to get the box back to Granny's so she could have the flowers for old man Cole's casket spray tomorrow. This was my daily responsibility to Granny's business and I didn't mind doing it. In fact, I enjoyed driving to the bus station, getting a bag of boiled peanuts from Fireball, the town kook, and waiting for the Trailways to roll in from Montgomery and Rosemont Gardens.

A daily ritual. A systematic pattern of behavior like getting up in the morning and going to bed at night, or going to Boutwell's Market daily for the fresh chicken and staples that Gladdy Mae concocted into a delicious dinner everyday at noon. A reminder five days a week that we had work to do and, for the recipients of the floral arrangements, this was considered serious business. Folks for miles around, in both the city limits and way out in the country would call Granny and place their orders for prom corsages, wedding bouquets, gifts baskets, and casket sprays.

I think every girl around here sooner or later came to Granny for their corsages. I saw them arrive this same time every year to pick up their flowers smiling from ear to ear that they would, indeed, go to the prom with their chosen boy. Some of the girls in town ordered fancy, expensive rose corsages to pin on their dresses. Others from the country spent less and pick up their carnation arrangements to strap on their wrists. In both cases they are going to the same prom on the same night with the same intentions. They feel on top of the world.

While waiting for the arrival of the always slightly late bus I thought of the floral arrangements and the rites of passage they signify I have witnessed dozens of times and it has never sunk in that they symbolize a loss. After the dance, the party is over. After the funeral, the dead are buried and life continues. After the wedding, the bride and groom get on with their lives. After the christening, the baby continues to cry. The flowers are a significant aspect of these rites. They symbolize all of my feelings of joy, sadness, respect, honor, loss, beauty, love and all things wonderful and sad.

I saw the bus coming over the knoll from Brantley as it makes the long upgrade from the hospital. Time for one more bag of boiled peanuts before I get to work. People here were waiting to board as soon as the driver unloaded the buses and luggage. Only one or two passengers ever got off here. Opp was small and not too many folks considered it a destination point. The driver unlocked the side compartment and I saw the long, corrugated waxed box slide out. I picked it up by the hemp string and dragged it over to the trunk of the Ford.

The box arrived safely. I never wanted to return to Granny's with the news that they forget to ship her flowers. Now that the box is in the playhouse I ask, "Granny, how many of these casket sprays do you suppose you have created? I was just curious how many caskets have been draped by the maestro of Dean's Florist?"

As she stood there working the fragrant flowers around sticks and foam her reply was, "Panky, I couldn't even begin to count all of them. All I know is it seems like someone dies everyday around here 'cause I keep getting phone calls to make one more spray for someone who just passed away. The phone rings as true as blue, and I know it will be either a glorious occasion or a sad one. I suppose some folks think of a passing of their loved ones as glorious but I can't bring myself to think that way even though I consider myself to be a religious person. Panky, hand me another bunch of those pink gladiolus please. And quit asking me all these questions. I'm trying to get this done." She looks down and away from me displaying her disappointment with my verbose behavior.

The smell, the fresh aroma of the cut flowers remained with me throughout the year, even when I was back at school far away from this here town. Standing, I closed my eyes to heighten the sensation as I stuck in the sprigs of the green fern used as garnish for the arrangements. As a chore I swept up the cuttings as Granny finishes each of her daily orders. Piles of the stems, unsightly blossoms and the green fern that have been discarded found their way into the path of my broom and eventual destination of the garbage can back in the alley. Jesus Christ! That smell. Must pass by Donaldson's chicken coop. Whew! Smells like shit out here, chicken that is. Thank God the flowers mask most of the odor from that coup.

"Panky, I'll finish this casket spray around two. Can you deliver it to old man Johnson's place out near Kinston. I'm simply too tired to drive out there today. Besides, you'll do this for your old granny, now won't you, you old sweet thing?"

Without hesitation I say, "Sure, Granny, when do they have to be delivered?"

"The services are at four, so you be safe you should leave at two. It'll only take you about twenty or thirty minutes to get there. You may remember old man Johnson. He's the father of Judy, the girl you dated down at Grayton Beach that Spring break. Always did like her. She's so respectful and kind to me whenever we run into each other up town. She's been up in Birmingham studying to be a nurse. Her father died last Friday and they'll bury him today. "

"I remember her, Granny. Yes, we dated my freshman year at Auburn during spring break down at Grayton Beach."

"You'll see her again today, I'm sure. I'm doing a special arrangement at the request of Mrs. Johnson. The spray will be made out of pink and cream colored gladiolus, her two favorite colors and her favorite flower. It will be very large, not the normal size, so you'll have to be very careful loading and taking it out of the car, young man."

Granny had an incredible amount of energy for such a small woman. Over seventy years and under five feet two, she had been up since at least five this morning, long before Daddy Dean and me. Here she stood working away at her craft. The long, green sponge-like pieces of hard foam slowly became covered with the flowers as each stem was wrapped with green wire attached to a small stake. Granny inserted the stake into the foam and moved onto the next gladiolus stem to repeat the process time and time again until the arrangement began to take form. She inserted leafy green stems of fern in between the long gladiolus stems for added color and to balance the symmetry. A look of intensity was always on Granny's face but not the stressful look I'd have if I were doing this task with my unsure hands and lack of expertise in this art form. She remained relaxed. She did not waste much energy in unnecessary movements.

It was approaching two as I return to the playhouse to see how the spray was coming along. It was just about finished so I pulled the Ford up onto the grass and backed up as close to the door as possible. "Granny, I'm ready to roll whenever you're finished. The car needs gas so should I go out to Benton's and charge some on my way out of town?

She huffed out the door, "Yes, but don't get Ethyl. Just get regular and charge it to my account. Go out Highway 16 towards Kinston, about three miles past Bob's Drive In. On the right you'll see an old red barn sitting about a hundred yards off the road. Just past the barn is a dirt road veering off to the right. Take that road. If I remember correctly you'll pass over three wooden bridges and then you'll turn left onto a tree lined lane that goes up to the house. They're burying old man Johnson on the family farm so the preacher and everyone will be there. Now, let me help you with the spray, and drive carefully, you old sweet thing."

I finally got the casket spray into the car and now I needed to get up to Benton's for gas. I tuned in WBAM on the radio and listen to some Roy Orbison wondered what I was going to do tonight. Sure would be good to see Judy but not under these circumstances. Haven't run into her for about two years. Maybe I'd ask her out for tomorrow night if she was still in town. Would loved to get my hands around her luscious body one more time in the back seat of the Ford. But, this was a day of sorrow and country folk, such as the Johnson's take losses very seriously.

I could appreciate losses. Been dealing with losses for as long as I can remember. That's why I hated funerals because they signified the ultimate loss. And the grieving that is attached with the death. I got enough sadness to last a lifetime and I don't want anymore today. My mind turns to sex, unadulterated sex whenever I get depressed. So, thoughts of Judy run rampant in my feeble little mind.

This old dirt road looked the same as the dozens of others I drive while delivering Granny's flowers. No road markers indicated where to turn off the main highways. How in the hell did Granny knew where all these people lived? I suppose she simply knew after living there for seventy years. The Alabama State Troopers could see my dust for miles while I barreled along this byway.

As for me, I would pass this way probably for the last time when I delivered the spray. No need to ever come down this road again unless Judy asked me to come on over later on another day. Nothing is common here and there was no common connection other than Judy.

There were rows of trees lining the path up to the main house and many trucks and cars parked along side. I went up to the front and parked so it would be easier to get the casket spray out of the back seat and into the house.

"Are you Mr. Miller?" Park here and we'll help you to unload the flowers. Bring it into the back parlor where Mr. Johnson lies in state."

Funerals and wakes, oftentimes more that life, were very important. Whaling, moaning, weeping, crying, screaming, sobbing, silence - all told the tale of the families surrounding the casket while the deceased rests thanked the Almighty he can no longer hear the mournful sounds permeating the otherwise peaceful countryside.

Folks came from miles around to partake in the ceremony by cooking for days as the preparations began. Food abounded - pan corn bread, fried okra, chicken pot pie, Brunswick stew, Alabama caviar, cakes and pies of every variety and taste, fried chicken, fresh oysters, raw milk, both sweet and buttermilk and, lordy, what have you on that table down the hall past the kitchen on the back porch while the flies circle and land on the mayonnaise soaked tuna salad. We ate all we could until we dropped or risked the wrath of a nanny who spent days preparing the dinner.

This was the part I always hated. I walked past the mourners sitting on the front porch rocking in the chairs and not saying one, single word. Two men came over to help me gently lift the spray out of the back and carried into the house. We walked past the women, all dressed in long black dresses with high top laced shoes, some with snuff in their lower lip, and some wiping their eyes with a fresh white lace handkerchief. The house was dark, totally quiet with the exception of our footsteps while we passed several children on their way back to the kitchen for snacks. Down the hall was the open door to the parlor. We carried the spray a few more feet and gently place it over the mahogany casket that contained the body of Mr. Johnson.

"Could you move it just a few more inches towards the foot and it'll be just fine. Mrs. Dean did an absolutely beautiful job for Mr. Johnson. Be sure to thank your grandmother, Panky. Now, come on into the kitchen for some treats the neighbors baked just for today. You know us southern folk love home cooking even on the day we mourn the loss of family."

Now for the anxiety attack that I had surpressed for the past half hour as I saw Judy leave the parlor and heading on down to the kitchen to just where I was standing. I was nervous and excited to see her after three years. Judy signified another loss as she disappeared to Birmingham shortly after Spring break. As Judy approached me she said, "Hi

Panky. Haven't seen you in several years. How do you like it up at Auburn?"

God, did she look good. She took my breath away for a split second before I answered, "Judy, I'm so sorry about your father. Are you doing all right today? Good to see you after all this time."

"I'm doing just fine, Panky. Daddy had been suffering for some time and this was no shock for us. We expected him to slip away several weeks ago but he held his own longer than any of us anticipated. Thank goodness he didn't suffer much and now we can finally put him to rest. Your grandmother told me that you were coming down to visit and I'm glad to see you. When are you ever going to put some meat on those skin and bones, Panky Miller? I thought that surely Auburn would fatten you up to where you looked normal. Anyway, you look the same as you did when we first dated during Spring break."

"Thanks, but I'm destined to a life of malnutrition, I suppose. Let me know if I'm talking too loud which I have a tendency to do. You must be ready to graduate from nursing school. I don't come home often. How about you?

"I usually come home on the spur of the moment. No, I never have enough time to write but I could call you. Have you ever thought about coming up to visit me in Birmingham some weekend? You've got a place to stay, you know. I have a small apartment near the medical center where I go to school."

"I'll think about it and thanks for the offer. I'm going to go back to Granny's now and let you all have time alone. Besides, I don't like being around funerals. Has nothing to do with your father. It is the loss and the grieving that I can't deal with. Anyway, is it all right to call you tomorrow and get together sometime this week?"

"Sure. Call me tomorrow afternoon and we'll go out to the country club for a cocktail."

We southerners love company. "Company's comin'," is heard up and down the street as we head towards the front door to greet those who we have known for years and who we see daily, but a visit to our house is special. Folks don't just drop in unannounced down here. It is rather formal albeit no engraved invitation is received in the post. "Lawdy, look who's here Ma. The Jacksons are coming up the front porch steps. Better hurry and get the door!" Like they're going to go somewhere else fast.

Back to reality. Time to leave this depressing place. I couldn't bear anymore crying and sobbing and dialogue about my parents and grandparents and other small talk that drove me up the wall. I said good-by to everyone and thanked them for their hospitality before getting back into the Ford for the drive back.

Thank goodness Judy was there to save me from the grips of the mourners. What in the hell am I going to talk about when I'm around them? Their crops when I'm not a farmer. The weather when I'm not a reader of Farmer's Almanac? Politics in the county when I don't even know the mayor?

So, at least I could fantasize about the time I spent with her down on the gulf that school break. I have a yearning for women with huge tits. I can remember slipping my hand under her sweater and feeling her nipples swell against my hand one night while the rest of the crowd was across the street dancing at Grayton's store. Judy's old boyfriend was down at the beach and warned others to keep me away from Judy or he'd kick my butt. Somehow I didn't give his threat a second thought as we embraced and proceeded to remove one more article of each other's clothing until we lay there naked.

After getting dressed we spent the remainder of the evening together across the street nursing my cousin, Rego, who was drunker than a skunk from guzzling white lightening supplied by one of the Opp locals. Staggering and tripping all over himself from one corner of the huge room to another while the sheriff eyed the crowd. The next day I left for Opp, and Auburn. That was the last time I saw Judy until today.

"Hey Judy, this is Panky. How about meeting me at the Parkmore tomorrow night around eight and we'll take it from there?"

"Panky, who's that on the phone? Would you please go down and pick up another delivery of flowers from Rosemont Gardens? The bus arrives in about thirty minutes. Thanks, you old sweet thing."

"Okay, Granny, just as soon as I get through talking with Judy."

What a day. I was bored to tears and I couldn't think of anything else but moving down the long lonesome road out of this place and back up to Auburn. Forget those goddamn gladiolus. Forget the funeral and the trip down that bleak country road. Before leaving, however, my plans took me to another place and time. My plans included Judy Johnson, the Parkmore and simple lust.

On second thought, perhaps a few stems of pink and cream gladiolus would pave the way for a glorious evening. What those flowers do for one person's ceiling as a casket spray become a symbol for what the flowers will do for another person's floor. Perhaps the dance floor.

Yes, indeed, I must truly be a southerner. Music is part of my mystique and I was born to sing, shout, strum and dance my way across the polished pine floors of the Opp country club ballroom or on the postage stamp area at Preservation Hall in the Big Easy. Gospel and blues is what I like best and the tune really doesn't matter. It is the lyric that makes me laugh or cry. Stephen Foster, Muddy Waters, Mose Allison, Elvis, or Queen Ida invades my sphere and starts that foot 'a tapping until the rest of my body catches up to the rythym, and I begin to flow, syncopate, and move without adherence to the tune being played. I begin to strut my stuff. The ladies begin to put some wiggle in that walk. Hips sway and legs move in rythym to the music.

No more grieving about old man Johnson. Done laid him deep in the ground today. Time for me to move into a more convivial frame of mind and away from thoughts of the grim reaper. I'd pick her up at eight. I suppose she'd be wearing a tight blouse as I remembered. She looksd good in tight blouses. Maybe I'd take her some gladiolus from Granny's stash in the fridge. Judy and I wouldn't be thinking about any flowers tomorrow tonight at the Parkmore as we tapped our tootsies and shook our hips late into the sweltering summer night.

"PINE HOLLOW" the William Thrower Shepherd home was at one time the latest, most modern and most respected home in all of Covington County. It was beautifully constructed around a courtyard and for many years was the social center for the surrounding area. It was built in 1908 but unfortunately was destroyed by fire in 1975.

Christmas in Poley

The weather had turned cold outside but the skies were crystal clear and I knew that our bad weather was still yet to come. Last night, the temperature dropped to below freezing and folks could count on having to go out to start their cars and leave them running for ten minutes before driving off. In these parts most of the trees are deciduous so the leaves have long since been swept from the ground leaving the skeletons of the trunks and branches silhouetted against the horizon. The big difference in this time of the year is the departure of college students to be with kinfolk during the Christmas break, and not the cold weather or thoughts of final exams.

Situated on a small knoll the great, white ante-bellum fraternity house faced north. Cars pulled in and out of the driveway as the exodus began. Auburn University, Magnolia Avenue, Delta Tau Delta Fraternity House. More feelings of emptiness as my friends began their departure. This hollow feeling was very unsettling and I probably suffer more than most because I am a true nomad, a vagabond, a charter member of the wanderlust society, and a Navy Junior who is used to a perpetual transitional existence. This scene always appeared to be an ending, a final chapter, a close, or a final curtain I suppose. Been through this scenario hundreds of times and each is no different from the last. I don't like being separated from my friends.

While gathering my belongings and textbooks I was thinking about Auburn playing Nebraska in the 1964 Orange Bowl, down in Miami. A group of my best friends were forming a car pool and they were saving a seat for me for the drive. I simply needed a few dollars for gas and food. There was free room and board so this would be a damn cheap trip. However, I hd a problem that was two-fold: Money for the trip and, more importantly, permission from my parents, who presently lived in Pearl Harbor, Hawaii, one hell of a long way from Opp, Alabama.

In the meantime, Auburn was about to receive one more visitor among the hundreds arriving today, who had made many previous trips to collect me, her oldest grandson, at the completion of Winter final exams. Granny's reputation precedes her by about a mile a minute. Mrs. A.T. Dean, alias Birdie, came screaming up the driveway, grinding through the stick shift gears of her two-door, 1960 Ford Fairlane, with just a memory of tread showing on all four tires. She was the only person I knew who drove the one hundred and twenty miles up from Opp through Elba, Troy, Perote, Union Springs, Tuskegee, and on to Auburn literally in a cloud of dust, seventy miles per hour, flat out. All of the attendants at the general stores along the way knew they were in trouble when she pulled up, and stormed into the store, and demanding that someone fill 'er up with Ethyl, because she was Mrs. A.T. Dean of Opp, Alabama, and, "By the way, sonny, give me a couple of bags of those boiled peanuts you have posted two for a dime. Hurry up. I don't have all day, y'hear?"

Granny gave me a big hug and says, "Panky, hurry up, you can drive but let's get going before that storm coming turns the sky black. The weather forecast calls for rain, rain, and more rain."

Granny's old Ford, and several of her predecessors, made the back road journey that always remained the same; corn and cotton fields, two-lane blacktop narrow roads winding over the dales and between the tall banks of red clay soil fighting the age old battle of erosion. The emerald green color of the kudzu vine covered everything in its path. And, the occasional barbecue stands usually adjacent to the owner's houses. Classic farm houses with gleaming tin roofs, narrow brick chimneys, front porches with a glider, and a shady lane winding up to the barn dot the countryside. Farm houses with occupants we'd never know but who seem to become part of our lives each time we made this trip.

Most of the landscape during our trip was bleak save a few landmarks depicting different towns and parts of the county. We southerners are a visual people. Water tanks signal where you are. I see the small dot on the horizon that signals our portends arrival in Opp. The bulbous gray monolith rises above the trees and low buildings and becomes the monument for high schools boys to utilize for significant rites of passage, such as hand-painted epithets. "Beat Kinston Eagles!", "Go Bobcats, beat those little fuckers on the football gridiron or my name painted here will be mud for another 365 days. Annual ritualistic misdemeanors, never enforced, surround the permanently embossed names of the towns, followed by a comma, then the abbreviation of the state, like we don't really know where we are here in this county. A boldly painted OPP, AL alerts me to my pending arrival home. The juices in my body begin to flow more rapidly and my eyes widen with anxiety and anticipation of greeting family one more time. I am a southerner who cherishes friendships more than ostentatious wealth. My pleasure is measured by kinfolk, fresh greens, scratch biscuits, raw buttermilk, and Mrs. Bird's lemon cake. Just can't wait to taste some of her delicious dessert I consider a real treat when home.

Coasting up the driveway I saw Daddy Dean come out of the front door to greet us. I loved my granddad so I jumped out of the car before Granny pulls to a complete stop, ran up the front porch steps and gave him a big hug. "Panky how do you do boy? So good to have you home. If you don't mind I need a ride uptown to the club when you have a moment. No hurry. Just let me know when you can take me."

"Sure will Daddy Dean. Let me go into the house, take a leak, and I'll be right back out. You go ahead and get in the car while it's nice and toasty. Be right back."

After I returned I told Granny about wanting to go down to Miami for the Orange Bowl. Granny was sympathetic so she volunteered to help me find a job. She proceeded to make several phone calls one of which was to a lady whose husband owns a cotton gin in town. This family, also, owned a brick foundry and they need temporary help to unloading a few thousand bricks for old man Cole's new house. Cole was a good friend of Daddy Dean. She told me to come down and begin work tomorrow. I thanked her and thought about work at seven o'clock tomorrow morning on one hell of a cold winter's day.

The day was crystal clear and freezing. I put on the warmest clothes I could find and headed out. As I approach the vacant lot just about three blocks from Granny's I spied two other workers on the job site and observed that I was, by far, the youngest and definitely the whitest. Two old blacks worked steadily to unload sixteen thousand heavy, red bricks from that truck, and onto old man Cole's lot. My body was rapidly deteriorating as we approached the noon whistle and my arms felt like Franco American Spaghetti - limp as noodles. My clothes were sticking to me. I gather every last bit of strength and manage to drive home to Granny's for our noontime dinner.

Her first words to me were, "Panky, you're a mess. Why can't you lift your arms? And, your hair is soaking wet from perspiration."

"Granny, that's the hardest work I've ever done. I am exhausted and dread going back this afternoon. Gotta eat something fast, then rest." I ate dinner for about five minutes and slept for about twenty-five more before driving back to work. The blacks looked as fresh as could be as we proceeded to put in another four hours of the hardest damn work I'd every done, only to return tomorrow for another day of slave labor. When we completed the second and final day's work we reported back to the office at the cotton gin. The owner thanked me and handed me thirty dollars. The other two fellows bartered for sacks of coal so they could heat their houses during this exceptionally cold winter's spell. Now, I had enough money for the trip to Miami.

When I returned to Granny's she was preparing another casket spray for one more funeral in town. Just as Granny and I were talking up came a driver who yells out the window, "Mizz Dean, Mizz Dean, yu whoo!"

Granny recognized her immediately and quietly said, "Panky, here comes Van Shepard. Do you remember her? She knows your folks and the Shepard family has been friends of ours for a mighty long time. Quiet, here she comes."

What a sight to see. A seventy plus year old lady drove up in a brand new, fire engine red 1964 Chevy Impala, with four on the floor, and Hollywood glass pack mufflers blaring away. This lady even had the unmitigated gall to wear slacks in public at her age. I loved her from the very first moment she drove up over the curb into Granny's backyard so she didn't have to walk another thirty feet. Van was part of the Shepard clan which hails originally from Poley, then from Opp. Mrs. Shepard, the grand matriarch, had several offspring, and Van is one.

"Panky, haven't seen you in ages. What a pleasant surprise! As a matter of fact you were about ten years old, or something like that. What are you doing now, you handsome young man?"

"Going to Auburn, Mrs. Shepard, and loving every minute of it. How are you and Mr. Hickey doing? I usually see him when I take passengers over to Andalusia for Sunday mass."

"Son, we're just fine, and Mr. Hickey sure enjoys your company when you're in town. On another subject Mrs. Dean, we want you, Mr. Dean, and Panky to come on out to our house, in Poley, for Christmas dinner. Don't need an answer just now, but."

Granny quickly replied, "Van, we'd love to come. Just let us know the time and what we can bring. Perhaps I can conjure up one of Mrs. Birds lemon cakes to bring out. I know Mr. Dean would like to visit the town where he has so many fond memories as a young man. Panky, you were at the Shepard house many years ago so this should be a real treat for you."

"You just bring yourselves, Mrs. Dean, and come on out for a relaxing day in the country. Please plan on being out around three o'clock. By the way, can I get some carnations from you? Can't seem to find any and I know that you always have some fresh flowers, even in the dead of Winter." Granny took her into the playhouse and proceeded to make the most beautiful arrangement for Van.

As I wile away the time winter grows colder, the sky grayer, the days shorter while I await word from my parents on whether or not I could attend the Orange Bowl game. Anger, loneliness, despair, frustration and a multitude of other feelings conjure up thoughts about my entire reason for being in Opp in the first place. Oftentimes, I wonder why in the hell am I stuck in this town when my friends are preparing to leave for Miami. Not to mention that my fiancé, Sharon, is among the troupe heading down. Christ Almighty! This is no place for a twenty-one year old original college preppie who wants action, women, crowds, music and football. Opp. Seems like I was eternally stuck in Opp. Besides, Jenny Hayward, another Navy Junior and my friend from Hawaii had invited me to spend the holidays with her in Atlanta. That was my ticket out of this place but my naiveté and my girlfriend, Sharon, would have no part of this arrangement.

Don't get me wrong. I love the memories of Opp, and the times shared in my early years but I have matured. I am 65 now and this place is a drag especially since my friends are in Atlanta, New York, or out on the West coast. This cowboy, on the other hand, is stuck in the land of the quintessential Falstaff sucking, truck driving, tobacco spitting, nigger hating, Parkmore Drive-In redneck heaven.

Christmas day finally arrived and my grandparents and I awoke to a crystal clear but very cold day. Each room in our house had the typical gas heaters, resembling ersatz log fireplaces, and the radiant warmth felt damn good as temperature outside hovered around twenty degrees. Granny, Daddy Dean, and I sat down for one of her typically southern breakfasts with farm fresh eggs, not over twenty four hours from the bottom of the hen to the bottom of our stomachs, biscuits made from scratch, and hickory-smoked bacon. I almost forgot the deliciously cold raw milk from just up the road. Lordy, it doesn't get much better than this.

After breakfast we opened our presents and took in the warmth of Christmas day. In a few minutes several of the old timers dropped by to wish us a merry Christmas and to pay their respects to two other pioneers, my grandparents. The warmth of today in the house that held so many fond memories feels very good to me. I suppose the house had nothing to do with it but I would bet money my grandparents hd a great deal to do with the feeling I experience this morning especially when friends came by to wish their Christmas best.

A few minutes later we heard another knock on the door. Granny answered and a dozen or so school children come in and the teacher asked if they can sing a few carols . Granny was delighted as they proceed to deliver their version of Winter Wonderland and Silver Bells. The teacher thanked us and the kids went next door to repeat the same for another older couple who just moved into the neighborhood.

We cleaned up the kitchen and now it was time to leave for Poley. I went around to the garage and got the car started and put the heater on full blast. "Daddy Dean, are you about ready to get going? Granny and I are bundled up and we have the car nice and toasty. Boy, do you look sharp in that new Christmas plaid shirt that Aunt Evelyn and Uncle Johnny gave you. Personally, I think that you'll drive those young gals wild looking that handsome on your way up town to the Domino Club. Anyway, let's get out to the car before Granny starts hollering." The three of us then proceeded to get into the car to spend the day with Mr. Hickey and Van Shepard out in Poley.

"Panky, don't drive too fast or you'll miss the turn-off. Now, slow down, young man, or I'll have to drive. You drive like you're running moonshine!"

My retort was mumbled under my breath.

Poley was historic, and lonely, and peaceful. Driving west from Opp, towards Andalusia, a dirt road jutted off to the right and appeared to lead to nowhere. After turning right what's left of Poley appeared in approximately one thousand yards. At one point this was a prosperous lumber mill town that had since faded from most maps. As a matter of fact, Daddy Dean got his start in the business world, as a young illiterate worker, in the lumber mill commissary. The Shepard estate was situated on the left side of the dirt road about one mile from the highway and it was rather spectacular, in a southern sense.

Sure enough, as we approached the side road, I was suddenly captured by the feeling of somehow stepping into a time warp, a slide into the past, a sort of deja'vu. Man, we were in the country driving down that red clay dirt road with the deep ruts carved from the tractors and the winter rain, tar paper shanties with pot-bellied cauldrons boiling in the yards, and an occasional attack by bloodhounds as they tried to catch us, and bite the tires off the car. Just a few minutes later we arrive at the Shepard estate.

Van directed us to come on in through the back door. This kitchen had a fireplace with racks for cooking, a huge butcher block island with wrought iron overhead storage for hanging pots and pans, a large gas stove and plenty of built-in cooler storage for fresh vegetables and bread. A young woman was working at the sink preparing our Christmas dinner as we pass through. She was young, white, appears to be shy, and didn't say a word as we greeted her on our way through. She wore no makeup to speak of, and her eyes were soft and gentle. Her sandy blond hair was in a typical German-style braid and she wore a dress over her slight frame with the familiar floral pattern off a feed sack . She did not speak a single word. Well, so much for her cheery Christmas day as she worked to prepare food for our enjoyment. I wondered what's going through her mind.

Mr. Hickey greeted us as we entered the living room before hanging our wraps. I mentioned my seeing of the girl in the kitchen to Van and I asked her why she was so quiet. Van indicated that she was fulfilling part of her obligation by preparing our Christmas dinner. Hell, she wasn't shy! This girl in the kitchen was embarrassed because I was about her same age, and that I was most likely from better breeding than she, which basically means I had more money. Bottom line is that she was a sharecropper's daughter with alot of pride, and very little else.

Much to my surprise I spotted a pint of spirits on the buffet. Could this possibly be some hootch, some fire water, some kickapoo joy juice, some bourbon? Immediately, I thought that dinner would not come to pass if the Deans saw that so-called drink of the devil sitting there prepared for consumption. My blood grew cold and a shiver went down my spine while I attempted to cover this bottle of alcohol from my grandparents view. Lord knows, the Deans are never, but never, seen drinking. Suddenly, out of nowhere, Van said, "How many of you would like a hot cup of coffee, with a little kick to it?"

"We'd both love some, Van. How sweet of you to ask. Now, don't put too much in Mr. Dean's. You can add a little more to mine though."

"Mr. and Mrs. Dean, let's go and sit down at the dinner table for our meal. Don't forget your drinks and we'll refill them if you want. Panky, please help your grandfather with his coffee."

I was shocked and amazed at the ease with which Granny and Daddy Dean consumed the entire bottle of bourbon with their coffee. Lord knows how much they could hold if given the opportunity.

The warmth of that room with the fireplace on our crystal cold winter day provided us with a perfect setting and ambiance for Christmas. Van said, "I'll be right back after I tell our little friend in the kitchen that we're ready to begin with dinner."

After saying the blessing we passed the bountiful food for all to share: Turkey, of course, with dressing prepared with the traditional liver, gizzard and oyster ingredients, pan fried corn bread, fresh cranberries, mouth-watering mashed potatoes and, I almost forgot, the raw buttermilk. One isn't truly southern unless they have witness the thick, sour, buttery substance sticking to the side of a Mason jar, waiting to dunk their cornbread into the chalky liquid.

Soon after dessert and coffee we extended some cordial "thank-yous," and we promise to not let much time lapse before we gather together again. God, how I hated to leave this house with all of its history and charm. It was so much larger and more splendid than my grandparents' house and I simply was not ready to leave, but Granny iwasgrowing restless. Sitting and talking with the Hickeys provided me with diversion and some time to forget about my ultimate objective - Miami.

"Panky, are those hot shot Auburn football players ready for this Orange Bowl game? You know, that Nebraska team is darn good and our boys from around here haven't had much experience against a northern team. They just might get intimidated, and blow the entire game."

"I think they'll do just fine, Mrs. Shepard, but I'd rather be in Miami, than here in Opp watching the game on tv. I'm saving a few bucks to hitch a ride with my classmates so we can all meet for the game and the New Year's celebration. So far so good, but I haven't heard from my folks whether or not I have permission to go. They had to think it over before granting me a pass to head that far South while leaving Granny and Daddy Dean alone during the holidays."

What my hosts failed to discern was the anger and the disappointment pent inside me because I felt that approval from home is totally unnecessary. I was pissed.

"Say, Mr. Hickey did you paint all of those scenes hanging up in the living room? I never knew you were such an artist. When did you start and how did you learn to get so good with your technique?"

At this point Van took the center stage by replying, "Mr. Hickey is originally from Ireland, and I met him on a sojourn in New York city. When we met he was a painter of sorts, but not an artist. When I wrote home to my folks that I was in love with a painter my family took it to mean a painter on canvass. An artist! Suddenly, I was confronted with a potentially humiliating situation and what was I to tell my family? The truth I deduced. So, Mr. Hickey began to paint, to paint pictures, scenes, images, to become a fledgling artist in New York. Hence, the beginning of an aspiring artist sprang forth in the Big Apple. Paintings of seascapes, of Coney Island, of landscapes. Mostly primitive in style, but good."

"Panky, please let me know if you ever want to pose for a portrait. I'll be glad to immortalize you on canvas one of these days."

"Thanks anyway, Mr. Hickey, but I'm sure you can find someone willing to pose and smile for hours upon end. I never could sit still so I would probably be a lousy subject. Granny and Daddy Dean let's head 'em up and move 'em out, so we call my folks, in Hawaii. Van and Mr. Hickey, many thanks for a great dinner and for having us into your home. You are special people and we love you to death."

Van said, "Panky, I sure hope that you get to go down to Miami, with your friends. You'll have a ball down there and you'll never forget the experience of that big old bowl game and the weather which will be quite warmer than it's been here. Please don't forget to say hello to your parents the next time you speak with them. I haven't seen Lucy and Hank in years, and I love them dearly."

"Sure will, Van, and thanks again for a wonderful dinner. Mr. Hickey, would y'all please say thanks and good-by to the gal in the kitchen?"

Back to East Ida Avenue we drove, warm of spirit and full of food. Once back at the house the phone call that was to ensue proves disastrous. No go on to the trip to Miami. No explanation. No regrets. A Christmas celebration on one hand, and a wake on the other. Another chapter in my life down the tubes and, with regret, I remain in Opp for the duration of the holidays, depressed and angry. Meanwhile, my compatriots from Auburn were heading down from Dothan, and I called to inform them that my space in the car can be taken by someone else.

I recalled that clay road off the main highway leading to Poley. Tall oaks and fields of cotton already picked. And grazing pastures with cattle exhaling warm foggy air as they mosied around the empty fields. And, an unnamed peasant girl working in the Shepard's family kitchen. My boredom wasn't anything like how she must feel. My life was alright and I had lots to be thankful for.

She was illiterate and destitute. Most folks don't understand what it's like to be destitute. I sure didn't especially on Christmas day.

***

"I am the daughter of a southern tenant, a sharecropper, a man with one mule or with none at all. We live on seventy-five dollars a month and some free crops to feed our family. We must pay interest on the income advanced for planting the crops and for medical costs. We rent the house on the Shephard's property. We have never owned anything new. We only receive hand me downs and discarded articles. Now and then, I make a dress out of the pattern on a Ralston Purina feed sack. The children go barefoot and sleep together in one room on the floor. I never went to school. I cannot read or write and I do not own a television or radio. I have been to three movies during my life of 23 years and never seen the state capitol. I live in the south today. People don't want to recognize this but I exist and I will for another three hundred years. I can't seem to work my way out of this hole. A dollar for me, and two for the man. Don't seem right, I know. Don't want to cook for the Shepards on Christmas day, but we need the money"

THREE

Mister, You Have a Definite Attitude Problem!"

or,

Excerpts From Navy Fitness Reports

Regarding My Military Performance

We are hung over! New Years Day 1966, Alameda, CA

"A RECENT COLLEGE GRADUATE, AND VOLUNTEER"
1964

ENSIGN MILLER PERFORMED HIS DUTIES AS A STUDENT AVIATOR IN AN EXCEPTIONAL MANNER. HE FINISHED THE U. S. NAVAL SCHOOL, PRE-FLIGHT, OFFICER INDOCTRINATION COURSE STANDING 24 IN A CLASS OF 43. HE IS RECOMMENDED FOR PROMOTION.

Have minor weaknesses been discussed with officer? ___yes___no X__not applicable

"EIGHTEEN MONTH'S LATER AND NONE THE WISER" - 1966

ENS MILLER IS AN EXCELLENT OFFICER WHO DEMONSTRATES A HIGH DEGREE OF ENTHUSIASM TOWARD HIS PROFESSION AS A NAVAL OFFICER. HE READILY ACCEPTS RESPONSIBILITY AND ACHIEVES EXCELLENT RESULTS IN ALL ASSIGNED DUTIES. HIS MILITARY BEHAVIOR AND BEARING ARE EXEMPLARY. HE CONDUCTS HIMSELF IN A MANNER AS TO INSTILL CONFIDENCE IN THOSE AROUND HIM. ENS MILLER EARNED HIS STANDARD INSTRUMENT RATING ON 2 FEBRUARY 1966 AND CARRIER QUALIFIED IN THE TS-2A ON 25 FEBRUARY 1996. ENS MILLER WAS DESIGNATED A NAVAL AVIATOR ON 11 MARCH 1966.

Have minor weaknesses been discussed with officer? ___yes___no
X__not applicable

The author's self portrait at Lemoore Naval Air Station, CA, 1966

"YOUNG, ARROGANT, AND HORNY" - 1966

LTJG MILLER HAS SUCCESSFULLY COMPLETED REPLACEMENT PILOT TRAINING IN THE A-1 AIRCRAFT AND IS CURRENTLY DAY AND NIGHT CARRIER QUALIFIED. HE ALWAYS PRESENTS AN EXTREMELY NEAT AND SMART MILITARY APPEARANCE AND BEARING. HE GETS ALONG

WELL SOCIALLY WITH HIS CONTEMPORARIES. HIS ABILITY TO FLY THE A-1 AIRCRAFT WAS NEVER IN QUESTION. HOWEVER HIS INATTENTIVENESS TO PRE-FLIGHT BRIEFINGS REFLECTED ON HIS "HEADWORK" PERFORMANCE IN THE AIR. LTJG MILLER WAS GIVEN A PILOTS DISPOSITION BOARD ON THIS BASIS, AND WAS RETURNED TO TRAINING STATUS BY THE REVIEWING BOARD. LTJG MILLER POSSESSES SIGNIFICANT ABILITY AND NATURAL TALENT. WHEN LTJG MILLER REALIZES HIS POTENTIAL, HIS WORTH AS AN OFFICER AND CONTRIBUTING MEMBER OF A SQUADRON WILL BE OF UNQUESTIONABLE VALUE.

Have minor weaknesses been discussed with officer? __X__ yes __ no not applicable

Diane and Fran, Peace Corp Volunteers, aboard USS Oriskany
Christmas 1967, Hong Kong

"SAN FRANCISCO, OPEN YOUR GOLDEN GATE" - 1967

DURING THE BRIEF PERIOD LIEUTENANT (JUNIOR GRADE) MILLER HAS BEEN ABOARD, HE HAS EXHIBITED AND INTENSE DESIRE TO BECOME HIGHLY KNOWLEDGEABLE IN HIS PRIMARY DUTIES. ON HIS OWN INITIATIVE HE HAS SOUGHT OUT EXPERTS OUTSIDE THE COMMAND TO DISCUSS HIS RESPONSIBILITIES AND GAIN THEIR ADVICE. HIS EFFORTS WERE RECENTLY REWARDED WHEN HE RECEIVED THE OUTSTANDING GRADE OF 95 FOR COMMUNICATION IN THE ADMINISTRATION AND MATERIAL INSPECTION. HE IS AN EXCELLENT AVIATOR AND IS EAGER TO LEARN FORM THOSE WITH MORE EXPERIENCE. HE IS ABLE TO EXPRESS HIMSELF EXCEPTIONALLY WELL ORALLY.

Have minor weaknesses been discussed with officer? __yes __no X__ not applicable

"ON THE 'BOAT' IN TONKIN GULF" - 1967

LTJG MILLER HAS DEMONSTRATED PRONOUNCED INITIATIVE AND ZEAL IN THE PERFORMANCE OF HIS DUTIES AS COMMUNICATIONS OFFICER. HE READILY ADAPTS TO ANY SITUATION AND ENTHUSIASTICALLY ENDEAVORS TO LEARN AS MUCH AS POSSIBLE ABOUT ANY TASK ASSIGNED. HIS LOGICAL CONCLUSIONS AND THOROUGHNESS TO DETAIL ENABLE HIM TO STAND AND EXCELLENT SQUADRON DUTY WATCH. HIS EXCELLENT AIRMANSHIP AND COURAGE IN THE FACE OF THE ENEMY HAVE BEEN RECOGNIZED BY A RECOMMENDATION FOR AN AIR MEDAL DURING A PILOT RESCUE MISSION OVER NORTH VIETNAM. LTJG MILLER'S SMARTNESS OF APPEARANCE IS EXCEPTIONAL AT ALL TIMES AND REPRESENTS A FINE EXAMPLE FOR HIS CONTEMPORARIES TO EMULATE. HE IS RECOMMENDED FOR PROMOTION WHEN DUE.

Have minor weaknesses been discussed with officer? __yes__no X__not applicable

The author with Tokiwa Stand Bar girl, Sasebo, Japan,

sukiyaki lunch, 1967

"YOKOHAMA MAMA, THE LIGHT CAME ON, AND I WANNA COME HOME" 1968

LTJG MILLER'S PERFORMANCE HAS GREATLY DETERIORATED SINCE HIS DECISION TO CHANGE HIS 1300 DESIGNATOR IN OCTOBER 1967. PRIOR TO THIS DECISION

HOWEVER, LTJG MILLER'S PERFORMANCE WAS EXCELLENT IN ALL RESPECTS. HIS AIRMANSHIP PRIOR TO OCTOBER WAS EXCELLENT AND IS APTLY REFLECTED IN A PENDING AWARD OF A SINGLE FLIGHT AIR MEDAL AND A NAVY COMMENDATION MEDAL FOR HEROIC AND MERITORIOUS ACHIEVEMENT IN AERIAL FLIGHT. DURING THE RECENT DEPLOYMENT HE REQUESTED A CHANGE OF DUTY, PROFESSING A LACK OF ABILITY AND FEAR OF INSTRUMENT AND NIGHT FLYING. A FIELD DISPOSITION BOARD CONVENED IN HIS CASE RECOMMENDED REMOVAL FROM FLIGHT STATUS. SINCE THIS TIME LTJG MILLER'S PERFORMANCE OF DUTY HAS DETERIORATED DRASTICALLY AND HIS OUTLOOK TOWARD THE NAVAL SERVICE HAS CONSIDERABLY CHANGED TO ONE OF APATHY.

Have minor weaknesses been discussed with officer? _X_ yes ___ no not applicable ___

The author with cast painted by Sue Slusher, San Francsico, 1968.

"A BROKEN LEG AND NINE MONTH'S OFF, WITH FULL PAY" - 1968

DUE TO SHORT PERIOD OF TIME ATTACHED TO THIS COMMAND, NO EVALUATION CAN BE MADE.

The author and Sue Slusher dressed as hippies, San Francisco, 1968

"LT. MILLER, I NEVER CAN FIND THAT BOY"

3 FEBRUARY 1969

MEMORANDUM FOR LT MILLER

SUBJ: WORKING ARRANGEMENTS

1. YOU WILL WORK UNDER THE DIRECT SUPERVISION OF CDR PAUL UNTIL FURTHER WRITTEN NOTICE FROM ME.

2. NORMAL WORKING HOURS WILL BE FROM 0730 TO 1630 WEEKDAYS, WITH ONE HOUR OFF FOR LUNCH BETWEEN 1130 AND 1300. COMMENCING NOT EARLIER THAN 1200 FRIDAYS, YOU MAY BE AUTHORIZED, ON A CASE TO CASE BASIS BY CDR. PAUL, TO TAKE THE AFTERNOON OFF PROVIDING THERE IS NO OUTSTANDING WORK TO BE COMPLETED AS DETERMINED BY CDR PAUL.

3. YOU ARE NOT TO LEAVE THE BUILDING FOR <u>ANY</u> REASON OTHER THAN LUNCH WITHOUT THE EXPRESSED APPROVAL OF CDR PAUL OR, IN HIS PROLONGED ABSENCE, OF MYSELF OR THE SENIOR OFFICER IN THE SECTION IN THE EVENT OF MY PROLONGED ABSENCE.

4. IN THE EVENT YOU CANNOT REPORT FOR WORK AT THE SCHEDULED TIMES YOU WILL CONTACT CDR PAUL OR MYSELF AT THE EARLIEST POSSIBLE TIME AND EXPLAIN THE SITUATION.

5. THESE WRITTEN INSTRUCTION ARE FOR THE PURPOSE OF AVOIDING ANDY FURTHER MISUNDERSTANDINGS AND ARE NOT CONSIDERED TO BE IN THE NATURE OF A REPRIMAND.

        RESPECTFULLY,

HADAWAY

D. L.

ASW OFFICER

COPY TO:

CAPT. W.E. SHARP

CDR J.E. PAUL

FROM: LT MILLER

TO: CDR HADAWAY

1. I ACKNOWLEDGE RECEIPT AND UNDERSTANDING OF THE ABOVE INSTRUCTIONS.

RESPECTFULLY,

LT H. MILLER

LIEUTENANT MILLER HAS BEEN ASSIGNED AS THE ASSISTANCE AIR ASW OPERATIONS OFFICER. HE MAINTAINED AND UPDATED THE INFORMATION NECESSARY FOR PROVIDING CONTINUOUS ANALYSIS AND EVALUATION OF THE EFFECTIVENESS OF THE OCEAN SURVEILLANCE PROGRAM IN A SATISFACTORY MANNER. HE ASSISTED IN THE PREPARATION OF EXCELLENT VP AIRCRAFT FLIGHT SCHEDULES FOR EASTPAC, ASW, OCEAN SURVEILLANCE, AND RECONNAISSANCE PATROLS. IN ADDITION, LT MILLER PROVIDED USEFUL INPUTS WHICH MATERIALLY ASSISTED IN DEVELOPING THE UTILIZATION AND PROGRAMMING OF AUTOMATIC DATA PROCESSING IN CONJUNCTION WITH THE ASW FORMATTED MESSAGE SYSTEM. LT MILLER WHEN UNDER DIRECT SUPERVISION, SATISFACTORILY ASSISTED IN THE RECONSTRUCTION AND ANALYSIS OF HOLDEX'S (HIGH PRIORITY COORDINATED AIR, SURFACE, AND SUB-SURFACE ASW EXERCISES). HE IS RECOMMENDED FOR RECALL IN THE EVENT OF A NATIONAL EMERGENCY.

Have minor weaknesses been discussed with officer? ___yes___no X___not applicable

"FREE AT LAST, THANK GAWD ALMIGHTY, FREE AT LAST" !

RELEASE FROM ACTIVE DUTY - 1969

"WHERE IN HELL IS MY HONORABLE DISCHARGE" ? - 30 NOV 1970

From: Commanding Officer, Naval Reserve Manpower Center

Bainbridge, Maryland 21905

To: LT Henry Louis MILLER, JR., USNR

3650 Broderick Street, Apt.104

San Francisco, CA 94123

Subj: Acceptance of resignation from the U.S. Naval Reserve

1. Forwarded.

2. Current directives require that an officer's service record be delivered to him upon resignation and discharge. Accordingly, enclosure (2) is forwarded for your retention.

3. The Commanding Officer, Naval Reserve Manpower Center, desires to add his expression of appreciation to that of the Secretary of the Navy and offers his best wishes for success in your future endeavors.

4. You are requested to return your identification card to this Center for proper disposition.

E. R. HANNON

II

BY DIRECTION

Copy to: BUPERS (Pers-E222)

Diane, Hank, Fran and Gabes, Hong Kong,

Christmas Day, 1967.

Peace Corp Volunteers and Nasal Radiators

<u>Our Very Own Yacht Club operating very large boats in Tonkin Gulf!</u>

The 39 Main Bar, Tiburon, CA, 1968

What Happened to The 39 Main?

Suzie is what I call a poor man's Joanie Mitchell. She is blond, slightly freckled, short, and nicely built. Her lips have a sensuous pucker, and she is indeed a good kisser. Both women have blond hair, and lots of it. Both have freckles, and lots of them. Both are rather short in stature, but tall in presence and it really doesn't matter, because we are all of the same height especially when lying down! One of Joanie Mitchell's record album jackets portrays her in the nude while she is standing on the rocks, probably near Big Sur, by presenting us with a moon as she peers out to the horizon. Suzie's and Joanie's moons are incredibly similar, with symmetrical dimples in each cheek, slightly pear shaped, and not out of scale to the rest of their nicely proportioned physiques. Joanie's mouth is harsher, while Suzie's is less severe, and more inviting for some serious smooching, and perfection of the butterfly technique.

Both are flower children, sexy, multi-talented, and they remind me of the '60's, which is when I met Suzie, and heard Joanie, for the first time. Suzie introduced me to novel and unique physical pleasures, and Joanie to her renditions of audible sensory perceptions. And, we both listened to Joanie while enjoying one another's sensory perceptions......if you get my drift.

My flight school buddy and road trip warrior Butch had made the conscious decision, as opposed to most of our decisions, which were consummated in the totally unconscious state, to abandon Lemoore Naval Air Station for the weekend, and to motivate up to our favorite city for so-called rest and relaxation away from the Navy types, Spads, and the constant chatter about war in Southeast Asia. Instead of shacking up with our TWA stewardess friends, down in San Mateo, he thought it best to check in at the Bachelor Officers' Quarters, on Alameda Naval Air Station, for relative peace and quiet as we pieced together our game plan for the weekend. Butch was still without wheels and he was waiting for the parts to arrive in Del Rio, Texas, so that he could fly down, retrieve his car, and report back to Lemoore. His Aston Martin pooped out during the first phase of our trip from Corpus, to our new duty station out in the San Joaquin valley. So, we traveled as a team most of the time when we were off duty from the assigned areas of responsibilities, such as flight operations, survival training, escape and evasion schools, altitude simulators, weapons delivery training exercises, POW debriefs, in addition to our collateral duties Butch had borrowed a set of wheels this weekend but he decided to leave them at the BOQ, and he would drive back down to Lemoore late Sunday night. My MG-B was a two-seater but we somehow managed to squeeze four into the front two seats if that was the only way we could transport two honeys back to our pad. Survival was the name of the game and we constantly strove for better and more efficient ways in which to get laid. Hence, our lady friends adapted rather quickly to the center parking brake lever and the rather confined regions close to the dashboard of this ersatz sardine can on wheels

We had heard some scuttlebutt about this terrific bar over in Tiburon, called The 39 Main, and that the place really jumped on Sunday afternoons with a Dixieland sing along band, and hundreds of sweet young things jammed around the piano. "Butch, even though you have to be back at Lemoore for your flights tomorrow let's try going over just to check it out, and maybe we can have lunch at Sam's. What do you think?"

"Hankus Pankus, sounds great to me and it's about time we weaned ourselves off Harriet and Donna down at the Royal Pines, in San Mateo. Harriet's going back to Corpus, and Donna's pregnant, so you best not show your face around there, kiddo, even though we all know it wasn't your fault. Seems like she got knocked up by one of those totally untrustworthy airline captains, probably another charter member of the Mile High Club. Anyway, I'm up for a Sam's Ramos Gin Fizz and cheeseburger so I'm ready to go anytime you are. Got a call from Del Rio the other day, and my Aston Martin will be ready to roll next week. How sweet it is! Shit. I've only had to wait four months for the goddamn thing to get parts sent from up in Pennsylvania, down to that border town in southern Texas. Then, I won't have to bug you anymore for rides when I come up to the Bay area."

'It's never been a problem with me, shithead. We make a good team and I'd hate to see it broken up, so my car is your car until whenever, okay? Anyway, glad to hear that your machine will be fixed and out here on the coast soon. Bet that makes you feel awfully good. Let's see if any of the rest of the guys want to motorcade over to Tiburon so we can rendezvous. I'll meet you down at the bar."

We hopped into my car, blasted through the Webster Street Tube, up the Nimitz, and over the San Rafael bridge to head south by San Quentin towards Tiburon, and eventually towards more and more fillies temporarily corralled in, yet, another commercial stable of love. After a few Ramos Fizzes we ambled over to The 39 Main restaurant and lounge, two doors down, just in time for the music to begin, and for the honeys lined up at the door trying to get into an already packed house. Butch and I joined up with a couple of our squadron mates and some other gals who we recognized from prior parties over at the Alameda Officers' Club. As the crowd began to dissipate a couple of hours later I spotted these two cutie pies sitting over in the corner at a tiny table gawking at the men and sipping some suds. Eventually I strolled over and asked the girls if they had ever seen my soft shoe number performed to the tune, "Tea for Two," to which they replied

"No." Why should they have seen my dance number? Hell, we'd only met them for the first time twenty seconds previously!

The blond didn't hesitate in replying, "No. So why don't you show us?"

I looked at Butch. Butch looked at me. We smiled. I jumped up onto the table, which was about the size of an overgrown silver dollar, and proceeded to do a soft shoe for their entertainment. A few seconds later I felt this hand around my arm and a voice said, "No dancing allowed on the table, sir. Please get down and be a little more respectful of our place?"

The gals broke into laughter and I retired to the ground level of the establishment as the introductions commenced. "I'm Hank, and this is my buddy, Butch. To whom do we owe the pleasure of our company?"

"I'm Suzie and this is my roommate, Marilyn. We think you are crazy, Hank, and Butch must be also, if he hangs around with you! How did you possibly get up on that table, dance, and get down without killing yourself, I ask?"

"Ladies, we're "Nasal Radiators" from Lemoore and Alameda, so we can do the impossible now. Miracles take a little longer. Where y'all from, and is this the first time you've been here on a Sunday?"

"First of all, what's a nasal radiator and, yes, we're from San Francisco. This is our first time here, and look who we meet. Just our luck to almost get thrown out with you by the manager. Your hair is awfully short, so you guys must be in the military. Right?"

At this point Suzie was doing all of the talking which was just fine with me. I had my sights set on her, while Butch didn't really have a strong hankerin' for Marilyn. Isn't this usually the case I ask you? One's a winner and one's a dog. In this case, however, Marilyn was no dog. She was average and that simply wasn't good enough in San Francisco during the '60s, when hundreds of thousand of eligible men invaded the Bay area to be literally outnumbered ten to one by female denizens. Butch's heartthrob was in Atlanta, so this was strictly sport fucking for him. On the other hand, I was in a perpetual search and destroy mode for the perfect hum job (the perfect what?), the perfect pair of breasts, the perfect ass, and the perfect legs - all to go with the perfect face. From the neck up, Suzie met my criteria. Soon, it would be determined while on a covert reconnaissance mission that, from the neck down, she, also, fulfilled the remaining criteria for an eventual cornucopia of copulative ecstasy.

"Not just any military, my petite parcels of palpitating piscatorial promptitude but the United States Navy, specifically Attack Squadrons One Fifty-Two and One Fifteen respectively. And, we are the two best Spad drivers you'll ever want to meet. Can we buy another round for you before we all get thrown out of this joint? Besides, we have big plans for you later on this evening.

"Sure, we'll have another beer. But what makes you think we're yours for the evening? We're in the driver's seat because, face it fellas, we know the ropes around here and, if you like seafood, we'll take you to the very best in San Francisco. Or, if you like to dance, we know those spots also. Besides, don't you like us? Two cute, sexy eligible women looking for a good time?"

I knew she had us on the hook at this point in the conversation. Yes, Suzie was cute, and I was horny. Marilyn was okay, but Butch was horny. We left the bar and proceeded to follow Suzie and Marilyn over to San Francisco, and down to Fisherman's Warf where we would rendezvous at a restaurant, unknown to either Butch or me, called Pompeii's Grotto. When it is cold outside and you have two cutie pies like Suzie and Marilyn along side then the only appropriate entree is steamed clams, clam chowder, sourdough bread, and a bottle of Blue Nun Liebfraumilch wine to capture the mood. And, we captured the mood by getting slightly drunk and even mellower as the evening progressed. Suzie was a recent graduate of Berkeley in pharmacology, and she found employment with Cutter Labs, in Berkeley. Marilyn was working as an administrative assistant in a stock brokerage firm, down on Montgomery Street. Both were what we would now refer to as upper mobile professionals, or Yuppies. As we completed our meal and returned to the parking lot I asked the gals if we could give them a call tomorrow. Suzie grabbed me by the arm, pressed those symmetrical I would guess-34 C cup boobs deep into my chest and said, "You'd better call me tomorrow, or I'll be real upset, Navy Lieutenant Hank Miller."

Butch and I departed company as he headed back down to Lemoore and his squadron for flight operations that commenced bright and early on Monday morning. I, on the other hand, had only a few miles to drive back over the Oakland Bay Bridge to Alameda, and the BOQ for some serious "Z's." I couldn't get this cute blond out of my mind. As I fell asleep I remember having thoughts of Suzie, wishing she was there to share my bed.

I possessed the hottest tickets in town. I was the envy of the squadron. People were talking about me. People I'd never met. Perhaps it was because I had in my wallet two, center row seats for the premier performance of the pop singer of the decade. Nothing could stop me now! I called Suzie at work the following day to ask if she would like to go with me to see Trini Lopez, at the Circle Star Theater, in San Carlos. How could she refuse such an offer? How could she deliberate for one, single second about this proposal? Shit! People were waiting in lines for tickets to see Trini. Just so happens I had the foresight to ask Special Services on the air station if they had tickets for sale, and the answer was yes. And, a resounding yes, at 40% less than standard issuing prices, I might add. Anyway, Suzie replied, "It's about time you called, Lieutenant Miller. Been thinking about last night and I was concerned that you wouldn't call. Sure I'd like to go, so when will you be by to pick me up?"

"The concert starts at 8:00 so I'll be by around 7:00 if that's okay with you." I've been having some electrical trouble with my MG-B lately, so I'll try to be on time.

Electrical problems with an MG-B is total redundancy! Those bastardly bastions of British incompetence stopped running in wet weather, and there's never any wet weather in Great Britain, of course. One would think that these descendants of former Anglo Saxon world dominance would solve electrical and ignition problematic situations with their automobile marques, since it must rain 364 1/2 days out of a possible 365 in the Empire. Seems like the MG-B would act up and refuse to operate whenever it was running smoothly the day before. Somehow the little bugger always knew it was time to let the shit hit the fan again…and the radiator…and the carburetors…and the water pump…and the…!

The weather outside was rather nippy as was most of the weather in the Bay area this time of the year but it wasn't raining which was a good sign since I had to constantly worry about my car starting. One way to do this was to give it a push, hop in, shift into first gear, pop the clutch, and jump-start the little sonofabitch. This was always lots of fun especially when dressed up or with a date, as one can imagine. I found myself going through this ritual for the past week or two and I knew that it would reoccur unless I tended to the problem so I simply lived with the reality. I arrived at Suzie's apartment in the Marina district around 7:00, and she greeted me at the door with a big smile and a hug. At this point in the evening I just wanted to plant the wettest of wet kisses deep down her lovely little throat but, discretion being the better part of valor, I thought it best to let nature take its course later that evening. We rode off and barely made in onto Lombard when the little sonofabitch stalled at a stoplight in front of the Doggie Diner, as dozens of drivers beeped their horns and shouted profanities for me to clear the roadway. "Suzie, just a minor problem that can't be fixed if you'll kindly help me push this thing so we can get it started."

She was dressed in a beautiful fur-trimmed wool suit, with color coordinated shoes and purse. She was not dressed to perform mechanical repairs of this piece of shit we used as so-called transportation. She hopped out of the car and put a shoulder into the rear trunk as I steered from outside in order to gain the necessary momentum and speed for a jump start, which we accomplished with relative ease.

"Lieutenant Miller, why don't you break down and get this car fixed before it breaks down again, while you have a nervous breakdown?"

"Suzie, you have a flair for the obvious, and such a way with words! You're so sweet helping me and I do apologize for this mess. I've been meaning to replace the generator for sometime and now it looks like I have no other choice. Still, you shouldn't have to push a car on your first date, right?"

"I thought it was kinda fun. My brother has an MG-B and he's constantly having problems with it, so I can appreciate what you're going through. Let's just get over this hill on Gough, and head down the Bayshore so we won't be late for the show."

What can I say about a Trini Lopez show that hasn't been said before?...Next subject.

We arrived back at my apartment in Alameda just in time for my roommate Pete to sign off for the evening by going to his room after a brief introduction to Suzie. Suzie and I put on some slow music and proceeded to slow dance and do a little smooching. "Do you have to be back to San Francisco tonight, or can I take you to work in Berkeley tomorrow?"

"Suppose I can stay if you promise to get me to work on time, Lieutenant."

As I mentioned previously, we were about the same height while lying down and, as Suzie massaged my bare chest, I massaged her fully dressed breasts. She had opted to remain fairly aloof on this, our first date, while I capitulated by agreeing to remain clothed from the waist down. So, she provided me with a right-hand only chest and stomach massage as her left hand was buried somewhere under my back. The massage proceeded to head south below my belt line and under my skivvies as her hand gently enveloped my rigid member while Suzie whispered in my ear, "How does that feel, big boy? I'm embarrassed for being so forward but I thought you might enjoy a little extra for such a great evening, like having to push your car, a Trini Lopez concert, and keeping me stranded here, in Alameda. God, what do you do for an encore, or for the girls you really like?"

"I promise never again to take you to hear Trini Lopez. I promise to have my car fixed today. I promise to get you to Cutter Lab on time. Don't stop now, because that feels sooooo good! What are your plans tonight, sweet thing? Can I pick you up after work and take you back to your apartment so you can shower and change?"

"I'll think about it and, in the meantime, get your hand out of my skirt if you don't mind. You promised not to take advantage of me on our first date, remember?"

"Sorry, it totally slipped my mind."

Sorry my ass! If I didn't think I could get away with it I probably still would have tried to seduce this nymph. I suppose she liked it as much as I but just couldn't break down and surrender the first time out of the chute. Even Berkeley women had a set of morals that weren't to be tampered with until they thought it was correct for modifications, however slight or compelling.

We, both, slept soundly and almost missed Suzie's deadline for reporting to the lab, in Berkeley, for her day's work. Suzie and I left it where I would pick her up after work and return her to the apartment in the Marina so she could freshen up for dinner at our apartment back in Alameda. I was late for the All Officers' Meeting (AOM) at the squadron but camouflaged my tardiness by using that sonofabitch car as my excuse for being late again. Not one single officer doubted my word because each and every one had been the victim of either riding in the "B", or by having to tow me somewhere, or by coming to provide transportation when the sonofabitch broke down.

Five o'clock sharp, and I was parked in front of the lab as Suzie walked towards my car. "Hey, sailor, how's about a lift to nirvana, or, if that's just too much to ask, a ride to my apartment?"

"You're on, my little handful of happiness. We'll be at your place in thirty minutes and I'm going to catch a few winks while you change, if that's agreeable. My eyes are rolling in the back of my head for lack of sleep and I only need a catnap to charge the batteries."

Suzie changed into casual clothes as I slept. What seemed like hours later, and was actually about 45 minutes, we roared out of San Francisco for my apartment, and for some home cooked spaghetti that Suzie cooked up. I sprung for the Paul Mason Pinot Noir that I purchased at the commissary and warmed the sourdough bread in preparation for our supper. We located the station where Wolfman

Jack was expounding the virtues of rock and roll, and taking requests from callers all over the West coast. His gravely voice and capricious style made him the hit of millions, thus barely a night passed without listening to segments of the Wolfman Jack program, from Los Angeles, California.

Night number two or, should I say, date number two, so no holds barred in my repertoire of naughty seductive techniques, practiced and perfected over countless years and numerous regions of not only the female anatomy but, also, the fifty States. Suzie and I finished our meal and decided it was time to retire to the room with no view as we kicked off our shoes and slipped between the sheets, which hadn't been changed since I moved in a month earlier. A certain yellowish beige patina was begging to develop and distinct olfactory sensations seeped from the percale warp and weft, so time to replace them with freshly laundered fitted bottom and loose top sheets was in order for the evening. Now, that necessary chore was out of the way, and so was Suzie's bra at this point. As I slipped out of my Navy issue skivvies she accommodated my unspoken request by removing her civilian I. Magnin panties.

Suzie asked, "Did I satisfy you?"

"Oh, yes, yes, yes! How's about you, love. Are you feeling good?

"Don't you worry about me. I am fulfilled! Do I have a surprise for you tomorrow. It's a book called The Love Book, by Lenore Kandel, and it discusses all sorts of sexy things. Don't you dare let Pete see it or tell him that I bought it for you. He'll think I'm a real slut. Anyway, you'll get a kick out of it, I'm sure."

We both were asleep in two minutes.

"Lieutenant Miller, I simply can't be late again for work. Dr. Hidalgo will have a fit if I roll in thirty minutes late again today so get your fanny in gear, boy, and let's get me to Berkeley on time for a change."

Suzie and I had become an item so it goes without saying that my bed was her bed. Her bed was my bed, and so on. Often when I arrived at the apartment after a late flight exercise Suzie would be steaming some clams, or baking lasagna, while listening to the omnipresent Wolfman on the stereo. Suzie introduced me to good wine. Suzie introduced me to good food. She introduced me to Lenore Kandel, and *The Love Book,* that I still keep in my library as a one of a kind memoir of the '60's. This thin little paperback depicted several fornicating positions along with the dialogue between two flower styled karma sutra love children.

This was my kind of book! Lordy, I didn't think you could purchase anything like this outside of a brown paper wrapper in a stall down the alley behind the pool hall. Berkeley had everything. Berkeley had this book for sale in the drugstores. Berkeley published the *Berkeley Barb* newspaper that advertised for couples to "Get it on," including graphic photographs to arouse the reader. I love this place. I love the Bay area. Suzie asked if I enjoyed the book and my only reply was that we should read it together, aloud, some evening. She didn't buy into that scene, unfortunately.

After several months most of the members of my squadron had met Suzie and they considered her to be one of the elite group, to be part of our family. We attended formal Navy inspections together, dined at the "O" Club numerous times, double dated, fought the crowds at Kezar Stadium to witness the '49er's get their butts kicked by every team that came to town, close down the Buena Vista after consuming eight Irish coffees apiece, one night, and stumbling out the front door into the path of the Hyde Street cable car as we led the passengers in a chorus of Christmas carols, toured the Buena Vista (no relation to the bar) Winery, in Sonoma, with my roommate, Pete, and his gal, Sandy; and more practice of those techniques taught in Lenore Kandel's masterpiece of quivering carnal copulation.

As the Christmas holidays approached my roommate, Pete, indicated that he would be going home to Nebraska, and that I had the entire apartment to myself if Suzie wanted to move in. I thought this was another stroke of Pete's never-ending contribution to genius. Without any warning however, one of our former squadron mates, stationed at Lemoore, called and said that he was coming up, asked if I had a place for him to stay; and that Jeanie and Loree would be arriving a day after him. Without hesitation or mental evasion I replied, "Get your butt up here, boy. Sure you can stay with me. Pete's going home, so you'll have a bedroom to yourself. *Suzie who?* Jeanie was the five foot pixie who I'd met while down in Long Beach, for Navy carrier qualifications. Loree was the tall, thin brunette, and the two shared an apartment down in a southern California beach community. Just the thought of the two of them coming up for a couple of weeks was terribly exciting. *Suzie who?* In the next couple of days Tom arrived and settled in Pete's room as we awaited the arrival of two more Navy groupies.

Around noon the following day we heard a knock on the door and Tom answered, "Ladies, it is indeed our pleasure to welcome you to Poggi apartments. Good to see you again and I bet you had a long drive. Come on in and let us help you with your bags so we can get on the road for happy hour over at the club."

"Hank, Tom, we had one hell of a long and horrible drive because our car broke down twice, so can we take a bath first? Why don't you guys go and get some beer and munchies while we bathe, okay?"

First date. Jeanie came to bed with a terry cloth sarong covering her beautiful and fully developed frame. Tout de suite, she was down to her bra and panties as we caught up on old news, and how she was doing in school. Then, sleep.

Second date. The top and bottom sheets of my bed assumed their role as her only wardrobe for the night. They were quickly discarded as we concluded the small talk and proceeded to more lofty subjects, such as who preferred to remain on top.

We moved to third date status the next evening which entailed eroticism that is best left to the reader's imagination.

I had made plans to host the New Year's Eve party at our apartment, so everyone in the squadron was coming over as we prepared to entertain approximately 25 couples, all who would eventually become drunk and disorderly. Jeanie and Loree helped to clean the apartment while Tom and I shopped for your basic hors d'oeuvres, such as Cheez Whiz on celery sticks, Lays Potato chips, Spanish olives, salami, bologna, and American cheese on Ritz crackers to round out the Epicurean fantasy. Tom heard the phone ring, answered it, and said, "Hanky Panky, it's some female on the line."

"This is Suzie. When do you want me to come over to the party?"

"I got a real problem. These two gals just arrived from L.A., and they're staying with Tom and me for a few days. Okay?"

"You've got to be kidding me, buster! I'm serious. It's New Year's Eve and here I am sitting and waiting for you to come over, and pick me up. I'm really hurt and I'm going to cry."

"Now don't go and do that! What do you expect me to do in this situation? Kick them out? Sorry I didn't call you to let you know that I had other plans this evening but there's nothing can do about it now. So I'm a real bastard."

"You said it, mister. I'm shaking all over and I am not going to take no for an answer.

"I'm going to hang up the phone now, Suzie. You'll simply have to make other plans for the evening, and I'll talk to you tomorrow."...*Click!*

"Hey, honey, who was that giving you such a rough time? Come on over here and I'll get you another drink. Suppose it was an old flame who feels left out on New Year's Eve. Right?"

"Not to worry ladies. Just another one of thousands of sweet young thangs waiting to beat down our door here at the Spad Driver's Love Palace!"

Several interludes occurred between the time Suzie and I met, and the time just a couple of month's before we were scheduled to board the carrier for Southeast Asia. One was Jan, a stewardess for TWA. I always wanted more of her TWA tea than her TWA coffee. Another was Lisa, a real bombshell and an even bigger tease. She was short lived in the Bay area, as were all teasers during this era. A couple of "Go ugly early" types from the "O" Club sneaked in between, and they shall remain nameless. On again. Off again. Seems like Suzie and I always had a wonderful time together, and God only knows why I was off on another quest for the ultimate orgasm.

"That was Suzie who thought she was coming over to the party tonight. Hell, I didn't ask her but then again who else would I have asked if it weren't for Jeanie. How do you suggest I get out of this one, asshole?"

"You don't, shit for brains. There is no winner in this situation. Only losers, and you're going to realize it long after Jeanie has gone back down to Long Beach. My recommendation is to forget it for tonight, and just have a good time. Who knows? Maybe you'll bump into some sweet young thing, so you can use the copyrighted and world famous Spad Driver's introduction, 'Excuse me. I thought you were a fucking tree!' "

It was one hell of a party that lasted into the wee hours of the morning. After the pilots, their wives, and dates had left, Jeanie retired to the bedroom where she reappeared in this magnificent red lace gown that clung to her luscious frame like Saran wrap. An unforgettable image that stands out in my mind was the sight of her perfect breasts. And, I soon discovered where Jeanie's heavy breathing could only be calmed by spontaneous and repetitive orgasms. It was one hell of a night, and an even more unforgettable entree not only to Jeanie but, also, to the year, 1967.

Jeanie was wonderful. Jeanie was magnificent. Jeanie was sensuous. Jeanie moved like a snake, both in and out of the rack. She was almost as beautiful from the rear as she was facing while our bodies moved in unison. Jeanie possessed the perfect body for the cornucopia of copulative fantasies, and she was simply wonderful to behold, from every conceivable angle. Still, Jeanie had absolutely no idea of how to perform a hum job. And, if this lass, with the simply magnificent ass, didn't know after spending two weeks in the Spad Driver's Love Palace, there would be no hope.

Two days later the two gals hopped back into their car, and split for the long haul down Highway 101, to Long Beach. We bade farewell to these sweet young things, Jeanie and Loree, and thanked them profusely for being our guests for the Christmas holidays. We waved good by as they rambled off in their rambling wreck towards southern California. Then, Suzie called to inquire about the status of my fidelity and if I was interested in coming over to enjoy some steamed clams and wine. Of course I replied in the affirmative, so we were back on track just the way she wanted it to be. Not a word was mentioned about New Years Eve, or Jeanie. Not one word was mentioned about my disastrous phone conversation with Suzie regarding the party, and the reason for her exclusion. Nor did I ask her where she wound up that night, on 31 January 1966. Back to the sack. Back to the sack for some recitals of Lenore's chapters on love. More tardys for Suzie at Cutter Lab, and late entrances for me to the AOM's over at the squadron hangar.

Suzie wasn't there on the Alameda pier to wave good-bye as we sailed for Southeast Asia, on 7 June 1967. However, she and I corresponded regularly for seven months and we remained close through our letters.I anticipated rendezvousing with another fair maiden named Cindy when we returned form Vietnam but, surprise, surprise, Suzie was the one person, however, who accompanied Sandy, my roommate's new spouse, to that very same pier, at Alameda, as our carrier sailed under the Golden Gate and Bay bridges on that cold day, in January. She looked simply terrific dressed in a tailored Harris Tweed suit, trimmed in fur, as she entered our squadron ready room Suzie hugged me and whispered, "Hi, sailor. Long time no see. How about some chocolate and I'll show you a really good time?

The three of us departed the Oriskany and went directly over to the "O" Club where hundreds of spouses and girlfriends had congregated for long deserved celebration for those who lived through this terrible episode in our history. I presented Sandy with a pewter cup and plate for Pete, Jr., my godson, which I purchased and had engraved while shopping in Japan. Pete could not join the festivities mainly because he was on a flight training exercise, so he would join us later that afternoon back in Alameda. While on one of my numerous buying sprees in Hong Kong, Subic, Sasebo, Tokyo, and other ports of call, I had purchased this beautiful jade ring that was mounted in a raised gold setting. For the paltry sum of forty dollars it could be anyone's, so Suzie couldn't resist as she proceeded to dish out four crisp ten dollar bills while I slipped the ring onto her finger. I must admit that it looked terrific on her hand and the pale green of the stone matched the color of her eyes perfectly.

Later that evening, while back at Sandy and Pete's apartment, Suzie and Sandy initiated a procedure whereby I had to pass the "Float test." This required my getting into the bathtub and having a panel of expert witnesses testify that my testicles hung in the vertical position in the water. This meant I passed the float test. However, should my testicles had floated, that would indicate I failed the float test. You may have guessed the determining factor used as the criteria for passing or failing. If one's balls were full of sperm, then they would sink, thus indicating that there hadn't been any sex for some duration. On the other hand, if the bather's balls floated, then one could assume the bather had emptied his sack with a maiden recently. Suzie and Sandy concluded that I, indeed, passed the float test. (I had been admiring where Suzie had lost around fifteen pounds since I last saw her seven months previously, and she was now entitled to the highly acclaimed title "Spinner", which we'll describe later.) Having satisfactorily passed that rigid float test exam Suzie and I recited Lenore Kandel's postulates, (from memory) while she proceeded to undress leaving only her recently acquired bikini panties on her substantially reduced derriere, as she walked over to the bed. I proceeded to doff that unnecessary undergarment with my teeth as we perfected the middle-fingered jade ring technique, yab-yum, (or yummy), karma sutra, and plain old slightly modified missionary positions before we fell asleep from sheer exhaustion.

Soon after our routines had begun to settle down at the squadron Sandy suggested that we go skiing up at Lake Tahoe one weekend. During this time I met another honey at the same place where I met Suzie, The 39 Main, on the first Sunday after our arrival home. Kathy was a student nurse, originally from Nebraska, and you know how those student nurses, from Nebraska, require constant updating and practice regarding the human anatomy. I was merely there to help Kathy make it through her final exams as a consultant willing to subject himself to the physiological oral and written observations necessary for this fair un-maiden to achieve an "A+" for her final grade. And, I might add, the rigors were never painful, often pleasurable, but always predictable.

So, I responded to Sandy's suggestion and informed her that I was bringing this nursing scholar along with me since neither of us had previously skied. A major hitch had developed in the scheme, however. Sandy and Pete invited Suzie along as their guest to assist with the baby-sitting chores for Pete, Jr. Didn't make me no never mind, I told them, and that I would be checking in at the El Rue Motel that Friday evening with my petite parcel who would, indeed, learn the true meaning of nursing during the course of this weekend.

Kathy and left San Francisco for the Sierras around 5:00 that evening and found ourselves checked in at the motel awaiting the arrival of the other contingency of skiers. Funny thing is that I didn't feel awkward about Suzie's anticipated presence. Perhaps this was a result of our being so close, almost like siblings, or simply lovers. Nonetheless, that night Kathy and I assumed her studies, and she received a very high mark in the oral portion of her preparatory final exam. Bright and all too damned early we were up and standing in line at Heavenly Valley's ski rental concession. Sandy and Pete had skied previously, so they knew the ropes, while Suzie, Kathy, and I were fumbling around just trying to carry the long and awkward goddamn skis into the tram for the ride up the face of the mountain.

This was one hell of a long day for us in that the stamina required to ski all day long was simply overwhelming. We literally skied until the operators instructed us to either board the tram for the ride down, or get our butts onto a chair, or to ski down the face towards Gun Barrel. I rode the chair down which, in itself, was the parallel to an "E ticket" ride at Disneyland-scary! We met for dinner at Harvey's for their famous buffet, and then I indicated to the group that this cowboy was headed back to the bunkhouse to sleep, sleep, sleep. Suzie and Kathy wanted to party. Pete and Sandy wanted to screw. I just wanted to sleep. We each headed off in different directions to accomplish the aforementioned objectives, and I was asleep in about two minutes. Sometime, late that evening, there was a knock on my door. I opened it to discover Suzie and Kathy, obviously high as Lake Tahoe 4000 foot elevation kites, entering the room as I blurted out, "Come on, I'm exhausted and I need to get some sleep after I pee." I could hear their giggles while they could hear my piddles, and, as I reentered the bedroom, I suddenly found two bodies, one on either side of mine. Was I interested? Shit no!

Suzie said to Kathy, "Do you think he could take us both on at once?"

Kathy said to Suzie, "Why don't we try to find out?"

I said to Suzie and to Kathy, "Just forget it, and Suzie, you can go home anytime now."

My opportunity of a lifetime, and an experience that men of all nationalities, religious beliefs, colors, creeds, and sexual persuasions had dreamt about for centuries: The Oreo cookie scenario. The ménage 'a trois. The two against one scene where the man could indulge himself with two women, and the two women could indulge one another, if that's their bag, or they could simply enjoy watching the man with the other woman. Never before had I been presented with this quandary of quail on a lubricated platter. Never again during my next twenty-five years would the same situation be repeated. I blew it. Simple as that. I simply blew it!

Back to the slopes on Sunday and then a long, silent drive back to San Francisco, as Kathy refused to talk to me because I left her in the motel room that morning while going off to ski with the rest of the gang. Obviously, I tried my damnedest to get her up to no avail. She had really outdone herself the previous night and nothing I could do would prepare her for the day's rather vigorous activities. Hence, I left Kathy in the room as I went off to hit Broadway and Patsy's Run on the beginner slopes, at Heavenly.

That was the end of my relationship with Kathy. Hell, if she couldn't take a joke! What can I say? What was I supposed to do? Sit around the motel room all day trying to sober her up to the point where she could put on a pair of skis and head on down the mountain? My time was precious and there wasn't a single woman on the planet who was permitted to obstruct my daily goals and objectives, including my very own mother. So, after the four-hour drive back to San Francisco, in total silence I might add, I let Kathy off at her apartment in the Castro, and headed back to Alameda for a long sleep, alone for once.

Why did Suzie keep coming back for more abuse? What was it that drove her to accept my invitations for social dates, and for official Navy events where she was a guest of honor? Was there something in her makeup that would indicate she was a masochist? Or, was it simply a case where she felt a strong connection to me? I never stopped to ask.

Our attack squadron was disbanding and the pilots were being reassigned to other units, from the Atlantic to the Pacific. I was given orders to COMROPDIVFOUR, *(no civilian translation because it was a top secret unit)* in Panama, but turned them down because I would have to extend my obligation to Uncle Sam for two years. Hence, I got revised orders to report to USS Hancock, as Assistant Flight Deck Officer no later than 7 March 1968. Three months turnaround before going back over the pond to Vietnam. How generous our government was with their warriors in allowing them to visit with their families and loved ones for three, whole months before risking the chance of adding their names to the daily obits broadcast globally by Dan Rather and friends. This meant I had approximately one and one-half months to live in reckless abandon because the shit would hit the fan on 7 March, as I boarded the Hancock for flight deck training. Lots of skiing to accomplish in the meantime, so Suzie and I, (Kathy was history at this point), made a weekend ritual by meeting at Spenger's, in Berkeley for steamed clams, chowder, sourdough bread, and Blue Nun wine as the commute traffic subsided on the Nimitz before we smoked up the hill to the El Rue Motel, at Stateline.

Suzie would ski on one particular run while I, the more adventurous one, would head off to the top of the mountain and tackle the moguls on the Ridge Run. We'd meet for lunch, then back to our routines before rendezvousing at the bottom for an Irish coffee at the lodge. Suzie looked hot, hot, hot in her tight fitting ski apparel of the day. She looked like an example of the perfect southern California ski bunny with her blond hair, freckles, white lip gloss, tight wool sweater, and skin tight ski pants. Lordy, sometimes we barely made it back to the room.

One day, while skiing, I twisted my knee very badly and the pain was excruciating so we stopped at the pharmacy for the most effective pain killer allowed by law. Then, we stopped at the Christiana for several cocktails that were the most effective pain killers allowed by law. I liked the cocktails effect much better as we returned to our room. I undressed and wrapped my knee with the Ace bandage purchased earlier while I sat on the bed contemplating my orders to the Hancock. Suzie appeared wearing a negligee that was a new and welcomed addition to her wardrobe - a full length pearl colored silk gown, scooped neck, sleeveless, and opaque, with two sheer exceptions; and those magnificent exceptions were nipple pink and rigid as I stared and said, "What are you trying to do? Turn me on?"

"That's the main idea, sailor. Just be quiet, and get into bed while I polish your German helmet."

The gown had assisted Suzie with the accomplishment her primary objective, and that was the total and repetitive seduction of her favorite Spad Driver.

7 March 1968 fell on a Monday. On 4 March Suzie and I ventured once again to the mountain to try our hand at the ski runs of increased difficulty. On 5 March they carried me off that ski run of increased difficulty in a wire basket and down to the first-aid station at the foot of the face where I was greeted by the manager, and a warm brandy, prior to Suzie being located to transport me to the nearest hospital. My doctor noticed where I was a Navy-type, and he indicated that he was formerly an orthopedic surgeon in the same branch of the service. Dr. John asked where I was stationed and I indicated that I was to report to the Hancock on or before 7 March for duty. The x-rays were returned to Dr. John, and his smile widened as he said, "Lieutenant Miller, you ain't going to the Hancock, you lucky sailor. You have what we call a spiral fracture of both the fibula and the tibia, so you're out of action for at least six months. Glory Hallelujah, praise the peaceniks! You didn't really want to go back over there now, did you, especially since

you've done your time and lived to tell about it?"

"Oh, the pain feels so good. Hell no, I don't want to go back this soon especially as Assistant Flight Deck Officer, which, you know, is one, important and demanding assignment. Do I have to stay here overnight? Where do I go from here?"

"Yep. One night, and then Suzie can drive you down to Oak Knoll Navy Hospital, in Oakland. Congratulations, Lieutenant, you broke your leg just in the nick of time. Suzie, we're going to put him in room 101, so why don't you go back to the motel and grab his things, like his Dop kit, and make sure his skis get put into the trunk of your car. Hank, are you hungry? If so, Suzie there's a MacDonald's just down the street."

"I am famished and I would love a burger, fries and a shake, Suzie."

The Demerol that had been injected in my butt was in full swing, and the trip was wonderful. No pain, and a warm and fuzzy feeling all over culminated by an enormous appetite. I shared a room with a fellow who had busted his thigh bone into a zillion pieces while tobogganing down one of the local hills nearby. He was in bad shape and had been a resident of room 101 for a month already, with another two to go. We both enjoyed a picture window view of the mountains, conifers, and of the cute nurses who tended to us. Suzie returned with the grub and I proceeded to quaff down the contents of the bag until I realized that the Demerol was responsible for my eyes being larger than my stomach. One or two bites and that was it. Suzie proceeded to open her purse and hand me a Coors that had been approved for prescription. The Demerol and the Coors signaled lights out until tomorrow.

Our trip down Highway 50 was not without pain. Dr. John allowed me to have a couple of sleeping pills for the road, but no more pain killer. I still felt every single bump in the road while Suzie drove exercising extreme caution and diligence. We put plan "C" into action, and that was a quick pit stop to purchase more Coors to go along with the sleeping pills. The sleeping pills and the Coors signaled lights out until

Oakland.

I liked Oak Knoll Navy Hospital a whole lot more than the USS Hancock, I might add. After a couple of days in my orthopedic ward getting acclimated to the quiet life, as an in-patient, Suzie dropped by after work and proceeded to get out her various paints to decorate my full legged cast in psychedelic colors embellished with peace symbols, and other colorful marques. My newly decorated cast was the talk of the hospital and I hobbled with pride as the staff and patients commented about the creativity of the artist. The doctors and nurses wouldn't permit me to leave the grounds until one week, and one bowel movement, had successfully passed. Within seven days both objectives were accomplished. Suzie and I went out for our usual crustacean delicacies of steamed clams bordelaise, accompanied by sourdough bread, rose wine, and numerous Irish Coffees.

When we returned to her apartment she helped me out of my trousers, since this was no easy task as the plaster cast covered the tips of my toes up to a couple of inches from my groin. Suzie said, "Lay back and enjoy this," as my head began to spin from the mixture of the coffee with the whiskey mixed with the whipped cream. . . to be continued.

Barry, Donna, the author, 1966

One Hell of a Marathon Week

I hate youth! I hate those who can work all day at their vocation, and then boogie the night away at their avocation. I hate those who can put everything into their work and then put everything into their sex. Do I appear to sound bitter? Do I appear to have a chip on my shoulder? *I certainly hope so, Ollie!* Well, perhaps I have some remorse in the fact that I was a master marathon party animal several years ago, and now I am an "Under ten second, three-yarder" to the chair seated in front of my Macintosh. Still, I vividly recall the times when I would fly two training flights daily, and then hit the bars down in Fresno, or San Mateo, or San Francisco, until I scored and took some local honey back to my room, or hers.

No reason to argue about it, goddammit!

I'd really get pissed off when I put out three or four dollars for entertainment just to discover where she would rather think of me as a friend, and to reconsider my proposal so I would respect her in the morning. Fuck respect! If she wants respect she can sleep with a theologian.

The '60s was the decade of the sure thing. The '60s was the decade when one would be virtually assured of a soft, warm pad to crash every night of the week, regardless of the situation, or the honey in question, be it a "Go ugly early type," or a "Let's have just one more Irish coffee before we blast off for my pad, you sweet petite parcel of palpitating piscatorial promptitude."

After receiving my Navy Wings of Gold, in March of 1966, I received orders to report to Attack Squadron 122, at Lemoore Naval Air Station, San Joaquin Valley, California, for flight instruction in the A-1H Skyraider, affectionately known as the Spad. After four months at Lemoore I would report to my squadron, in Alameda, for deployment aboard the USS Oriskany, for Vietnam. Until then, however, I was stuck in Lemoore, and the San Joaquin Valley. Lemoore is four hours away from civilization. The San Joaquin Valley is sparsely populated, hot, flat, and boring, which reminded me allot of the entire State of Texas. Lemoore was squarely situated in the hairiest part of her armpit. All it took was one week in Lemoore before I found a thousand excuses to blast off for the Bay area. My friend, Butch, and I had discovered a covey of stews living up in San Mateo who were on call, constantly. We had been with them for good times in San Francisco, Sausalito, Carmel, for the Laguna Seca car races, and many other locations far away from Lemoore. Eventually, our relationships with these gals had worn thin, so I had contingency plans in effect while Butch concentrated on his childhood sweetie, back in Atlanta.

I had met this stew who lived on Gough Street, In San Francisco, and she had my undivided attention for at least 24 hours, at a stretch. Jan was a cute blonde, small physique, with a northwestern ethic that took me longer than anticipated to subvert before she hit the silks with this cowboy, and I don't mean skydiving. As the Thanksgiving holiday week approached I made plans to escape the doldrums of Lemoore for the excitement of San Francisco, once again.

Monday, beginning Thanksgiving week, was routine in that we were scheduled for two hops a day in preparation for carrier qualifications in our newly assigned, but technologically ancient, aircraft. Day and night we practiced take-offs and landings, called Field Carrier Landing Practices, (or FCLP's), until we thought we were going to die, so the thought of having several days off was helping us to get through the next two days of intense instruction and flying. Trouble is that we really didn't have two full day and nights of liberty before we could split away from the armpit. I had my mind made up that, regardless of the flight schedule, I was going to take advantage of every single minute of the time away from Lemoore, and FCLP's. Jan was scheduled to fly on Wednesday and she wouldn't return to her apartment until Thanksgiving day, so on Tuesday I ventured North to visit with my friend Barry, who lived in Redwood City. I arrived late that afternoon and Barry suggested that we head up to the City to a newly discovered night spot called the Lemon Tree, on Bush Street. We changed into our party clothes, hopped into our respective sport cars, Barry, in his Austin Healey and I, in my MG-B, and blasted off for our ritualistic race up the Bayshore, at speeds in excess of 90, to rendezvous at the Lemon Tree for a planned attack on the clitoral cuties in the confines of the club, affectionately known as the "Four C Strategy."

Soon after our arrival we proceeded to single out some single women as we consumed our single beers for some serious chest to breast juxtapositioning and other grinding of the genitalia on the dance floor. My newly discovered cutie, named Gail, suggested that we head back to her place, just around the corner on Green for some late night hugging and kissing. Barry and his squeeze headed off for parts unknown as Gail and I entered her apartment while she proceeded to put several LP's on the stereo. Then, Gail showed me her bedroom which was my introduction not only to her floor plan and living arrangements but, in addition, to her sexual preferences, which were diverse. We consummated our newly formed short time relationship before I left her apartment for the four-hour drive back to Lemoore, and the armpit, in order to make the All Officer's Meeting (AOM) at 0800 Wednesday (that's 8:00 am for you draft dodgers!).

I flew my two hops and was given a reprieve by the squadron Landing Signal Officer (LSO) in that I didn't have to report back to

Lemoore Friday night for FCLP's because my flight proficiency was above average. A few other pilots in the squadron had to fly additional hops because they were having difficulty with the flight pattern, altitude, airspeed, or all of the above in getting the Spad to accurately simulate actual carrier approaches and landings. As usual, my Bingo bag was packed in the trunk of the car so I blasted up California Highway 33, through Dos Palos, Mendota, Firebaugh, Los Banos, Gilroy, San Jose, up the Bayshore, and to San Francisco where I met Gail for a resumption of where we left off the previous evening for more dancing, space planning, and tenants improvement of her bedroom as we screwed our way into Thanksgiving day. I left her apartment later that morning and stopped to take a whiz on the facade of the Catholic convent adjacent to her building.

While I sprayed the stucco of the corner of the structure I reflected back on several nuns or Christian Brothers who I wished were physically there instead of the inanimate wall, so I could piss all over their heads for retribution for the wonder years spent in Catholic Catechism classes and schools back on the East coast.

Bladder empty, car warmed up, KFRC tuned in on the monaural radio, and this cowboy was heading down that highway towards the hairy armpit, called Lemoore. By now, I was in a survival mode. By this time, I had a cumulative total of about ten hours of sleep, six or seven orgasms, a dozen gin and tonics, two dozen Irish coffees, one badly overcooked and scalded turkey, and one serious case of heartburn. My body was running on empty as I sped through the early morning tulle fog towards the main gate of N.A.S. Lemoore. I arrived just as the chartered Greyhound bus drove up to the front of the BOQ with a full contingency of sailors and pilots for the long ride away from the hairy armpit to Long Beach. I asked the driver if he could wait for five minutes as I dashed up to my room for my flight gear, civilian clothes, guitar, and uniforms. We departed at 0900 sharp (that's 9:00 for you commies) on this Sunday morning as we left Lemoore towards Hanford, Visalia, and California Highway 99 South. Before we had gone a mile the sailors pleaded with the driver to stop at a store for a full load of beer, tequila, smokes, and munchies for our four-hour trip to southern California to which the driver acceded. I made it through one sip of Coors before my eyeballs crossed, and rolled in the back of my head for what was to be a three-hour siesta through the scenic San Joaquin.

We arrived at Long Beach Naval Base around 1600 (that's 4:00 pm for you perverts) as we proceeded to unload the gear and proceeded up the gangplank to the officers' brow for stateroom assignments, and I drew the short straw by getting Tom Dush as my roomie, who we called Tom "Bags" for short (douche bags, you idiot). This four walls of steel, with one measly porthole, would be our home for the next week as we qualified for carrier operations in the Spad while launching and recovering from the pitching deck of the huge horizontal floating monolith off the California coast. Tom had indicated during the ride down that he had two honeys who were going to meet us at the "O" Club for dinner that evening. My retort to Bags was simple. My retort was without hesitation or mental evasion. My retort to Bags was that there was absolutely no fuel left in the tanks of one, empty and exhausted Hank Miller…That his body was no longer a weapon…That he was whatever you wanted to call him, be it a pussy, a wimp, or even a jet puke! That he simple didn't give a shit about women this particular night and he simply wanted to have a nice dinner, enjoy a Grand Manier, and head back for an early retirement, and numerous hours of refueling his tank. In other words, "No, no, no!" Bags refused to accept my answer because he was looking after his best interests in attempting to find an escort for his girlfriend's roommate. Again, I impolitely refused his offer. Again, I told Bags to stick it where his afterburner didn't shine. Again, I emphatically told him that I was simply too exhausted from the previous week's activities in and around San Francisco to have even the slightest interest in women. During cocktails we discussed it. Before dinner we discussed it. During dinner we discussed it, again! The answer was still, "No."

Loree and Jeanie walked through the door into the dining room of the club, and *stutter stammer* I said to Bags, "Which one's the spinner?"

Tom replied, "That's Jeanie, my gal's roomie, the one with the pixie haircut and the big tits!

"Good evening ladies! I'm Hank and it's awfully nice to meet you!

Tom was telling me all about you two, and he sure wasn't exaggerating. I had no idea until now what a couple of cuties he was describing. Jeanie, come on over here, sit down next to me so we can get acquainted, you petite parcel of palpitating piscatorial promptitude! Lordy, do you smell so sweet! Do you taste as good as you look? What's that perfume you're wearing, anyway?"

"Hank, it's called 'Passion,' and I wore it for the first time tonight, so I'm glad you like it. Hey, when you guys finish your meals why don't we get going out to Mama's, in Inglewood, for some dancing? Hank, do you like to dance?"

"Darling, do I love to dance and, now that my batteries are recharged with this meal, let's get into your car and move 'em on out."

What do you mean tired? What do you mean fatigued? What do you mean exhausted? You're putting everything out of proportion. You're misunderstanding what I've been trying to say for the past several paragraphs. You have absolutely no fucking idea what you're talking about! So, shut up and keep on reading.

All it took was just one look, and I was in love, in lust, in heat, horny, and having a white out. Jeanie was a total woman, a bombshell ready for my fuse. She was about five feet tall, one hundred pounds, huge brown eyes, and perfectly proportioned body with the exception of those huge tits. And, her large mouth was perfectly shaped for some serious deep-throated tongue tag. My spirit was in first gear, albeit my body was in park

Into the back of Loree's car, and off to Mama's as Jeanie and I snuggled to one corner while I slipped my hand under her overcoat to massage those big, beautiful, magnificent mammarys. She immediately planted one hell of a French Louie half way down my throat, and I knew for sure that we were in for one hell of a marathon evening, to go along with my marathon week. Mama's is in Inglewood, near the Los Angeles airport, about fifteen minutes away as Jeanie and I continued the exploration of one another's semi-private parts while Tom and Loree rode in the front seat-eyes straight ahead.

What can one say about Mama's that hasn't been said of every other beach bar situated up and down Pacific Coast Highway One? One big flat expanse of terrazzo floor, dozens of linoleum topped tables, metal chairs, a rectangular bar situated squarely in the middle of the room, a juke box over in the corner next to the often occupied stage, numerous blonde-haired, tan-skinned men in their baggie shorts hustling the numerous blonde-haired, tan-skinned honeys in their super tight shorts making their way through the front entrance. Jeanie walked over and put several quarters in the juke box and punched in C-9 for the Beach Boys new hit, "Good Vibrations." Tom and I loosened our ties, threw our coats over into the pile with the girls' jackets, and proceeded to boogie, boogie, boogie! Jeanie displayed the same sensuous moves on the dance floor as she did in the back seat while I proceeded to inquire about her social status beyond Hank Miller and Sunday night at Mama's. She was in her last year of college and she planned to apply with the airlines for a stewardess position after graduation. We danced and danced, and drank and drank until the bar closed at 0200 (that's 2:00 am for you Peace Corps volunteers!).

Then, back into the back seat of the love mobile for some serious crotch grabbing, nipple enhancement, and deep throated kissing as we contemplated consummating our relationship right in front of our two friends, in the front seat. She decided against our fucking our brains out while going down the 405 towards Long Beach which was a discretionary good move. Nonetheless, we made plans to see one another later that year when the gals would come up to visit us, in Alameda, close to San Francisco. Tom and I bade the Laura lovelies adieu as we attempted to navigate the officers' gangplank up to the carrier quarterdeck, without stumbling or tripping over the foot guards as we made our way back to our stateroom below.

I did not go to sleep this morning. I did not crash onto my bunk. I literally went into a coma for the following 12 hours. Thank God flight operations were canceled due to poor visibility or else this cowboy would have been unable to man his aircraft for the ensuing catapult shots off the bow and into the low hanging fog as we sped towards the Channel Islands. While the remainder of the squadron was having breakfast I was sound asleep. While the remainder of the squadron was having lunch I was sound asleep. While the remainder of the squadron was...Well, Tom decided this was enough so he got me up for dinner. My sin was forgiven by the LSO since there were no flight operations this day and evening. I felt much better now spiritually, physically, mentally, and sexually, thanks to a long rest, Jeanie's ability to arouse me to stiffened heights and hardened resolve, and to a delicious dinner with my compatriots.

To summarize my week thus far I would say that, never again, would I put my body through the endurance test that be felled me Thanksgiving week, in 1966. Between the thousands of cumulative miles driven between Lemoore and San Francisco, the various one-nighters with Jan, Gail, and Jeanie, the mad dashes between the aircraft carrier and the local bars, I had surely passed the primary test of becoming a full-fledged Spad pilot. However, tomorrow I would be confronted with, yet another, test of mental and physical endurance as my aircraft would be strapped to the catapult harness, and propelled via means of hydraulics from the bow of the carrier, at speeds in excess of a hundred miles per hour.

Been down this carrier qual road before on two different occasions, and I dare say that none ever gets used to the thought of controlled crashes and five G shots only 64 feet above the ocean from the bow of a boat moving at 20 knots. My first qualification was down in Pensacola while flying a T-28 Trojan during primary flight training aboard the USS Lexington. The primary difference in this initial qual was the weather, which was beautiful, the flight deck was stable, and there were no catapult shots. We used the deck launch technique instead, for we were still flight students and the aircraft wasn't suited for catapult shots. My second carrier qualification was down in Corpus Christi, in the S-2 Hawkeye, as an advanced flight student. The S-2 was a twin-engine prop aircraft used for anti-submarine activities. Again, the weather was clear, the deck relatively stable, and no cat shots, only deck launches, and absolutely no night operations.

Somehow, I didn't cherish the thought of going off this carrier's bow while strapped to a huge slingshot and immediately entering the gooey fog, with virtually zero visibility, only to return to land aboard the pitching deck, with virtually zero visibility. And, to top it off, we had FUCKING NIGHT OPERATIONS to look forward to! What a hell of a deal! I must admit the taxpayers were getting a big bang for their buck.

After our briefing we left the ready room and rode the escalator up to Flight Ops and then out onto the flight deck to begin the pre-flight checklist for our aircraft. If there was in as much as one drop of hydraulic fluid, or a minor oil leak, or a leaking strut, or a missing ashtray I would down the bird. I would not fly that sucker off the carrier and put my life in Harm's Way. My mother didn't raise any dumb kids, I'll tell you. Shit! No excuses to down the aircraft this go around so I strapped in my seat, completed the checklist, started the engine, and followed the deck hands' directions and taxied up to the bow as the crew engaged the harness under the fuselage while I applied full throttle, place my head back against the headrest, glued my eyes on the instruments, and saluted the catapult officer to indicate that I was ready to launch. As I was literally pinned to the seat my plane shot down the track towards the bow and attained a speed in excess of a hundred knots, and I was airborne. My eyeballs were caged in the back of my head from the acceleration and, suddenly, I was in the fog, only a hundred feet from the ocean waves. Immediately, the instruments of the aircraft became my savior, my soul, my spirit, and my only salvation in order to maintain the aircraft in a safe flight attitude. Holy Christ! Noone prepared me for this experience, which is an understatement. I vividly remembered when I prepared for my first carrier landing back in Pensacola, when an instructor indicated that the experience we would feel resembled a combination between the first piece of ass and the first automobile accident we had in our lives. Too bad he failed with his description of this giant sling shot into virtual reality! Now, I was at 400 feet as I turned downwind to set up for the recovery phase of the qualifications. Recovery. Now, there's a word that is almost appropriate for the life experience, in that if one failed to successfully recover, one would never recover from the splat his body made against the stern of the carrier in a screaming ball of fire. So, recover techniques were uppermost in my mind, still unable to see the water, the carrier, the landing area, or the "Meatball." The LSO had us on his radio and he asked us to report as we turned onto final and left the four hundred foot preassigned flight altitude.

"Locket thirteen, ball, four hundred pounds," was my initial contact with the carrier as I proceeded to pull back the power, drop my tail hook, lower the flaps, three green indicators of gear down and locked, and check all the instruments for accuracy and for vital information. The ocean was rough and the deck was pitching like a bucking fucking bronco at the rodeo so we had an additional problem to cope with on the final approach. We had to ensure that we didn't overcorrect and exaggerate our manipulations of the controls. In others words, we had to remember everything our instructors had told us, and everything we learned during the past two years of flight training, or we would become another proud consumer of the well known petrochemical product known as the Zip Loc body bag that would contain what little remains that could be scrapped off the carrier's vertical, extremely solid, and always fatal, fantail.

"Roger, Locket thirteen give me some power. Line up is okay. You're below glide slope. Power, power, power!"

I applied power, power, power, for God's sake, as the LSO signaled the green landing lights to indicate that I was now to reduce power, power, power, as my landing gear slammed onto the deck while I continued to roll towards the edge of the angle and off the edge to Davey Jones Locker. Suddenly, the tail hook had done it's job and caught one of the four arresting cables stretched across the deck as I simultaneously slammed forward into the shoulder harness while the aircraft stopped about ten feet from the edge.

Shit! Just think. I had to repeat this feat at least five more times today as I looked forward, with glee, to night operations! No thoughts of Jan, Gail, or Jeanie at this time, I might add. Pussy was the farthest thing from my mind.

By the end of the week we had individually refused engraved invitations from the Grim Reaper to join him as his guest in virtually reality as we packed our bags and reboarded the same Greyhound bus for the ride back to the hairy armpit, Lemoore, and to thoughts of more amorous experiences that would develop with Loree and Jeanie up in Alameda, later in the year.

Now, for some serious sleep as we made our way up California Interstate Five towards the Grapevine, down the mountain towards Bakersfield, and back to the reality of the San Joaquin Valley, albeit unvirtual. I gotta tell you that chasing poontang was one hell of allot easier and more fun that slamming that Spad onto the deck of a huge hunk 'a hunk of screaming metal floating around the Pacific ocean. I'd much rather have been pursuing a petite hunk 'a hunk of burning love somewhere around San Francisco, or Long Beach, for one more attempt at breaking my own personal record for a marathon week.

My weary legs barely propelled the rest of my exhausted body up the stairs of the BOQ, and the attempt to insert my room key into the door resembled that of a Parkinson's diseased cripple. Stumbling out of my clothes and taking a last minute piss I finally crashed onto my very own bed devoid of what we referred to as "Strange," which was a euphemism for lusty women.

This is Locket 13, over . . .

Spad formation Tonkin Gulf 1967

The author at Cubi NAS Philippines Beach Detatchment

Cindy and Cher in my MG-B June, 1967

A Covey of Quail

Say, why don't we hum a little tune that has since become the national anthem out on what we refer to as the Best Coast?

If You're Going to San Francisco

If you're going to San Francisco,

Be sure to wear some flowers in your hair.

If you're going to San Francisco,

You're going to meet some gentle people there.

For those who come to San Francisco,

Summertime will be a love-in there.

In the streets of San Francisco,

Gentle people with flowers in their hair.

All across the nation such a strong vibration,

People in motion.

There's a whole generation, with a new explanation,

People in motion.

If you come to San Francisco,

Summertime will be a love-in there.

Scott McKenzie sang it *as no other could.*

John Phillips wrote it, 1967

"Hanky Panky, you are not even going to begin to believe what just happened to me over here in the city...Goddammit, operator, I just put in two dimes and you're telling me that my time is up. Go fuck yourself, operator! . . . Hank, call me back over here in the city at PL3-4567. Hurry!"

That smooth talking Boo always had a way with words, but the telephone operator saw no humor in his verbal abuse, so she cut him off smack dab in the middle of his call from San Francisco over to the BOQ at the Alameda Naval Air Station. I was soon to discover that I should be mighty proud that he called me instead of some of the other pilots in our squadron, however, because I was about to fall into a situation that had eluded me for over twenty years. That glorious sequence of events consisted of Boo's inadvertently discovering what I refer to as a covey of quail - a bunch of sweet young "thangs" living together in the same San Francisco flat, and damn proud of the fact they loved to party especially during this summer of peace and love, 1967 style.

Hallelujah! Haight Ashbury, the Doors, Gatsby's, the Latitude 38. Turtle races at Zack's every Wednesday night, the Swiss Village, Pierce Street Annex, and the Camelot, that we referred to as the golden triangle (and I don't mean the pussy of some unnamed lass from Kansas), blowing a doobie at the grandstand in Golden Gate Park during Sunday afternoon concerts, Inez Jones at the Rainbow Room on Union Street, steamed clams at Pompeii's Grotto, Irish coffees galore at the Buena Vista, hall parties at the BOQ where girls would flock to show off their braless ensembles with "matching pairs of raisins" to horny Naval aviators ready to depart for Vietnam; and those glorious Navy nurses from Oak Knoll Hospital who truly understood and appreciated the male anatomy. If one had the distinct fortune of running into a group of nurses sharing a flat with some airline stewardesses, then one's dream had come true. Party, party 'round the clock, between flight schedules and shifts. Somehow there must have been an underlying current, an unwritten creed that we lived by, and that was to eat, drink, and make Mary, for tomorrow we may no longer be here.

Up until now, I had been working my ass off by flying twice daily and preparing for a 12th Naval District ADMAT Inspection, plus my collateral duties as Communications Officer and RPS Custodian but, in my off time, I found pleasure in close affiliations with Suzie. Suzie and I had been an item for over a year as we intentionally remained fairly independent, each with his/her own agenda.

Sarah, Lisa, Jan were other numerous nameless one-night stands; and I was beginning to prematurely age from flame-out. My life seemed rather empty and I was growing tired of these same Laura lovelies whose amorous surprises varied from sustained daily abstinence to that of my leaving late for the squadron AOM's (All Officers' Meetings) on certain mornings. Sensuous blonds like Suzie and brunettes like Lisa, to red shades like Jan, to the "go ugly early" types found hanging around the bar at the Alameda Officers' Club during Friday happy hour searching for primeval pleasures. I needed consistency. I needed a place for one-stop shopping. I needed Harriet, Cindy, Cher, and Melody. And, Boo provided them for our added enjoyment and viewing pleasure. A covey of quail whose sole mission in life would soon be to provide ecstasy to the stalwart sailors just about to enter their Quadra lexical sphere.

If you're going to San Francisco,

You're going to meet some gentle people there.

I had just completed my flight operations for the day and, as the Communications Officer, I had ensured that all of the confidential and secret messages received at the squadron that day were routed accordingly. Now, it was time to hit the road, go back to the BOQ to change into civvies, and goose that MG-B in the ass for the city. Boo had left a message at the front desk of the BOQ that I was to meet him at 1001 Union Street, and to be prepared for a dream come true. As I approached San Francisco the first exit off the Bay bridge was Broadway, and that would eventually lead me past the strip joints and through the tunnel, by Chinatown. An immediate right turn after the tunnel before Polk Street, onto Larkin, then a quick left onto Union, as the hill dropped abruptly towards Van Ness. God, was this a beautiful city when you could see the Farallons and the Marin Headlands, the clear panoramas of Alcatraz, Angel Island, and the magnificent Presidio from atop Russian Hill. I found a place to park in front of the rendezvous point and I proceeded to enter the apartment building up to the third floor, and knock on the door of apartment No.301. All of a sudden this sweet lass opened the door and asked if I were Hank, and my reply was, "Darlin' I'm anyone you want me to be!" This first encounter was with Melody, and she was a TWA stewardess. As I entered the flat three other petite parcels of palpitating piscatorial promptitude came over to introduce themselves, and to offer me a cold

Coors.

"Hi, Hank. I'm Harriet and these are my friends, Cindy and Cher. I fly with TWA and so does Cher."

"Cindy, what do you do? Are you a hostitute at 35,000 feet, also?"

"No, Hank, I'm taking time off from my job in Portland, where I am a dental assistant. I simply couldn't refuse the offer of my old friends to come down to San Francisco for this fantastic music and weather. You know that it rains all of the time in Portland, and the weather has been absolutely beautiful since I arrived. Besides, isn't this the summer of love, so don't you want to participate?"

"D'a'aaarling, you have no idea about the degree of interest I possess regarding this subject!"

"Harriet, I detect a southern twang, honey child. Where are you from, you little devil?"

"Boys, I'm from Arkansas, but you have no room to talk about my accent. Boo, you have to be from Louisiana, and my guess is that you're a coon ass from the way you talk, and because you wanted to cook us up some of your world famous gumbo. After all, that's how we met you."

"Boo, old buddy, where did you have the fortune of meeting these fantastic ladies?"

"I was sitting down at the corner bar minding my own business when Melody came in and asked the bartender if she could borrow a large pot to use for some cooking, and that she'd clean it and bring it back tonight. Besides the fact that Melody was one, great looking chick my curiosity got the better of me so I asked her what she was preparing to cook. Melody replied that she was cooking some stew for her roommates and she didn't have a kettle large enough to hold the ingredients for the four of them. Then, I asked Melody is she'd ever had any really good gumbo, or jambalaya, and she replied 'No.' One thing lead to another and, before you knew it, she asked me to come up and to cook them a good Cajun supper, so here we are and ain't you glad, Hanky Panky!"

Words cannot convey my emotions at this point and I'm certain that this dream was about to end; and that I would awaken to a nightmare in the cockpit of my Spad in a cold sweat as I approached the run-in on a low level napalm run 25 feet above the ground with the target illuminated only by the nocturnal moonlight during exercises above the high desert at Fallon, Nevada.

"Ladies, it's a pleasure to be here and I'm thrilled that you met Boo down at the corner pub. By the way, his gumbo and jambalaya are killers and you'll need lots of beer to put out the fire. It just so happens that I brought a few six-packs with me, and if you want some wine I'll go down and get some of that, too."

Harriet. Definitely, the least attractive of the four, but well above average. Beauty is in the eye of the beholder, or the one with the hard on, so let's not be too critical of superficial beauty at this stage. Who knows? Perhaps Harriet was one of those southern women who had been deprived and who could go all night with some "nasal radiator" stud, from Alameda. I loved her southern accent and her effervescence, so she was my first candidate of choice. In turn, Harriet loved my little MG-B roadster, and she had never been to Sausalito, to Gatsby's, or The 39 Main, so I could do no wrong at this point. Life to her was one, big adventure and total hedonism was her creed. Still, Harriet found a sustained necessity to eat, so she ensured that, wherever she bedded down, she would still find the time to make the TWA scheduling for her flights out of San Francisco International.

All across the nation,

Such a strong vibration.

Harriet and I dated once. Harriet may have preferred this but neither of us will ever know since we didn't openly discuss how we felt about one another. Good times were our motto and we suppressed our emotions due to many factors, some which may relate back to old boyfriends and other places in time. San Francisco was the escape clause in our personal contracts. San Francisco was the perfect location and time for superficial relationships albeit some were consummated here and many endured the separations resulting from boy meet girl but girl must remain here while boy goes off to the war in Southeast Asia.

Melody was engaged to some guy from Portland, and she was not considered fair game in the machismo eternal conquest for some strange. Too bad, because Melody was absolutely beautiful but forbidden fruit and the lure of conquest remained omnipresent in our fragile libidos. She loved to go out with Boo and I when we piled into my car for the PSA for dancing and beer until the joint closed at 2:00 am, but that's as far as it went. No shenanigans and no false pretenses with Melody. She enjoyed our company on the bar scene but she would quietly proceed to her bedroom upon returning to the flat, on Union. But could Melody dance! Lordy, this gal had moves like a snake, and my skinny little body developed growing pains just moving with her to the sounds of the Beach boys or Jefferson Airplane. Sensual was the proper term for Melody and we envied her fiancé up there somewhere in Oregon. Her bright blue eyes and sultry smile would melt any man's heart. Melody was seldom around during her off time because she would fly up to Portland to see her flame, or they would rendezvous down in Monterey, just to get away from the likes of us.

There's a whole generation,

With a new explanation.

Cindy. Cindy reminded me of the girl next door. Cindy wasn't beautiful but she possessed a certain radiance that eventually got to men, such as me. Her stature was not petite and, at the same time, she wasn't what one would consider a large physique, but somewhere in between. Cindy possessed that Campbell's Soup Kids allure, and our male competition at the local pubs took to her like a Trojan to a stiff phallus. Cindy loved to dance, dance, dance, and she would literally undulate until your uncontrollable perspiration demanded that you step up for another cold Coors at the bar. Boo took a fancy to Cindy but the feeling wasn't mutual, as I would discover later. Suppose I wasn't astute enough to perceive that Cindy had her eyes on another lad, close by. Nonetheless, I loved taking turns in cutting in on Boo and Cindy, and she truly understood the meaning of the Beach Boys suggestions in their rowdy songs. I almost forgot to mention that Cindy had what one would refer to as the perfect toilet which, in civilian terms, means she had a beautifully pear-shaped derriere.

Cher. Now, Cher was a spinner. Spinner is slang for a petite "chez chez la femme" who loved to assume the dominate sexual position on top. In other words, one could take a spinner and turn her around rapidly thus creating a circular motion and a geometrically induced orgasm. Cher was my squeeze and I suppose that one of my attractions to her were her magnificent large brown eyes. Remember in the late '50's and early '60's Walter Keene's paintings of people with disproportionably large eyes? Well, Cher had beautifully large eyes that reminded me of Keene's subjects. Cher had sort of a French aurora to her and she also reminded me of Edith Piaf, the famous French singer. And, Cher possessed beautifully pointed breasts that were neither large nor small by any standards; and her wearing a bra was strictly a matter of conscious rather than of necessity. Perhaps TWA wouldn't let her get away with that summer of love attitude while hostituting aboard the airplane. Cher wore her hair in a modified pixie cut, and she looked simply terrific in Levis. Plus, she had moves on the dance floor similar to those sexy gyrations of her three other roommates.

It would appear that I was about to repeat the same scenario and play "eenie, meenie, minie, mo" with the ladies and find myself in more shallow intimacies that had been my preoccupation for some time. I would soon determine that there was more to this situation than presently met the eye. This group of ladies became synonymous with our daily routines and existence, and us with theirs. We bonded together as if we were siblings albeit we were not of the inclination to sleep with members of our true families. Nonetheless, Boo and I found ourselves with these ladies daily, nightly, and virtually constantly when we weren't preparing for flying operations across the bay on the naval air station. In turn, the stewardesses and one hygienist allocated more than their fair share of time to us and I wanted to believe that the primary reason for this was because they felt a sense of security, a sense of belonging, and a wee bit of adoration for the likes of Boo and me.

During the mid to late '60's in San Francisco you had a situation where young adults from all corners of the globe congregated to participate in the now famous summer of love, where hippies, soldiers, businessmen, and students homogeneously melted into one, big mass of humanity for the sole purpose of finding some soul. Your job didn't matter. Your background didn't mater. Your social strata didn't matter. What really mattered was your attitude. And, that attitude is what separated the good guys from the bad guys. You didn't necessarily need to participate in LSD, acid, or other drug experiments to have the right attitude. As a matter of fact, thousands of participants never touched drugs, even pot. This contradicts many of the press releases induced by the so-called objective media to those non participants sitting in their mid-western living rooms and watching the evening news who were coerced into believing that the world was going to hell in a hand basket. As a matter of fact Boo and our covey were abstaining from everything unnatural, and that included drugs. An occasional doobie was enjoyed by the gals but this was much more the exception than the rule.

For those who come to San Francisco,

Summertime will be a love-in there.

Mostly, our group lead a rather hedonistic existence in that fun, sex, and time off from work were considered priorities over all other interferences in our lives, and that is the primary reason why Boo, Cindy, Cher, Melody, Harriet, and Hank relocated to San Francisco from places like Salem, Portland, Milwaukie (Ore.), Little Rock, Abbeyville, and Opp.

These local hangouts that I previously mentioned, such as the Swiss Village, PSA, and Camelot were local pubs that were riding high in this era and there was no such thing as an off-night. Throngs of the working class jammed into these pleasure palaces nightly and it was a situation where one could get into a whole lot of trouble without even trying. The gals loved men in uniform and whose big line of seduction proved to be, "Honey, I leave for Vietnam in a few days, so let's party!" Ironically, the women didn't feel the same way about us warmongers as the civilian men. Perhaps, the jealousy factor should be included in the formula of why most of the Laura lovelies preferred us to those of the three-piece suit variety, down on Montgomery Street. And, perhaps it is because we simply had more money than our civilian counterparts. Hell, I made three times what a beginning banker or insurance peddler was bringing in. I didn't mind spending it, either.

Most Naval aviators drove cars that were ersatz reminders of the planes they flew - Corvettes, Jaguar XKE's, Shelby Mustangs, MG-B's, Austin Healey's, Dodge Daytona's, and other machines suited for the egocentric maniacs who maneuvered down the avenues of life. The bigger and faster the auto, the larger the psyche and libido connected with the machine. At the time none of us were perceptive enough to understand why these little tie-dyed, leftist-commie, pinko-pig, hippie-squirts drove beat-up Volkswagen busses when they could pilot a highly mortgaged racy two-seater with the top down and tonneau cover securely buttoned at speeds in excess of the posted limits. Little did we realize that our perceived social outcasts were getting laid in the back of the often graphically decorated love palaces on wheels. They drove portable houses, with all the accoutrements of home, less the bullshit, such as stereo systems blasting Janis Joplin and Richie Havens, musical instruments, drugs, organic munchies to nibble, psychedelic artwork, a porta potty, sometimes a solar shower, and, last but not least, a wall to wall, silk-sheeted, futon bed soaked in Eastern Indian patchouli oil. These truly ingenious owners had moon roofs installed for those damsels who enjoyed celestial views from the prone, or perhaps, the Karma Sutra position. Meanwhile, those of us who were brilliant enough to buy two-seater cars had to strategically pre-plan our next moves, and where we would eventually bed down for the night. However, these tie-dyed gypsies simply skirted the traffic and police, and just pulled over to the curb along Ocean Beach, or the Embarcadero, or atop Twin Peaks, slapped that sucker into park, and commenced negotiations with their amorous companions. I always said that, when I grow up I want one of those VW Vanogons, fully loaded!

Boo had been a bad boy one evening over at the Officers' Club during happy hour when he enticed a senior Naval officer into a fist fight out on the back lawn. Well, this fool of a Lieutenant Commander took one swing at Boo, and then Boo proceeded to smash his nose, cut his lips almost in two, and nearly blinded him in one eye before the fight could be stopped. Boo was sent before a hearing where the Naval Board determined where LT Ashton L. Langlinais, Jr., alias Boo, was guilty of assault on a senior Naval officer; so he was restricted to his quarters in the BOQ for two weeks. We were being deployed to southeast Asia immediately at the end of his restriction. Thus, Boo would not see "daylight" until he reached the shores of North Vietnam. The only exception to this quarantine was that Boo could report to the squadron each day for his daily flight operations, then head straight back to his room where meals would be delivered to the door by the Filipino stewards assigned to the Officers' Mess.

Cindy, Harriet, and Cher felt real sorry for Boo, and so did I. After all, we were now one short for dancing and drinking at the local bars, and the girls felt a certain sense of insecurity in not having Boo around for that added dimension that precluded them from trying to explain to potential seducers why they didn't particularly want to dance with anyone other than Boo and me. Time and time again we would be at the PSA when some civilian stranger would approach one or two of the girls, and ask them to dance. The girls would reply to the aggressors that they were spoken for, and that we were their dates. Obvious looks of confusion would grow on the men's' faces and they would ask how in the hell could the two of us handle three of them or possibly even four, when Melody was in town. Boo and I would look at each other and try not to exaggerate the shit eating grins on our faces. One by one the fellas would capitulate and slink back to their tables confused and bewildered about the situation, and how Boo and I must have been truly endowed to keep these fine looking ladies from wandering out of the corral in search of other interesting stallions.

So, the girls and I came to the same conclusion that, since Boo couldn't come to party with us, we would bring the party to him. I picked up Harriet and Cindy to head for the BOQ and this particular evening Cindy was going out with Melody to a movie, so we were down to two quail in the covey. Cher and Harriet gathered some belongings and beer then we hopped into my car to blast across the Bay bridge for Alameda. Shortly, we arrived on the base just in time for several hall parties given by squadrons and the crowds were beginning to grow. Poor Boo was confined to his room and little did he realize that, within seconds, two of his favorites would appear knocking at his door. The surprised look on Boo's face is one that I will always remember and he said, "Lordy, my prayers have been answered, so let's celebrate by playing my saxophone and please hand me a cold Coors, Harriet. God love you and, Hank, thanks for bringing the girls over to the base and up to my room. You have no idea how it's been cooped up here while y'all are over in the city partying to Joe Cocker down at the Swiss Village, or swinging to Good Vibrations at the PSA. Harriet, darlin' you look fine tonight and I thought of you when I took the mattress off the box spring and threw both on the floor, so we could have a wall-to-wall bed later. I'm always thinking of you honeys and, for your added enjoyment, I will play you a tune of my sax. Hank, throw on that record I have on top of the turntable and crank up the volume."

In the streets of San Francisco,

Gentle people with flowers in their hair.

Boo hooted and tooted on the sax and people from down the hall at another gathering couldn't but help hearing the be-bop, and dozens suddenly appeared in Boo's room to watch him wail away. The crowd started to go crazy and couples danced in the hall, in the small bathroom adjoining the officer's suites, and on top of the mattress that Boo had so thoughtfully placed on the floor for Harriet's benefit later down the road. What a party! If the Naval board that judged where Boo should be confined to his quarters for behavior unbecoming an officer and a gentleman they would have shit. This was not what they had in mind. This was a perfect example of incompetence because they failed to stipulate no booze, no women, no parties, no music for our friend Boo.

As the hour grew late I made an offer to Cher that apparently she couldn't refuse, and that was to spend the night in my quarters at the BOQ. I proposed a caveat whereby Cher could sleep in my bed, and I would sleep in the adjoining room on the sofa. By this time Boo and Harriet had their own designs and had suggested that we depart quietly and quickly unless we wanted to practice voyeurism by observing them on the wall-to-wall love pad. Cher and I told them that we'd rendezvous for breakfast the following morning, and good night.

When we reached my room Cher wanted to slow dance, and I could tell that this was going to be a pre-consummation ritual that she needed in order to loosen up and relax. Cher could slow dance. Could Cher slow dance! In no uncertain terms, Cher could practice the art of slow dancing. Cher dropper her arms from around my neck and she placed the palms of her hands on my thighs, so she could also enjoy the sensuous feeling sandwiched between our four lower extremities. I got to tell you that I was getting excited and Cher could obviously sense this when she asked me if I had an extra tee-shirt for her to wear. I obliged and she disappeared into my bathroom and then reappeared minus her shoes, slacks and blouse. In their place Cher had donned my white tee-shirt over her braless frame, with her bikini panties extending below the tail of the shirt, exposing her cute little insie belly button. Cher's beautifully prepared packaging immediately prompted me to suggest more slow dancing, and Cher obliged by unzipping my pants and suggesting that I would be more comfortable without them as they dropped to the floor. Our feet moved ever, ever so discernibly slowly around the room.

Cher and I lasted about an entire thirty seconds on the dance floor before we walked hand in hand into my bedroom and slipped between the official U.S. Navy cotton sheets on my gunmetal gray metal U.S. Navy issue single framed bed. As Cher gently removed my last piece of U.S. Navy issue skivvies my eyes rolled in the back of my head, and we immediately realized that this was going to be a special evening.

People in motion ... ...

Certain folks were meant to go together, and certain physiques were meant to fit together, and Cher and I were meant to go and to fit together. The preceding night turned out to be sheer eroticism and Cher was a wonderful lover albeit a moaner whose sounds surely permeated the foot thick concrete walls separating my suite from that of another Naval aviator who immediately understood the origin of the lusty noises choreographed with the mood of the evening.

... ...people in motion!.

Neither Cher nor I had said two words to each other as we sat on the lawn the next morning before joining Harriet and Boo for breakfast. Suddenly, Cher broke the silence and said, "Little Hanky Panky, you're a damn good lover, and I still feel your spirit inside me."

"Cher, I can't remember a night like last night."

"Hush! Let's go eat breakfast," Cher said.

We catered breakfast up to Boo's room where Harriet had bedded down with the Cajun animal of Attack Squadron 152. The room was a total disaster and Harriet's underwear was strewn from the hanging light fixture to the blinds. "Well, kiddies, looks like we had ourselves one hell of a frolic after Cher and I left, wouldn't you say? Here's some breakfast, and from the looks on your two faces, you need nutrition! Harriet, come on down the the lounge when you're through eating and I'll take you and Cher back to the city. No hurry. Cher and I will be watching the TV."

Little did I know it at the time but Cher was engaged to be married to a Marine who was stationed over in Hawaii. This almost blew my mind but I wouldn't let it, and I never let onto Cher that I knew about her planned betrothal to this jarhead. Her ultimate plan was to continue to fly up to the last minute for TWA, give her two week's notice, and split for Honolulu to meet this unnamed jungle bunny. As those of us in the Navy used to say, "Eat the apple, fuck the Corp." Cher would never let onto the fact that we had knowledge of her plan that was leaked by her roommates, and she simply enjoyed her time with us as if nothing covert was planned for later in July.

While Boo was still on restriction and confined to his quarters, on the Alameda Naval Air Station, this cowboy was out gallivanting around with Cher and Cindy, and Harriet, whenever she was in town. On one particular Saturday, only three days before we would board the USS Oriskany for the Far East, Cher and Cindy were my guests in and around the Japanese Tea Garden in Golden Gate Park, Sam's, in Tiburon, for brunch, and the Buena Vista for more Irish Coffees than should have been legally permitted, but weren't. This was one of those glorious days and I found that the more I drove this MG-B with the top down the better I liked the Bay area. California and convertibles are synonymous as far as I'm concerned and this day protected my theory completely. As long as the sonofabitch ran and didn't require pushing to get it started, we were all right! I was proud to accompany these two lovely ladies around to my favorite places and to watch the boys gloat with envy over my dual situation. Just about dusk we headed back to the girls' flat, and Cindy disappeared into her bedroom with nary a sound, leaving Cher and I prone on the living room floor. One thing lead to another and before one could say, "Last one in bed is on top," we were in bed, and Cher was on top, surprisingly enough. Without repeating myself and blueprinting the details of that evening I will desist and leave the particulars to the reader's imagination, which I trust will remain true to form to the vivid descriptions presented during our previous time together. Suddenly, about sunrise, I felt a tap on my shoulder and a voice saying, "Cher, time to get up and get dressed. Did you forget that you are scheduled to fly out today to New York? Anyway, you still have time to make your flight if we get you a cab in about ten minutes."

It was Cindy whose voice whispered into Cher's left ear, and into my right, that told me it was time to hustle and to get Cher dressed, and into my car for San Francisco International. Cher arose and proceeded to walk from the bedroom to the bath in her au natural, and I told Cindy that I'd take her to the airport, and guarantee that she would make her flight. I said, "Cindy, do you want to come along now that you're up? I'll treat you two to breakfast if you want."

"Great idea Hank, and I'll take you up on the offer. Let me go and get some clothes on and I'll make sure that Cher is ready to go in ten minutes, or she'll miss her flight."

There's a whole generation,

With a new explanation.

The three of us piled into the front seat of my damp-with-dew MG and I proceeded to set a land speed record from Union to Van Ness, over to Gough, and onto the freeway that would put us at the airport in fifteen minutes. Sure enough, we made it with plenty of time to spare, and we found the coffee shop for breakfast. I said to Cher, "I'm very upset that you're leaving so close to our sailing for Vietnam.Is there anyway that you could call in sick because I wanted to take you up to Lake Berryessa for a couple of days before we depart."

"Hank, I'd love to go but I've already taken so much time off and, besides, I'd have to stick around the house in case the flight scheduling officer calls to check up. I've got an idea. Why don't you ask Cindy if she wants to go? Hey, babes, what do you think? I don't mind if you don't mind, and you'll have a good time with old Hanky Panky, I guarantee."

"Cindy, what do you think? Do you want to go up to Berryessa for a day, or two.?"

"Oh, Hank, I'd love to go and Cher, you are my best friend so don't worry. I won't steal him away from you. How long will you be in New York, anyway?"

"Most likely a two day turnaround and then back to San Francisco for a week off. And, boy, do I need it with the way we've been partying this past month. My body no longer feels like a weapon, to steal your phrase, Hank. I am exhausted and there are five hours on this flight to the Big Apple. How in the hell will I ever make it?" Anyway, you two kids have a real good time and, Cindy, I'll check in with you on Monday, okay?"

We walked Cher to the flight crew entrance and I bid my last farewell to this dynamite lady who I would not see again. She was visibly upset and so was I. I always hated good-byes, and this one in particular, because Cher and I had truly enjoyed our brief time together during this summer of love. "You take care, darlin', and you know who loves you. Boo and I do."

Such a strong vibration.

Cindy and I drove back to the flat so that she could throw some clothes together, along with her make-up bag. Does a woman go away without a make-up bag, ever? Boo, Cindy, and I met at the BOQ for lunch, and Boo indicated that he would be up at Lake Berryessa tomorrow. This whole idea of going up to the lake was his idea in the first place, and I had never even heard of Lake Berryessa, and Steele Park when he mentioned these places. Cindy and I were heading up there blind not knowing what to expect but at least we both knew it was going to be fun, fun, fun and I was beginning to get a wee bit apprehensive about our relationship in the absence of Cher. What should I do and how should I behave regarding sex and sleeping arrangements? Naturally, I'd let nature take it's course, which it did, in time. After touring the squadron and showing Cindy the aircraft cockpits we went over to the Acapulco restaurant for some Mexican food, and we brought a bag chockablock full of tacos, burritos, chimichangas, and sapodillas to Boo since he was becoming sick and tired of the BOQ menu, which changed semi-annually. Boo had indicated that he would arrive at Steele Park in the afternoon so we could get a little waterskiing in before he headed back for flight deck duty watch that evening aboard the carrier. In other words, Boo was sneaking out for a little liberty during our final hours in the continental United States and he was looking forward to meeting us up there where the weather had been extremely hot compared to our moderate climes day and night, by the Bay.

Cindy and I shared the same Navy issue bed and sheets that had provided her best friend Cher with previous creature comforts, and I have to tell you that the thought of this juxtaposition never crossed my mind once I felt the softness and warmth of Cindy's nude body next to mine. Lordy, Cindy was of the same exact school of love professed by Cher-hedonism and adoration of their men of the moment was their self-anointed preamble, and Essalyn-styled bill of rights. Cindy and Cher were true flower children albeit they seldom wore flowers in their hair, as the song depicted.

On a beautiful Saturday morning Cindy and I threw very few belongings into the rear seat of my two-seater and bolted down the road, past Berkeley, Crockett, Vallejo, Cordelia, and off the interstate onto a rural country road as we wound our way up the hills towards a manmade reservoir called Lake Berryessa, and specifically through the gate of a community resort named Steele Park. After check-in, Cindy and I unloaded our gear and proceeded to walk down a dirt path to our room which turned out to be lovely accommodations overlooking the lake, so we put away our stuff and sat on the deck to enjoy the view as we hummed a tune, probably by the Mamas and Pappas, Loving Spoonful, or the Beetles. Cindy proceeded to remove her jeans and change into a silky blouse as I was engrossed in observing the small white-tailed deer grazing beneath our balcony. As I turned around, Cindy was sitting in the deck chair minus her jeans, and wearing, instead, a pair of pink bikini panties. She had my immediate attention, as our conversation turned away from fawns, fauna and flora, to fucking. We soon realized that Boo would be arriving any minute and that we both could wait until sunset when the mood would be greatly enhanced by our magnificent environment, and by solitude, and no Navy types wandering the passageways of the Alameda BOQ.

Sure enough, Boo came walking up, so the three of us proceeded to introduce ourselves to a couple of chaps who were living at the resort. These men were Air Force enlisted men stationed at the nearby base, called Travis, and they had just returned from a tour in Vietnam. Coincidentally, they owned a small runabout boat and offered to take us water-skiing, so we took them up on this most egalitarian invitation. Hour after hour, we enjoyed the warm water, sun, and water skiing but the thought we'd be parting company across the big pond called the Pacific lingered in the back of my mind. After Boo left for Alameda Cindy and I fell asleep on the dock, only to awaken and discover that I was badly sunburned. Cindy had the foresight to don (usually she was doing just the opposite) her clothes a lightweight smock that protected her from the ultraviolet rays that had destroyed my epidural layer, as I attempted to have Cindy rub some Noxema over the affect areas, such as my shoulders, chest and back. God, was I in pain! The thought of having to wear some clothes turned me off completely because of the abrasion that resulted from putting on a pair of jeans, or even a soft tee shirt. Cindy suggested, in her infinite wisdom, that we simply sit on the deck in whatever clothing suited our mood to enjoy the sunset and the deer arriving to graze beneath our deck by the lakeshore. I had on a bath towel wrapped around my bottom as Cindy proceeded to gently rub more and more Noxzema onto my scalded shoulders. She was wearing the exact same wardrobe as I in the form of a bath towel wrapped up around her breasts in the typical female fashion.

I must capitulate and admit that the thought of sex at this time was not foremost in my scheme. All I wanted was more Noxzema, more aspirin, and a couple of cocktails to kill the pain.

Cindy and I had a very brief dinner at the resort dining room, and then we proceeded to walk back down the moonlight path to our love nest, humming a tune all the way. The sunburn had subsided to the point where I could almost endure the pain of wearing a soft cotton shirt and slacks up to the dining room, but now I felt the compulsion to remove these unnecessary items of clothing as we entered our room. And, Cindy felt the same compulsion as she removed my shirt, pants, and began to perfect her mastery of applying the omnipresent Noxzema, and by gently massaging parts of my skinny physique that weren't too badly sunburned. After what seemed like hours she quietly left the room and returned in a sheer silk nightie that radiated the moonlight as she stood silhouetted on the deck. The night was sheer ecstasy if you'll excuse the pun.

"That'll be $15.63 for the night, Mr. Miller," said the manager at the front counter. "We certainly hope that you and your wife enjoyed you brief stay with us at Steele Park and that you'll return soon."

"This is a beautiful place and we especially enjoyed our dinner last night in your dining room overlooking the lake while the deer fed just outside our window. Do you take Carte Blanche?"

"No sir. We just take Diner's Club and American Express. Do you have a problem with that?"

"As a matter of fact, I do. Carte Blanche is the only credit card I have but I can write you a check, which is the only way I can pay for the room."

" We don't take personal checks so you'll have to find another way to pay."

'Let me go make a call to see if there's a way to pay. I'll use the phone outside and be right back."

Boy, was I pissed with this man's attitude, and the sunburn just added to my aggravation. At this point I tried to call Boo and ask if he could come back up with some money to bail me out, but I couldn't reach him, nor could I reach any of my other fellow aviators for the same request. Knowing Cindy didn't have enough to make a difference I approached the manager with this logic. "Sir, I've tried to find another way to pay but with no success, so a check will have to do unless you take an I.O.U. I am a Navy Lieutenant with identification and a driver's license so you shouldn't have to worry about whether the check is good or bad."

"You military men are all alike and I've been burned by the likes of you before. Suppose I have no other alternative than to accept your check but I'll contact your commanding officer if there's any difficulty, you hear?"

"Listen, asshole, I'm leaving for Vietnam day after tomorrow, so I frankly could give a shit what you think about me, or the Navy. Just give me the total amount so we can get the hell out of here. I'm going to do you a big favor. I'm not going to trash this place on my way out, and, furthermore, I'm not going to call Herb Caen at the Chronicle to inform him about your piss poor attitude towards those military men who put their butts on the line to defend your right to abuse people here in the States. Any questions?"

"The total is $15.63, including the tax."

I wrote the check, handed it to the manager, got back into my car, and proceeded to spray gravel all over the front of his office as Cindy and I blasted down the unpaved road towards the highway. I did not share this unpleasant experience with her simply because I didn't want to put a damper on the lovely time we had over the weekend.

Our ride back to the city was rather mellow and special and, as we approached the Bay Bridge, we both knew that it was time to pull off the freeway to embrace and to kiss passionately for a few minutes. We didn't speak much and we both knew that our time together was short, so our emotional ebb flowed strongly symbolic with the outgoing tide of the bay.

I dropped Cindy off at her apartment and I had to return to Alameda because I was assigned Flight Deck Duty Officer Watch, from 6:00 pm until midnight aboard the Oriskany. Boo had been released from his restriction, so he said that he would go back over to the girls' apartment and see that they were entertained, and to let Cindy know that I got off watch in a few hours.

All across the nation,

Such a strong vibration.

I reported to Flight Deck Control aboard the carrier and logged in only seconds before I was scheduled to begin watch. Even though the temperature had dropped considerably I was still burning up with this serious sunburn, so I brought my jar of Noxzema along for respite. The sailor who accompanied me on my four-hour duty watch was, also, in my squadron and he immediately perceived my agony, so his offer to rub more of this balm on my shoulders was graciously accepted. I removed my shirt and he began to apply the gooey white cream on my shoulder blades and, without warning, four of the most senior Naval officers who would accompany us on our cruise to Vietnam entered through the hatch. The Commanding Officer of the Oriskany, the Commander of the Air Group (CAG), the Commander of Task force 77 (an Admiral), and his Chief of Staff proceeded to walk over and inquire about my physical status and if it was appropriate for me to be on watch while out of uniform. My retort was that I would have my uniform shirt back on my back in two seconds and that I made a judgment call in having this sailor apply temporary first aid rather than desert my duty watch for sick bay. They agreed that I made a wise decision and that they would proceed to tour the carrier, and for me to "Carry on, Mr. Miller."

Probably the only thing that saved my little ass was the fact that my father was currently Chief of Naval Information, back in the Pentagon, and a Rear Admiral, to boot. This legacy was a cautionary flag to some Naval officers that permitted me to skirt some situations that, otherwise, would prove disastrous to my fellow junior Naval officers. I never gave it a second thought but those with whom I was associated had an entirely different perception. Many believed that this relationship bought me certain favors and permitted me to receive special attention. This was bullshit, and the body count in Vietnam never differentiated between plumbers or politicians, roofers or Rhodes Scholars, seamen or Senators.

I completed my watch and returned to my room at the BOQ as fast as I could in order to remove the starched khaki uniform, pop a dozen aspirin, and try to sleep off the pain. Only a day and two nights left before we departed the pier at Alameda, and I just wanted to get a decent night's sleep before the onslaught of chores to complete later this morning. As if I were in a bad dream I awakened to this mad man jumping up and down on my bed. Boo had returned to the BOQ and he brought Cindy with him. I could barely get up and show Boo to the door and get back to my bed. My mood was terrible and I didn't appreciate what Boo had done in providing transportation for Cindy back to Alameda. Cindy proceeded to get undressed down to her bra and panties and to join me in bed, but the problem was her underwear scratched my skin as if several pieces of course grade sandpaper were wrapped around her lovely body. I couldn't endure the thought of amour now and sleep was the only thing on my agenda. It wasn't the only thing on Cindy's, but she had to wait until later for primal relief. We both enjoyed sleep until the countdown began and I had to proceed with numerous chores and check-outs before the big day arrived tomorrow.

Cindy decided to remain in bed and to simply relax as I ran around the base like a chicken with its head cut off. Over to the laundry to pick up my uniforms. Back to my room for a long, wet kiss. Raced over to the commissary for some staples, like smoked oysters, cheeses, milk, booze, canned chili, and other items not provided aboard the carrier. Back to the room for more tongue tag with my femme. Over to the squadron for last minute packing and moving of my Communications Officer and RPS Custodian gear that, hopefully, would arrive aboard the carrier and into our ready room later today. Back to my room for brief petting and more deep-throated kissing. A call to my good friend Barry regarding the arrangements he made for the storage of my car for the eight months I'd be over in Westpac.

Time for lunch, so I brought some gedunk food to our room. Cindy and I sat on the bed and enjoyed our hamburgers, milkshakes, fries, and each other. This was the first time that I had dined with a woman who was partially clothed in only her lace underwear, and admittedly, it was a most sensuous experience. Soon after we had devoured our burgers we devoured one another. Back to the squadron for more last minute contingencies and messages regarding our deployment. Over to the Club to pay my monthly charge account. Return my rental TV back to the Exchange. Buy some last minute survival gear, such as my Buck knife, beef jerky, more rounds of ammunition for my personal pistol, and other items that were highly recommended by Dieter Dengler in his debrief after escaping a Pathet Lao prison camp, in Laos. Back to my room to help Cindy get dressed so that I could take her back to the flat in the city. We would meet again that evening about 6:00 for and intimate dinner, consisting of candlelight, steamed clams, San Francisco sourdough bread, Sonoma white wine, and intense emotions; and an evening out with a squadron mate, Fred Guenzel, with his date.

Summertime will be a love-in there.

I removed my only suit from the closet; a suit that my parents had purchased when they came to visit me one weekend at Auburn, four years previously. A Botany 500 suit that would embellish me while residing on numerous Naval Air Stations, over many years, with many women, and eventually became part of my working wardrobe in civilian life. My wing tip cordovan shoes were, also, purchased at the same shop, in Auburn, four years previously. Funny how we remember these details in our lives....These insignificant details of articles of clothing that eventually became integral aspects of our personalities and character. Many scrapbook photos of places and times recorded on film depicted me wearing that same suit, and shoes.

Top down, long-range driving lights on, 25 cents out for the toll at the bridge, and plenty of Noxema soaked into my burning shoulders. This evening was star-studded and my eyes were full of moonbeams. The thought of leaving my friends and this city were deeply suppressed inside my libido, for there was absolutely nothing that was going to detract or ruin this mood. When I opened the door to the flat Cindy appeared in a deep midnight blue, and extremely sexy, cocktail dress, with matching high heels. We embraced, kissed, and stared into each other's eyes, not saying one, single word. After a few moments I removed my jacket and she kicked of her heels as we prepared supper. Harriet and Melody had made themselves very scarce this evening and we had the entire flat to ourselves for our last night together. The bay window provided a perfect setting for the two of us as we dined and reminisced about our experience at Lake Berryessa. Neither of us was very talkative tonight as we finished our meal. Cindy went to put on her heels and to get a wrap as we prepared to meet Fred at the Rainbow Room, on lower Union, and hear Inez Jones perform.

Fred met us at the bar and introduced us to his date for this special occasion. Cindy and I proceeded through the usual courtesies, and then found ourselves a booth in the corner. Fred and his date joined us and the evening began to slip away as we listened to Inez perform various songs from the past. She had a magnificent voice, similar to Sara Vaughn, Ella Fitzgerald, and Della Reese, all rolled into one. After about two hours Cindy whispered in my ear that we leave for the flat, but that same whisper was not extended to Fred and his date. So, the two of them remained at the Rainbow Room as we left for some last minute errands.

Up to Gough to pick up a jacket I had left with Jan several months earlier. Over to Lisa's to retrieve a portable radio on loan. Then, to Suzie's for several items I needed to return to her and retrieve some goodies I had left during our one-year romance. Suzie gave me something in return - a large bottle containing one thousand tetracycline tablets that she had procured from her job at Cutter Lab, in Berkeley. I would discover later that this was a very personal and much appreciated gift, and that Suzie had my best intentions and her personal thoughts in minds when presenting this illegally obtained and prescribed formula. God bless her little heart!......Back to the flat on upper Union.

I stretched out on the sofa while Cindy disappeared into the bedroom, and suddenly I found myself asleep. The aspirin, lack of sleep, and booze, had begun to take its toll, and I was on the verge of physical and mental exhaustion. After an undetermined period I awakened, and Cindy was nowhere to be found. I opened the bedroom door and she was sitting on the bed waiting for me to arrive. I removed my clothes and she undressed leaving her midnight blue French bra and skimpy midnight blue bikini panties so that I could finish the ritual under the sheets. I graciously proceeded to complete the removal of feminine accoutrement as we found ourselves together again for the last time.

The alarm was set for 5:00, and I barely heard it sound as Cindy helped me to get dressed. She remained nude as we gathered the items that were needed to complete my exit and return to Alameda. Suddenly but quietly, Harriet and Melody entered the living room and each gave me a big, warm hug and a kiss with prayers that Boo and I would come back one day, in one piece. Then they returned to their bedroom leaving us alone. Cindy and I stood there, silent, and then the time came to leave, to let go, to walk down the hall, and bid the fondest of farewells to this lady, her friends, and to Union Street. She promised to write and to keep me informed about her roommates who became integral aspects of Boo's and my lives during the past two months. Somehow, I knew that she would keep her promise.

As if I needed anything to remember her by she still gave me a memento as a good luck charm which turned out to be her lucky nickel that had been placed on a railroad track and flattened into a medallion by the oncoming train. I carried this medallion on every flight over North Vietnam during my seven-month tour.

The morning was cold, foggy, dreary, and perfectly fitting the melancholy mood for our departure from the pier at Alameda, while those of us stood on the quarterdeck as the Oriskany sailed full speed under the Golden Gate Bridge as loved ones stood on the span dropping flowers in their feeble attempts to say good-bye for the last time. Boo and I never saw Harriet, Cindy, Cher, and Melody again. After we deployed that morning in June, Harriet moved back to Arkansas, Melody got married and moved back up to Oregon, Cher left to meet her fiance in Hawaii, who unfortunately stood her up so she moved down to Miami to be with her mother, and Cindy moved back to Milwaukie, Oregon, to be with family.

I was deployed aboard the Oriskany from 7 June 1967 to 31 January 1968. Cindy wrote at least one letter every single day that I was gone. When we reached Honolulu, after four days at sea, I had five letters that she had written delivered during mail call to the squadron ready room. During liberty in the Philippines, or in Sasebo, Yokosuka, Hong Kong, or in Tokyo, Cindy would write even though I would miss sending her letters while I was out gallivanting around with the nurses, Peace Corp workers, whores, and geishas.

She never stopped caring about me. I thought about her every single day. I would love to see her now, many years later.

The catharsis continues, and I dedicate this remembrance to Cindy as we hear in the words and music that mesmerized me while reading her daily epistles that help to soothe the sporadic pain I endured for seven, long, and agonizing months, in Southeast Asia.

<u>*In My Life*</u>

There are places I remember,

All my life.

Though some have changed,

Some forever, not for better.

Some are gone and some remain.

All these places had their meaning,

With lovers and friends I still can recall,

Some are dead and some are living.

In my life, I loved them all.

But, of all these friends and lovers,

There's no one compares with you.

And, these places loose their meaning,

When I think of love as something new.

Thought I know I'll never loose affection,

For people and things that went before.

I know I'll often stop and think about them,

In my life, I love you more.

Judy Collins sung it

as no other could.

The Beetles wrote it, 1967

VT-1 Squadron Pilots Hanging Out, Saufley Field, Pensacola, 1964

The author with the Admiral, USS Oriskany, Yankee Station, 1967.

A4 Skyhawk being catapulted, 1967

VA -152 Squadron and Tokiwa Stand Bar Honeys, Sasebo, Japan

Zapper Lounge Cubi NAS BOQ Philippines

From Hums to Hymns

Bye bye Golden Gate, San Francisco, CONUS, Mom and Dad, brothers and cousins, fabulous ladies, my MG-B, good friend Barry, that little sexy Suzie, our covey of quail-Cindy, Cher, Harriet, and Melody. Good bye to Spenger's Fish Grotto, Scoma's, the Buena Vista, the Acapulco, Sandy at the "O" Club. Farewell to all those warm and fuzzy memories that disappear in the early morning fog as we blow under the Golden Gate and approach the Potato Patch, at full speed ahead for Honolulu, as the ship begins to pitch and roll with the oncoming sea. The visibility is near zero and we finally give up hope of seeing our friends wave from the Marin Headlands as we leave the quarterdeck and head down the ladder to the wardroom for some hot coffee.

Up until now it seems like a game, a charade, a farce acted out as we prepare for our ultimate missions aboard this battle bucket that was a holdover from the Korean war. Until recently, our mission has been the search for the perfect hum, the perfect spinner, the perfect covey of quail, and the Perfect Rob Roy! Little did we realize that this forthcoming engagement with a third-rate power is for keeps. All of the preparations, which include the briefings, training, escape and evasion schools, night carrier practices, weapons exercises at Crow's Landing and Fallon, and low level Sand blowers across the southwestern deserts lead up to this day. Well, not exactly this particular day, but one that would soon appear as we made Yankee Station in about 20 days. Now, we discussed our pasts over a cup of java and countless games of Acey Deucy in the ship's wardroom as we contemplate our futures, if we so dared.

Most pilots don't like to contemplate their futures because it conjures up "Screwing the pooch," or "Auguring in" or simply death, to nonpilots. Aviators are great procrastinators on the ground. Not in the cockpit, however. Talk of how many Distinguished Flying Crosses would be won by the young hot shots perforated the squadron ready rooms, while the veteran pilots of previous cruises to Vietnam remained silent and pensive. Personally, I could give a rat's ass about medals and awards because I made a vow to Cindy to return to the U.S. in one piece, and not part of a human jigsaw puzzle as a result of a cluster bomb unit air burst, or a SAM II missile launch, all wrapped up in a plastic body bag, with that ever-so-famous high-tech zip-lock construction.

Boo and I sat in the ready room and talked endlessly about the gals on Union Street who shared with us their most intimate moments. I wondered if Cindy would write as she promised, and if Cher would drop me a letter now and then. Boo didn't care about letters from the covey. All he wanted was photos of their nude bodies to keep him company on the flights over North Vietnam. Boo had the right idea. Problem is that the "Scratch and sniff" photos that would appear in Hustler and Penthouse several years in the future were not yet available, so Boo concocted his own versions by gluing small clips of different colors of pubic hairs onto the nude snapshots he possessed, and slipped them into protective heavy duty plastic sleeves - the same type we used to protect our aircraft emergency check lists. This way he could sniff Cher or Harriet or Cindy, depending on his mood and preference during that particular flight. I never thought to ask where he obtained these miniature muffs. What a brilliant idea! Why hadn't I thought of it so that a marketing scheme could be devised where I could mass merchandise muff photos to all of the pilots engaged in this conflict. I could make millions of dollars with this idea and no one had even thought of a long range plan to implement bush photos to those who flew combat missions off the carriers, or the bases in the Philippines, or South Vietnam.

After four days at sea and various flight operations we arrive in Honolulu for two days liberty. Problem was I was confined to the ship as a result of being AWOL, absent without leave, with Cindy, up at Lake Berryessa, just before we departed Alameda. My Executive Officer awarded the punishment, then he asked, "Henry, was it worth it?"

I replied, "You bet your sweet ass it was, sir! Would I do it again? No question!"

However, as I sat on board the carrier I could almost see my old house up on the hill above Pearl Harbor, and I could definitely see the Hilton Hawaiian Village, where I spent many evenings entertaining the honeys at the Garden Bar while we were enjoying summer vacation. Even though my action was a minor infraction of the Code of Military Justice I still had to sit out my time on board while the rest of the squadron enjoyed the pleasures of Waikiki. This makes me feel sad and I am very melancholy tonight. However, the next morning, after we had our briefing in the ready room, there was mail call for the first time in four days for the obvious reason we hadn't been able to receive the mail since we departed Alameda, four days previously. "Commander Headley, one letter. Lieutenant Watson, a postcard. LT Lewis. Oh, does this one smell like a French boudoir! LT Miller, you have four letters with the same address. Shit! You must have sat on her face that last night in port! Commander Willson, one crummy magazine"… and so on.

A gold mine! I struck a gold mine with Cindy. Four days out at sea and four letters, one written on each successive day. Carefully, I lined up the letters with the postmarks in ascending order, so that I can read them in sequence. Then I ripped open the first to find not only this beautifully edited epistle but, in addition, a photo of Cindy and Cher when they were, both, about ten years old, dressed in their tap dance costumes. Second letter: Words of love and lust that remain intimate, or simply put, none of your business. Third letter: Ditto. Fourth letter: …"We, all, miss you and Boo, and only hope that you will survive the madness over there. We think of you and pray that you will return safe and sound so that we can resume where we left off, in San Francisco. Hank, I am sending you the pair of my undies that you removed the last night we were together, so that you will have something to remember me by during those long, hot tropical nights. Yes, I did wash them! Cher, Harriet, and Melody send their best to you studs. Keep it in your pants, and don't 'Screw the pooch' over North Vietnam. We sure do miss you guys, all of the great food that Boo cooked up, the nightly dancing down at the PSA, and just your company. Melody had someone to keep her company but the rest of us shared you. Now, we have to rely on the local civilian types to entertain us."

Well, at least my pain has subsided to the point where I don't miss the Hawaiian Village Garden Bar too terribly much now that I had the solitude of these letters from Cindy as I read them over and over again, word for word, while my mind conjures up all sorts of fantasies, like her silhouetted figured against the moonlight, at Lake Berryessya. I missed all of the girls, however, and not just Cindy because we were family, if only for a couple of months. We ate together, played together, drank together, and danced together. We slept together albeit not with more than one quail at one time. We worried together about the outcome of this disaster in the South Pacific that saturated the news in all forms of media dissemination. We were family. We were warm and fuzzy towards one another. Let's talk about the expression "Warm and fuzz." These petite parcels proved to be warm and fuzzy not only in a spiritual sense but from the tips of their noses to those lustful regions where their thighs converged. There goes my imagination again: Can't seem to keep control over that little devil as it continues to play tricks on my mind, and my dick, which is, in effect, my mind since my brain is located in the head of my dick, if you get the drift.

There goes Miller again. Thinking with the head of his dick. That man is insatiably horny!

Back to sea and air operations almost around the clock as we made our way towards the Philippines, and Subic Bay, which lay ahead about ten days. No mail since our second day out and my depression was setting in because I truly lived for Cindy's letters after my experience in Honolulu. We are all in the same boat however, in that no one received mail until the carrier on board delivery plane arrived from Barber's Point, on Oahu, or from Cubi Point in the Philippines. Homesick and forlorn adult males traipsing around the passageways and ready rooms of the carrier looking like a bunch of "Little lost sheep that had gone astray,…baa…baa…baa." More briefing and tales of terror about the POW camps that faced us in the days ahead as well as the implementation of the newest super SAM II missiles shipped in directly from good old mother Russia for our added viewing pleasure. The ship kept humming right along while we passed the International Date Line as we proceeded to go on 24 hour watch for overhead flights of the Bear bombers, from Vladivostok, with those commie pinko pigs aboard as the flight crew. We are required to man at least one fighter on deck 24 hours daily for a ready launch in order to intercept the Russian bombers flying overhead, and I think the whole idea is preposterous because the Russians wouldn't dare bomb us since it would be a suicide mission for them. The entire game of international intrigue make some of us want to puke. Those of us who are honest with ourselves and not slaves of the military industrial complex theories constantly jammed down our throats never bought into the belief that the Ruskies are all bad guys out to conquer to world. Shit! They are territorial, just as we, and have as much right as we to fly anywhere they desire as long as it was in international airspace. Besides, this was terribly exciting for me to see an actual enemy aircraft, up close and personal.

After our fifth day at sea the COD flew aboard with supplies, medicine, and mail. I scurry down to our ready room just in time for the mail call to receive my six letters from Cindy. Checked the postmarks and arrange them in chronological order, first thing. Then, carefully open the first letter and savor each and every morsel of the written word. News of her daily routines and then the bomb dropped that Cher had been stood up by her fiancé, in Honolulu, after she quit her job with TWA, just to fly to Hawaii in order to meet this Marine jarhead bum. I felt so sorry for her. Cher had given up on the whole idea of returning to San Francisco, so she flew down to Florida, to be with her mother. Melody was still in love with her man up in Oregon, and Harriet was still in the active search mode for the right stallion, preferably Kentucky bred, and hung. In each of the five succeeding letters Cindy included a sheet of poems that she composed during the day back in Baghdad by the Bay. Short, sweet, very creative poems usually depicting lusty moments and life in the flower child era were her main topics, and that was perfectly agreeable with me, since I was the subject of some of the love portion.

Still more flight operations, day and night and day and night as we enter the final preparations prior to arriving at our first destination, Subic Bay. The thought of flying over the Marianas Trench didn't thrill me in the least since the bottom of the ocean in this area approached 37,000 feet below the surface of the water, the deepest known region of ocean on the globe. That statistic added to my flight altitude of approximately 10,000 feet means I was suspended at nearly 50,000 from the bottom. Psychologically, I was not prepared to accept this figure and I was extremely queasy at the mere though of it. Plus, we were so far from land that if there was any difficulty coming aboard the carrier we are unable to select an alternate field to fly to, and land our aircraft. That meant we ditch at sea. Over my dead body! In addition, this region sported tiger sharks up to 30 feet long, so if the controlled crash in the water didn't get you, the sharks definitely would. Miles and miles of smiles and smiles, I always said. What in the hell was I doing here at this point in time at this point on the map at this point in history? Boo and I constantly asked ourselves this question. Problem was that we never had a good answer that was acceptable to the draft board. So, back to the wardroom for more Acey Deucy, coffee, evening movies, collateral duties, guitar picking, and discussions about liberty in Olangapo and Subic .

I received a letter from home with news that Capt. and Mrs. Everett were stationed at Subic, and they were anticipating our arrival in port. I had dated Lynn, their oldest daughter, a few summer's previously while we lived in Honolulu. She and I worked at the Submarine Base Navy Exchange and we were definitely an item for the duration of the summer vacation. Unfortunately, Lynn wouldn't be meeting me at Subic because she had gotten married some time previously, but her sister Diane and her younger brother, Craig, would be home during their summer vacation. I looked forward to this reunion as the Everett's were great people who permitted my taking liberties with Lynn for almost three months that one summer she was home from Wellesley.

And an absolutely wonderful summer it was during those three months in 1962. Lynn and her family lived in temporary housing provided by the Navy located at the Royal Hawaiian Hotel on Waikiki that was like living in a surfer's dream world, only fifty feet from the beach. Lynn was a Yankee and you know what that means in terms of sexual promiscuity to a southern boy. Translation was that she liked to fuck. It only took me two months, twenty-nine days, and fifty-nine minutes to realize this patently obvious fact as I had held back my advances for fear of rejection during the previous two months. Little did I realize how horny she was during the summer vacation until she was almost ready to board her flight back to Massachusetts. Then, our last night together as we were parked behind the Ilikai, she let me know in no uncertain terms that she wanted to rhythmetically lock our suntanned bodies in the pretzel position until our moans could be heard out the car window for fifty feet, but we didn't. Damn!

When we docked at Subic I headed straight for the Cubi BOQ for a room, and Boo was right behind me. I call the Everett's and they ask me to come over that evening for a cocktail party, and to see Diane and Rich. I asked for the time and realized that we had several hours until the party begins. Boo and I had plans to go out into the sleazy town of Olangapo to check up on the local talent and to rendezvous with our squadron mates at New Paulines, or the East Inn Club for some bizarre rituals and burlesque. I lived in the Philippines ten years previously so the shock of the filth and the stench was partially acceptable to me while my fellow pilots attempt to acclimate to this non white bread, third world lifestyle. Words couldn't describe the Philippines. Only your nose knows for sure. Everything stunk! Some things stunk more than others, like the crotches of the whores at the East End Club as they strutted up and down our table picking up Coke bottles with their pussys, using the same vacuum technique that they would apply to sailors' dicks in the back rooms, and depositing them in front of some other young Navy-type down the bar. The entire place smelled like a rancid fish.

As I looked across the table I witnessed this sweet young Filipino hooker lifting her dress and exposing her pantiless bush as she proceeded to sit on the head of our skipper, Commander Willson. We referred to this scene as a "Skippered herring," and we promised our Commanding Officer that Mrs. Willson wouldn't hear about or see the photos we shot. "Another San Magu, please and keep your pussy to yourself, if you don't mind!"

That evening, I ask the driver to drop me off at the Everett's for the cocktail party and we proceed to reintroduce one another after a five - year hiatus. Diane looked good and so did Craig as they begin their evolutionary process of becoming acclimated to not only the tropical weather but to the customs and the ever present stench as well. Mind you, I had no intentions of taking either Diane or Craig to the East End Club. I promised the two of them that I will return tomorrow to take them into Olangapo, at the request of their parents, just to look around and to get a feel for the real Philippines. Diane was enrolled at the same college that her sister previously attended-Wellesley, and Craig was in high school on the naval base. Diane, a striking tall light brunette, with the genes of her mother, and Craig, a truly handsome young dude who could win the hearts of any young maiden, American or Filipino, so we would have to watch our step out in town for fear these beautiful kids would become targets of the local street hustlers, pimps, and whores.

We soon found ourselves out in Olangapo but not before I promise the Everett's that I would guard her chillun with my life, especially Diane. A couple of the ladies of the night who I met previously that day greeted us as we entered New Pauline's and I indicated, in no uncertain terms, that neither Diane nor Craig were for sale. Cokes at New Paulines, shoes at Fast Eddies, and guitars for Craig at a nameless hole in the wall on the muddy main drag, and then we returned to the main gate, and to the safety of Subic. I asked Diane to join us at the Subic "O" Club for dinner and dancing the following evening, and she obliged.

Her accompanying me to dinner becomes a ritual as we establish our platonic relationship as good friends, and as ones who would entertain one another until we returned to her school and my combat missions. Diane was just a little too young for my tastes and perhaps it's because I enjoyed my time with her sister, Lynn, that precluded any advancements on my part.

Boo and I meet the remaining members of the squadron up at the Cubi "O" Club where rowdy was the official word of the day. As I entered the bar area I felt a light mist falling over my head and neck. I looked up and saw a Marine squatting on one of the exposed rafters peeing down on our group. We immediately launched a beer mug salvo at his exposed nuts, and proceeded to gather into a circle while our voices ring "Hymn…Hymmmmmn…Fuck hymmmmmmn!" No sign of humming here but one hell of alot of hymns going around the bar. Do you suppose we have been somehow transformed from humming to hymning as a result of crossing the International Date Line? Several more Marines had the unmitigated gaul to trespass into our club so they received individual hymns or, ir they are accompanied by their families, we presented their group with our group hymn.

Every five or ten minutes one feels the vibration ringing throughout the club of the harmonious, (always in resounding bass notes, no tenor notes, and always cappella), hymns offered in tribute for everything from another free round of San Miguel beer to the entrance of an Air Force pilot, or a black shoe, non-aviator Navy type encroaching our hallowed halls. Special hymns are reserved for the Flag staff and other Commander Carrier Division personnel who deserved only our very best "Fuck hymmmmmmmn's."

Now, for a quick trip down to the carrier for my duty watch and to receive the mail that I longed for. Sure enough, there were at least eight letters from Cindy, one per day and she is batting a thousand percent. I always say that a letter a day keeps the Naval psychiatrists away, at least for the time being.

Our liberty in this port of call was ending and we are enroute to Yankee Station off the coast of North Vietnam, and Hynan, China. Daily briefings become more and more intense and detailed as we prepare for our initial flights over the most heavily fortified country in the history of warfare. That thought alone just plain scares the living shit out of this cowboy. Why me? Why this war just after I spent five years as a business major at Auburn? Couldn't the French just have held on for another fifty years? I was born to rock and roll, not pitch, roll... and yaw! Tomorrow morning will be an abrupt change in my life, or what is referred to as a major transition in that I will launch from the flight deck of the Oriskany for my first flight to Route Package One, down by the DMZ for some aerial strikes against the purported enemy of the United States, so says El Presidente Johnson, otherwise known as "Garbanzo breath." I have my magic nickel that Cindy gave me before we left. It is a special nickel that she had place on a railroad track, so the result was oval rather than round, and slightly thinner than before. I keep my lucky nickel in the left shirt pocket along with my college class ring. Freddie Guenzel, or Big Fred, (as we nicknamed him) would have the distinct fortune of becoming my section leader tomorrow because Fred was a veteran of previous cruises to Yankee but more importantly, he and I double dated the last night in San Francisco. I suppose he just wanted to perpetuate the legacy and relationship we established at the Rainbow Room, on Union Street. I never suspected that he had this strong feeling for little old me. Poor guy! With all due respect to Big Fred he was assigned as my wingman by the Operations Officer, Jim Harmon, who could literally give a shit whether or not we double dated, slept together, hummed, or hymned our way into history, written or oral. Just rack up those sorties, for MacNamara.

FLASH...CINCPAC MESSAGE, UNCODED 1159 TANGO 31 DECEMBER 1992

An uneventful flight over an uneventful country on an uneventful day as I record my first combat flight into the official U.S. Navy Aviator's Log Book. My lucky nickel did me good, and I write Cindy to thank her for her added good luck sachet of love juice that she applied to the nickel prior to giving it to me on that special occasion. The fragrance of the mystical secretion permeates my pocket in the heat of the cockpit and I thought my attention will wane as a result of my inability to concentrate on the combat mission at hand. We were here to destroy the enemy and not to simply fall into memory lapses while lingering along at 10,000 feet.

We landed safely aboard the carrier and, as a result of losing my "Cherry," the squadron veterans presented me with my very own special prayer later that evening while we stood in the Spad Driver's ready room listening to Tom Lull leading the chorus, "To Fats Miller, who lost his wad over Package One as he pickled his Zuni's at an abandoned Red Cross Hospital. At least we hope it was abandoned!"

"Hymmmn...

Hymmmmmmn...

Fuck hymmmmmmmmn!

Aerial view of North Vietnam coastline and Flak, 1967

"Bandits, Bandits, Bandits"

No one has his cherry intact. Everyone has his skivvies cleaned daily. Alka Seltzer is on sale in the ship's store, two boxes for a dollar. The games are over and we're a full contingency of aviators in the air wing, less those who augured in over the topography of North Vietnam. Daily reports broadcast by the Public Affairs Officer that the incessant Alpha Strikes were successful and that another dozen sorties are flown against the enemy resulting in more trucks destroyed along the Ho Chi Minh Trail. Ops! How could I possibly forget? One small detail is missing in his otherwise sterling report:

"We're sad to report that Lieutenant Williams is missing over the target. His aircraft was last seen in a dive over Tiger Island and we have not received a radio signal of his exact location. Father Duffy will lead us in the evening prayer. The movie for tonight is *Ocean's Eleven*, starring Frank Sinatra."

What in the fuck do they mean when they say that the Alpha Strikes were successful when the Bomb Damage Report Assessments are falsified and that we have aircraft missing in action? What do they mean the movie was "Ocean's Eleven" mentioned in the same breath as the evening prayer? Was I missing something in this equation, or was I simply too stupid to read between the lines of the encoded messages received by commander carrier division staff? God, I hated this place already and I'd only been over here for about a month, but a month seems like years when you fly a strike only to return to a sweltering stateroom located less than four feet under the number three arresting gear wire as the aircraft slams onto the deck of the ship, or the ceiling of your room, depending on your perspective. As I always used to say, "One man's ceiling is another man's floor." The noise was literally ear shattering and the sounds of the aircraft being recovered continued twenty-four hours a day, seven days a week, rain or shine. I slept with rubber plugs inserted in my ears through 24 hours of controlled crashes no more than a mere meter or two above my room to the point where I am now able to sleep through a nuclear holocaust, or an all-night rock party, take your pick. And, the heat! And, the humidity! If the temperature was 90 degrees, the humidity exceeded 95. Least we forget that Vietnam lies in the southeastern Pacific where mildew, leeches, malaria, and the bubonic plague were self-perpetuating realities of the way of life down here. If you were unfortunate enough to develop a fungus, like jock itch or athlete's foot, you were destined to become close friends with the malady until you either bought the farm or until you returned to the States. If you developed a skin rash, or an infected foreskin, the flight surgeon said," Tough shit, fella, no reason to down you for this flight, so get going and man your aircraft." My close friend and squadron mate, Boo, and I simply loved being over here and enjoying weeks of celibacy with thousands of men, locked up aboard this floating Zippo lighter waiting to ignite.

Most of our flights were over the water while escorting a chopper based on some destroyer running up and down the coast of North Vietnam for hours of relative boredom, interrupted by moments of stark terror. The anti-aircraft guns left their signatures all around us in the form of puffy black clouds and sudden jolts as the blast eventually reached the fuselage of our aircraft. Just another kick in the seat of the pants but I didn't like it one, goddamn bit. Shit! It's okay to see this sort of action in the movies but not for real as we maintained a safe distance from shore, and from the batteries of guns and surface to air missiles aimed our way. No medals for this cowboy. No medals awarded posthumously to my mom and dad back in the States as the official Navy Public Affairs representatives present them with the illustrious black plastic body bag with the zip loc closure that contains what little remains they could scrape off the cockpit interior. Thanks, but no thanks. Sure, I've had my fair share of shitty frights....I mean flights. But there was a limit to what I wanted as far as choreographed excitement is concerned.

My name is MacNamara and I'm the leader of the ...

Boo and I hd been on a dozen or more strikes in four plane formations, usually with senior officers, Jack Baker and Jim Harmon, as our fearless leaders who had two basic missions: One, to fulfill the strike assignment, and, the other to keep our respective asses in one piece. Several months ago, back in Alameda, we formed a cooperative union, a fraternal bond, to reassure one another that nothing out here in the southern Pacific was worth our lives. We have relegated the heroics to those who prefer night Alpha strikes to the negotiating of the services provided by geishas, in Japan. Lordy, our mothers didn't raise any dumb kids. We were professionals but not the career types who worry about their fitness reports and the relationship to any pending promotions. We, each, had our own survival gear, some of which was provided by the Navy and other devices of our own choosing, such as my Smith and Wesson Model 39 pistol that fires 9 millimeter hollow-pointed, soft-nosed, cyanide-dipped rounds as fast as I could pull the trigger. And, the Buck knife with the 8 inch blade sharpened to where I could shave with it. Boo carried enough morphine syringes to get the entire NVN army high as a Saturday night in the Haight Ashbury. Jack Baker carried money concealed in the heel of his flight boots. We each had our own little tricks that were tailored to suit our own personalities and weaknesses and phobias in case we became the subjects of the Walter Cronkite evening news broadcast during someone's supper in the States.

I stood for hours to practice firing my pistol from the quarterdeck at the porpoises swimming alongside the boat as we make our way up and down Yankee Station. Most of the aviators carried the standard Navy issue snub-nosed 38 revolvers that were as worthless as tits on a boar in a real life-threatening situation. As a matter of fact, one of the sailors offered to make me a silencer just in case I landed in North Vietnam and needed to shoot my way out of a potential hostage situation. I should take him up on his offer but I was none the wiser at that point during the cruise. I wore my Auburn class ring on every flight but not on my ring finger. Instead, I taped the ring, one of my most cherished possessions, onto my dog tags and slipped it under my flight suit. Along with the ring I also carried the coin – a memento of Cindy's relationship and of our times together back in San Francisco.

While we were out running up and down the coast looking for water born logistics craft, otherwise known as WBLCS, our fellow aviators were attacking the Than Hoa bridge, or the Tren Yuen depots, or the airstrips outside Hanoi, or the docks in Haiphong and the body count escalates, and the sorties escalate, while the statistics reported by our fearless leader MacNamara filled the airwaves and front pages of the evening news. And the news during supper in the wardroom became as routine as the weather forecast in El Paso, Texas.

"Now hear this! Now hear this! Attack Squadrons One Sixty Three, led by Commander Smith, flew twenty successful sorties against the truck depots in Package Five and recorded over fifty successful hits on the enemy while suffering only one lost aircraft. Lieutenant Stevenson was reported down over the coast, and there was no sign of a survivor. Father O'Reilly will lead us in a moment of prayer while we mourn the loss of our brother. The movie for tonight is *The Cincinatti Kid*, starring Steve McQueen."

Enough! All I wanted was to get laid, several times. Not just once or twice but several times in a row, in daily succession, in every conceivable position, with any conceivable woman. This incessant heat makes me horny and it was a constant reminder that I should be with some luscious thing as our bodies lather up in the tropical fashion allowing us to move together, in unison, on top of soaking wet sheets in a dank room somewhere in Subic, or Manila, or Bangkok. We've been out here on the line for forty days and my hormones are at full launch speed as I read my daily letters from Cindy with thoughts of her luscious thighs, and what it was like to be between them during our last few nights together before leaving Alameda for this God forsaken shithole. Now and then I receive an epistle from Suzie, in addition to the letters from Cindy, and then I'm in big trouble trying to balance my sexual craving with the reality of being aboard a vessel that houses three thousand men, and not one, single, woman.

Alas, this was about to change.

After dozens of relatively boring flights either in Route Package One, or along the coast while strafing the junks or tops of the small island fortresses, we were about to enter the sphere of reality and a pucker factor of nine on the scale of one to ten. A major Alpha strike was planned on Phuc Yen airfield and the entire Seventh Fleet was airborne in one capacity or another on this typically hot and humid clear day in the Tonkin Gulf. We had our briefing and now it was time to ride the escalator up to the flight deck and to pre-flight our aircraft. I'm mum, silent, pensive, scared shitless, and my eyes are glued to the deck. No eye contact. Stomach jumping and gurgling. My ass was puckering.

The photo reconnaissance birds were the first airborne, followed by the Zappers whose mission was to monitor and jam the enemy signals and missile sights located throughout the northern area.

All of these towns and hamlets sounded like baby talk. Fuk Yen, Ha Ho Yu, Hi Fong, Than Hoa!

Our four-plane formation consisted of Lieutenant Commander Jim Harmon - our Operations Officer, Boo, section leader Lieutenant Commander Jack (no middle name) Baker, and myself. We'd been up together on dozens of flights in preparation for this one, or so we thought. I had my trusty Nikon strapped around my neck loaded with slide film just in case we saw some action worth recording. Boo had been suffering from an extreme case of constipation for the previous two days so he loaded up on Carter's Little Liver pills for relief. No doubt he'd find it somewhere about five thousand feet above sea level.

We launched from the catapults and rendezvoused with a heading of due West as our radios were filled with reports of extremely heavy anti aircraft activity in the northern sectors around Hanoi, Phuc Yuen, and Haiphong. Eventually, we saw our accompanying helicopter, the

Big Mother as we affectionately called this bird, lift off from one of the SAR destroyers on station, and we headed over to provide escort service while we continued our heading towards the coast. The Air Force airborne early warning platform was called Puff and we always wanted to know what the Magic Dragon had to say as it maked its way up and down the interior of Laos close to the Vietnam border. One of Puff's primary missions was to report enemy aircraft activity that appeared on the radar screens. In order to put everything into proper perspective the code for MIGS in the air was referred to as Bandits. And, the relationship to our positions was called out in degrees of the clock, with Hanoi being the center of the hands. In other word, six o'clock meant the MIGS are flying due South of Hanoi. Three o'clock meant they are flying due East of Hanoi. And, when the baritone voice over Puff's airwaves indicatet thousand of feet this was an indication of the flight altitude of the MIGS. For example, "eight thousand" meant the MIGS were now at a flight altitude of eight thousand feet above sea level.

"Mayday, mayday, mayday! We have two aircraft down in Package Six, on the ridge, with two parachutes sighted. Childplay, do you have RESCAP in the air at this time, over?"

"That's affirmative, Puff, Lockets are with Big Mother on their way to sector five in Package One, and will be feet dry at four-five, over."

"Listen up, Lockets thirteen, five, and eleven. That's us, you guys. We're going in with Big Mother."

"Locket One, can you fly straight and level for five? I've got some business to take care of, over."

"What's the problem, Boo, got to go number one, over?"

"The Carter's Little Liver pills started to work. I've got to go number two, over."

Jesus Christ! How in the hell was Boo going to shit in the cockpit of a Spad while crossing the coast of North Vietnam? We started to rock our wings as a gesture of sheer hysteria when it finally sank in that this raging Cajun was going to try to straddle his seat, drop his flight suit down to his ankles, grunt and groan, and still maintain straight and level flight vis a vis his automatic pilot. This was my cue to drop the lens cap and get a shot of his aircraft as we cross the coastline. We maintained our flight altitudes and positions and we could see the canopy of Boo's aircraft open with several large pieces of paper flying out, disappearing in the sky. So, we assumed his in-flight constitutional was complete and now we can get back to the business at hand, and that is to proceed inland until we're vectored North towards Hanoi, and the crash scene.

I didn't especially like all of these small black puffs appearing ahead of our flight at the same altitude at which we were approaching the coastline. We began to spread out and fly as loose a formation as possible without jeopardizing the safety of the Big Mother chopper that is extremely vulnerable at this or any other altitude, for that matter. My mouth was becoming very dry and I was sure that my pulse was racing by this time. Light a Marlboro, smoke it down to the filter, snuff it out, and light another.

"Locket One, this is Puff. Are you feet dry yet? Report your position at feet dry so we can vector you to the area in Package Six that is the reported site of the two downed pilots from Childplay, over."

"Roger, Puff, we are feet dry at four-six, and eight thousand. Request you vector us for another few miles straight ahead until we get far enough inland and away from the flack here on the coast, over."

"Roger, Locket One. Proceed on course two seven zero at eight thousand until further notice, over."

"Locket One, affirmative, out."

"Okay, boys, this is the real thing. Hank, you are to split off to port and establish visual contact with the crew aboard Big Mother. Jack, hang close to me and Boo, you maintain visual to starboard. Any questions at this time? Do not, repeat, do not talk unless absolutely necessary. The airwaves are monitored by Charlie and there's too much garbage anyway, over."

"Roger, what's the poop? Do we have two down with reports of flares or are we going up just to see if there are any survivors, over?"

"Duthie and Hartman are reported down and there is activity on the ground closing in on them fast. No more chatter, out."

We flew for about another ten minutes towards Laos and then Puff instructed us to turn starboard towards Hanoi. We were deep in the heart of North Vietnam by now, and I was scared shitless! Why couldn't this goddamn chopper go any faster? Lawdy, it was literally crawling along as we meandered our way further North, and closer to a shit storm over the carst of this beautiful country whose denizens, in no uncertain terms, wanted to blow the living shit our of us. Words that I didn't want to hear ring out over the already crowded airwaves.

"Bandits, bandits, bandits. Bullseye, six o'clock, at one two thousand."

Time for a brief review! Time to see if I remember my homework. Bandits means enemy MIGS. Bullseye means Hanoi. Six o'clock means they're flying due South (while we are flying due North)! One two thousand means they're screaming along at 12,000 feet, which further means they're above us looking down for slow moving Spads with a creepy crawly Big Mother chopper. Lord God almighty! The recruiter never promised me this much action when I signed the papers to become the world's best - a United States Naval Aviator. Hell, I would have settled for second best at this point in my young life! MIGS flying down from Hanoi towards us. I have one eye looking towards the clouds above and the other at the ground below. Each eye has a specific mission. The left eye looks specifically for anti-aircraft flashes and SAM missile launches while the right eye looks for dark spots with signs of contrails against the blazing hot sky that indicates they're aircraft and not simply high flying birds cruising along at 12,000 feet, or thereabouts.

I was awfully tempted to call and ask Boo to repeat the procedure for defecating at 8000 feet in a Spad because I was about to shit in my pants. We have been flying for about twenty minutes on our northern vector and I could make out the area called Hanoi which, unlike our major metropolitan areas consisted of simply more dense buildings and housing than that of the countryside. We're not talking Empire State buildings, or the skyline of San Francisco, but rather simple one or two story buildings clustered close together approximately thirty miles ahead. Our mission lay just a few hundred yards ahead, however, and we could see the white phosphorous smoke of the signal flare against the dark green of the hill where the pilots supposedly were down. Jim Harmon took command as the flight leader began to issue instructions in a rather tenor voice compared to that of his normal baritone.

"Lockets five, eleven and thirteen, maintain your altitude and I'll go in with Big Mother for the pick-up. There're enemy troops moving up the hill towards the chute, so use a right pattern and roll in with your guns. Save your FFARS and ZUNIS for later, over."

"Roger, Locket One, I see them. Hank, you go in after Boo and me. That'll be our pattern and roll out to the right over the valley and not the hills. Watch your altitude and do not get low, over."

Low! Don't worry about me getting low! I feel just fine up here around 5000 feet where the air is cooler and the gunfire is minimal. Suppose I should roll in for a few runs just in case they have trouble getting the guys out, however.

"Locket One, we've been hit. Our hoist man is dead and our radios are going. Get us out of here now, over!"

"Hank, join up with Big Mother and take her back out to the SAR. Maintain your altitude at eight thousand, retrace our vector South, and await instructions from Puff, over."

"Roger, Jim, I'm outta here, out."

I thought my mouth had been dry before and I thought my pulse had been racing before, but nothing could compare to the rush I was-feeling now! Suddenly, I was entrusted with the safety of the helicopter crew and my own life somewhere over the interior of a very hostile enemy country where they would love to get their hands on my lily white, skinny young body for interrogation, incarceration, and anal manipulation. I flew up next to the chopper's open door and used hand signals to indicate to the crew that they were to follow my flight path and when I rocked my wings to the left they turned left. When I rocked my rings to the right they turned their course to the right. I applied full rich mixture, increased the prop rpm by 500 turns, checked out my circuit breakers to ensure the guns, missiles, and bombs were ready to go, and lite another Marlboro. We headed South as the impotent chopper lingered along at speeds that appeared to be at least half of that when we crossed feet dry sometime earlier. My adrenaline was running so fast that I even thought the chopper might be experiencing engine difficulty because of the terribly slow pace we were maintaining over the lovely but hostile countryside that I was anxious to leave behind, forever. Meanwhile, the airwaves were saturated with all of the commotion of the rescue back on the hillside, and the Alpha Strikes following ours from other carriers on Yankee Station. It sounded like a contest of who could talk the loudest, the fastest, and the longest which made it nearly impossible to decipher who was doing what to whom, and where they were doing it. Meanwhile, our flight was relatively quiet in that the chopper's transmitter was inoperative and I wasn't sure they were receiving my transmissions, so I felt like I was talking to myself as we made our way from the southern course towards the East, the coast, the SAR, and hopefully, back to the Oriskany, and to safety.

I flew up and around and over and below, to the left, to the right, to the rear, and forward of the chopper in order to let her know that I am in command of the situation albeit I am not of sound mind and body, because if I were of sound mind and body I would not have been flying this slow piece of post Korean war shit over the most heavily fortified air defenses ever recorded in the history of warfare. Now, I could see the water and meaning approximately ten minutes from feet wet, as the expression goes, and to relative safety but not before flying over the same anti-aircraft positions that greeted us on the way in this morning. "And a happy and healty good afternoon to you too, assholes," as I let my remaining ZUNI's loose from their pods to wind their way downward towards the trees that camouflage the fortifications where the short shits were shooting at us. More puffs of dark smoke as the artillery charges exploded around our two aircraft and the blasts close by would rock the wings in a hostile gesture that we were invading someone's elses territory. Well, fuck you! Take that, as I pickled the two remaining pods of FFAR's down the pike towards several junks meandering off the coast, and who monitored our activity.

We had safely reached to coastline and now were enroute back to the SAR that is homeplate to the chopper. The saliva glands in my mouth were active, and for the first time in hours I could now swallow. We began our descent towards the destroyer as the Big Mother entered her approach pattern and landed safely on the stern platform of the rocking ship. I giave a fly by at 50 feet off the deck and across the bow as a gesture that we did good for this was my salute to the blackshoes aboard just doing their job keeping us alive. I could see the crewmembers exit the chopper and a couple of them waved to me as the medics carried the wire stretcher containing one, lone body out the side door.

How did I feel? Shit hot! That's how I felt, to tell the honest-to-god's truth. My ass had made it out in one piece and I knew that without my assistance Big Mother would never have been able to return to her ship safely. I had done my job and now it's time to return to my carrier for the cut. Only hope that Jim, Jack, and Boo were okay.

"Childplay, this is Lockett Thirteen for landing, over."

"Roger, Lockett Thirteen, your compadres were successful in helping the Sandy's from Laos get one of the two downed pilots out safely. Congratulations on a job well done. Your Charlie time is one zero, over."

"Roger, one zero."

I could see the Oriskany ahead about twenty miles away and my pulse was literally jumping out of my body. The deck was clear and I was the first post strike aircraft to recover since the Alpha strike pilots had returned and were now on board awaiting the news of Duthy and Hartman. I entered the pattern, flew downwind, and caught the number three wire for a good landing.

While I taxied to the bow of the ship I can hear Boo radio for help as he approached the carrier for landing instructions. "This is Locket Eleven. I have hydraulic fluid streaming all over my canopy and I want the deck cleared for an emergency landing, over."

"Roger, Lockett Eleven, you are cleared for landing. Can you see to come aboard, over?"

"No sweat, paddles, but I am having trouble seeing the ball, over."

"We'll talk you down so get on your instruments and we'll start your descent now, Eleven. You call the ball if possible, over."

"Roger. If I bolter, I'll take it in straight ahead. Is the angel airborne, over?"

"That's affirmative, we have you on glide slope and your line up is good. Take off some power, maintain line up, and you're looking good."

"I've got the ball! I've got the ball! Give me the cut lights no matter what, over."

"Give me some power. You're low. Give me some power, power, power. That's it. Cut, cut."

Boo made it aboard safely as he taxied towards me on the bow. I was standing by my aircraft while Boo stopped and waited for the crew to chock his plane. A twin-engined Carrier on Board Delivery aircraft (COD) landed just a few minutes before us and is parked adjacent to our planes. As the hatch opens several crew members exit and one was wearing Army fatigues, had shoulder length hair, and tits.

Tits!

I signalled to Boo and he immediately walked out on his wing, turned his backside towards her, and presented her with a full, hairy, Cajon moon for her added entertainment. She responded with a big grin while I ran over, threw her into my arms, and presented her with a French kiss most apropos since she was from France, and a reporter with Paris Match magazine.

"Lieutenants Miller and Langlinais, report to Flight Ops immediately."

We were viewed on full 180 degree Cinerama with surround sound by the Air Boss, the Admiral, CAG, and numerous other big shots, and our antics were not appreciated by the mucky mucks, so we were instructed, in no uncertain terms, to behave like officers and gentlemen, a feat of extreme difficulty since we were neither, and damn proud of it, I might add.

I ran back for another squeeze of my little French squeeze but she was nowhere to be found. And, neither was Boo for that matter. All of a sudden she showed up with Boo as her escort. Little did the Commanding Officer, who despised Boo, know that he was fluent in French, and that he was the only crew member on board, out of a tally of 3000 able bodied men, who could speak the language. Being a Cajun from Abbeyville, Louisiana, was a blessing in disguise for this cowboy and our little French sparrow was relegated to our area of responsibility for the following three days as she began to report her story of the Spad drivers of Attack Squadron 152 to her editor.

Meanwhile, back in the ready room we heard the news of the successful rescue of Larry Duthie with our help and that of the Air Force Sandy's out of Laos. Hartman was still on the ground and the rescue attempt to retrieve him had failed. My job of escorting the Big Mother back to her base was the talk of the town, and word had it that the crew of the chopper was coming over to the Oriskany tomorrow to thank me personally.

I couldn't wait to get back up to my stateroom to write the world and tell them about today's episodes. I was totally euphoric and I hastily transcribed my thoughts onto parchment for Cindy, and Suzie, and

Jeanie to read, and hurried back to Boo's stateroom for some action with mademoiselle.

Frenchie wasn't even attractive. She had hairy arms. Her eyebrows had never been trimmed. Her teeth were crooked and smoke stained. Her hair looked like it hadn't been washed in days. However, after 40 days at sea, with 3000 men, and nicely scented letters from the States, she will do.

After an evening of drinking and carousing tomorrow has arrived and so has the remaining crewmembers of Big Mother from the activities the day before. I recognize the pilot as one of my classmates from pre-flight down in Pensacola, and he personally wanted to come over to thank me for the job I did in helping them get back safely to their ship. Sad to say that the wounded crew member operating the hoist died as a result of the enemy ground fire just as he was preparing to lower the hoist down to pick up Duthie. And, at the same time the ground fire knocked out their communications systems so it was a good thing that someone was around to help get them back out to the gulf. Our boss Jim, my wingman Jack, and Boo and I began to celebrate by getting out the medicinal brandy and slipping a few shots into our coffee mugs for the toasts that ensued, and the poker games that went late into the night. Time to celebrate. We lost our cherries about 35 miles south of Hanoi. We lived to tell about it.

While I was playing poker with the guys Boo was giving mademoiselle a free mustache ride up in his stateroom, and I wanted to think that I had the better end of the deal. Soon, we bid adieu to her as she promised to write about us in her magazine. Neither Boo nor I ever corroborated that promise.

Boo came down with a case of the clap a few days later, most likely from Frenchie who had probably screwed her way through the Third Marines, and other various unsundry regiments, down in South Vietnam. One of these days when I return to the States after this mess is over I'll go to the Library of Congress and look up the back issues of Paris Match to see if she's was for real or if, in fact, she merely wanted to fuck two Yankee Spad drivers while out in the Tonkin Gulf.

Back to the wardroom for countless games of Acey Ducey and more lies about who bombed what and who destroyed whom and who has the biggest balls.

I was grounded today because the skipper didn't want those of us who flew the last rescue attempt to get excited about going back in for Hartman. Soon we discovered via the announcement over the ship's intercom that the rescue strike proved to be a total disaster for our 7th Fleet, for Hartman, and for the same Big Mother chopper we escorted previously who had gone in for the attempted rescue of Hartman. The North Vietnamese had fortified the position where Hartman was shot down and they quietly and silently awaited the Air Force and Navy combined rescue attempts with an incredible barrage of weapons. We lost several aircraft in the strike, and the entire crew of Big Mother - the same crew with whom I had enjoyed the previous day's activities aboard the Oriskany; and, last but not least, Hartman, who most likely met his demise many hours earlier at the hands of the NVN.

The four of us retired to Jim's stateroom to contemplate the whole god dam ordeal, and to get drunk, real drunk. Now, I felt closer to these guys and I wanted to hear what Jim, our leader, had to say. He had been here before.

Such a shitty war. .

Big Mother after aborted rescue of LTJGDuthie

OPCON TOP SECRET MESSAGE

One little detail I failed to mention . . .

In November I had one hell of a scare during a night flight over North Vietnam where we dropped 250 pound bombs along the coastline in pitch black darkness. After completing the mission my section leader and I headed back towards the Oriskany to make Charlie that translates into when we were directed to land aboard.

After this harrowing experience I continued to chain - smoke on the return flight to soothe my terror and nerves. We entered the holding pattern for about one half hour, then were directed to enter the pattern and head downwind for the arrested landing. As I turned my aircraft into a left 45 degree bank I got instant vertigo. Total disorientation at 400 feet above the seas! Instruments instruments always rely and believe in your instruments kept calling to me. I looked outside the cockpit and saw the Oriskany in a vertical position sticking out of the water like it was heading straight towards Davey Jones Locker. I immediately scanned my instrument panel to see where I was flying straight and level and at the appropriate airspeed. This is what they call vertigo and I had it bad. I had to force my hand on the controls not to follow my instincts and to follow the instruments which don't lie. I was covered in sweat from head to toe. Even my cigarette was soaking wet! As instructed by the Landing Signal Officer (LSO) I maintained the glidepath for the correct lineup while adjusting the airspeed to ensure the Meatball was all Green. After what seemed like hours I trapped a three wire and came to the typical screeching halt safely aboard.

When I entered the wardroom for my debriefing I was as white as a sheet and about five pounds lighter from sweating. But I was alive! I told my wingman LCDR Jack Baker that I was going to turn in my wings. I was deathly afraid of another attempt of coming aboard the ship at night. Jack advised me not to turn them in but, instead, to request a change of duty station to a land base. He also was totally empathetic and said he didn't blame me at all.

After conferring with my Ops Officer LCDR Jim Harmon and Baker I advised our CO that I wasn't going to fly off the boat anymore at night. He gave it about five minutes thought then reported my action to the CAG who in turn called for the Kangaroo court to convene for the judgement.

The following documents are testimony of that board and our CO's pathetic follow up to same.

23 November 1967

From: Field Aviators Evaluaton Board

To: Commander Attack Carrier Air Wing SIXTEEN

Via: (1) Commanding Officer, Attack Squadron ONE FIVE TWO

Subj: Field Naval Aviatiors Evaluation Board; record of proceedings of

Ref:(a) BUPERS Manual, Article C-7318

Encl: (4) Appointing Order, CVW-16 ltr ser 319 of 18 Nov. 67

(5) Signed statement of purport of the Board

1. Pursuant to Article C-7318 of reference (a) and in compliance with appointing order, enclosure (4), the following information is submitted in the case of Lieutenant (junior grade) Henry L. MILLER, Jr. USNR, 687001/1315 of Attack Squadron ONE HUNDRED FIFTY TWO.

    a. <u>Summary of the Facts</u>:

        (1) Lieutenant (junior grade) MILLER has stated that his fear of night flying has reached a point where he feels that he may have an accident and/of endanger other pilots flying with him.

        (2) He has had a basic fear of night flying which is aggravated by carrier flight operations, instrument conditions and a combat environment. This fear has, by his own admission, increased throughout his flying career.

        (3) He states that if he is required to continue to fly from an aircraft carrier at night he would request termination of his flight status.

        (4) There is no apparent medical reason why he is not suited for night flying.

        (5) He has flown a total of 123 night hours, 76 night hours in the A1 aircraft and 27 hours of night carrier operations.

        (6) His flying performance with Attack Squadron ONE HUNDRED FIFTY TWO has been below average.

        (7) He is considered to be an average pilot, during daylight hours, by Attack Squadron ONE HUNDRED FIFTY TWO.

(8) He desires to remain in the aviation field regardless of whether or not he remains in flight status.

(9) He has no record of any flight violations or aircraft indicents.

(10) Lieutenant (junior grade) MILLER has stated that he has no intention of making the military a career.

Enclosure (3)

b. <u>Summary of flight statistics</u>:

(1) Total flight hours: 801.7
(2) Total hours last three months: 110.4
(3) Total hours by model for last three months: 110.4
(4) Type of aircraft presently qualified to fly: A-1 H/J

c. <u>Signed Statement of Awareness of purpose of board</u>:

(1) See enclosure (5)

d. <u>Statement of witnesses</u>:

(1) Lieutenant (junior grade) MILLER was accorded the priviledge of appearing in person before the board and making such statements pertinent to the case as he desired.

(2) Additional witnesses were not called.

e. <u>Findings and opinions of the Board:</u>

(1) The Board finds Lieutenant (junior grade) MILLER and average pilot during daylight hours, however it also finds a deepseated fear of night flying. This fear is aggravated by, but not limited to, carrier operations in a combat environment, and it is becoming progressively worse with each succeeding flight. His present situation is intolerable and has forced him to request a change in duty or termination of his flight status.

(2) It is the Board's opinion that a change of duty, remaining in a flight status, would not alleviate Lieutenant (junior grade) MILLER's problem, as night flying is an integral part of Naval Aviation. It is also the opinion of the Board that his desire to be downgraded to a limited flying status could be an expression of a compromise between a desire to cease flying altogether and a wish to avoid the stigma attached to terminating his flight status while in a combat environment.

(f) <u>Recommended classification:</u>

(1) Type "B".

(g) <u>Recommendation of the Board:</u>

(1) The board recommends a change in designator and orders to duty not involvingflying. It is further recommended that he be restained on active duty, assigned a billet in the aviafield.

R. G. SONNIKSEN, LCDR, USN

J.B. ROOSEN, LT, USN

G.F. SCHINDELAR, LTJG, USNR

B.S. EDWARDS, LT(MC), USNR

Copy to:

CO, ATKRON ONE HUNDRED FIFTY TWO

Enclosure (3)

FF12/5420VA-152:11:mSer 42727NOV1967

(NOW HERE IS OUR WHIMPY COMMANDING OFFICER'S RESPONSE TO THE BOARD!)

FIRST ENDORSEMENT on Field Naval Aviators Evaluation Board ltr of 23 NOVEMBER 1967

From: Commanding Officer, Attack Squadron ONE FIVE TWO

To: Commander, Attack Carrier Air Wing SIXTEEN

Subj: Field Naval Aviator Evaluation Board; record of proceedings of

1. The contents of the basic letter of the Evaluation Board are noted and forwarded with the following comment.

(a). The statement of paragraph one, a. (6) of the basic letter is one with which issue is taken unless qualified to state specifically, "during night operations and instrument conditions." Otherwise his performance has been average to above average.

2. The comments and recommendations made in the First Endorsement to Lieutenant (junior grade) MILLER's letter by this command remain UNCHANGED.

Spads and A4 Skyhawks parked on USS Oriskany flight deck, 1967

Notes from a Place Called Vietnam

1......Only 2 actual stand down days in over 55 days on the line. Our first line period of 25 days; the other was because WX *weather* was bad and we canceled. The next day was scheduled as stand down but that was canceled, and we flew. We should have had two (2) days in a row of no fly. Excuses given are lucrative targets. In one case of stand down 2 Alpha strikes were launched after one bridge and another strike on RR *railroad* cars. These definitely could have waited until next scheduled flying day.

2...Evidence of mail censorship. Two men in VA-152 had portions of two letters eradicated in which foul language was written. These letters were mailed to people in the U.S. from Yankee. This is 100% illegal since we are neither in a declared war nor in a restricted war zone. Extensive efforts by the two men to locate this infringement and prosecute those responsible to the fullest extent of the law are now underway.

3...PAO *Public Affairs Office* releases by Alpha strike pilots stating "All bombs on target and total destruction," constantly being sent to news media in U.S. A.I. *Air Intelligence* and pilots say just the opposite. This list of fibbing goes from CAG *Commander Air Group* on down to green Ensigns. PAO's on ships interested in one thing- dramatic tales of ravaging destruction over NVN *North Vietnam*. These are blown up to such proportions that it sounds as though the war may be "won" tomorrow.

People in U.S. have been reading this same garbage for three years and now wonder how could they possibly be waging a war if all we have said is true???

4...There had been much difficulty in procuring pilots' flight and survival gear mostly because of hang-ups in the supply line. Squadron's Para riggers submit a chit to S-6 Division for flight gear. If S-6 does not have it, which is usually the case with SEEK -II kits, MK-3C life preservers, and Nomex flight suits, they forward request to Cubi Point *Naval Air Station* Supply. There has been much difficulty in obtaining said items from both S-6 and Cubi. Cubi must then submit request to Alameda (?) *Naval air Station* for gear and the time required is very lengthy in obtaining single items or gross amounts. It is obvious that someone in the Supply system is dropping the ball due to the fact that most items are in short supply, and are very difficult to obtain in the desired sizes and quantities. Cubi Point should have an abundance of said gear and also means of rapid transport to the various ships and squadrons. At the present time the Supply system is UNSAT.

5...Flight Plan made up in War Room and TGT *target* and times are chosen from debriefs from pilots during that day. Flight Plan then submitted to Strike who then goes over finer details with respective CO's. Then, Air Plan is made and distributed to Squadron at about 0100. Squadron Schedules Officer tries to get info as early as possible in order to prepare next day's flight schedule from Strike. A flight schedule is then typed, distributed to all Squadron departments usually no later than 0500, but pilots usually know next day's launches before 0000. However Strike or Flag change schedule as much as twice during the early morning. Therefore, Maintenance, Ordnance, Ops, and the pilots are never totally aware of the day's schedule until it occurs, this entails literally as 24 hour job by respective Squadron departments and the Squadron flight Schedule Officer. An alternate could be to determine Alpha strikes for a week in advance (providing WX is good) and coordinating these strikes daily between carriers so that strikes, launch times, TOT's *time over target* are known well in advance of actual flights - like a day or two.

6...Various inspection teams and fact-finding boards come aboard CVA's *aircraft carriers.* However, these teams discuss problems at the Flag and CO level. They never make an effort to "come down" and get the real scoop from Squadron CO's and respective pilots and ground personnel. This is the age-old problem of those in responsible positions being leery to expose all the facts due to the fact their positions may be jeopardized. The only way to get the facts is for these teams to stay aboard longer, mill around where know problems exist, talk with men from E-1's on up to and including CDR's, evaluate the situations, and submit an unbiased, accurate report to their respective commands, such as NAVAVNSAFECER, OPNAV, CNO, CHINFO *who incidentally was my father at the time,* CINCPAC, CINCPACFLT, etc.

7...It is a known fact that R&R *rest and relaxation, or liberty, or leave,* does not totally exist when CVA's and other ships and squadrons pull into port. Proficiency flying, duty section watches, collateral duty responsibilities, etc evidence this. Some squadrons make an attempt to give each pilot 4 or 5 days in Cubi during the course of a line period so that said pilot can have complete R&R. Some squadrons do not even make an effort to do this. It ought to be a written law that each pilot in every squadron on Yankee and Dixie Stations to be given a minimum of three full days in an R&R port every line period. This law not being subject to compromise by CAG's, ship CO's, Squadron CO's, etc. ...Keep a man on Yankee for 30+ days and then require him to work when in port. Yet, some wonder why men literally are disgusted with this war and with the Naval service. A little antagonism goes a long way as far as careers are involved.

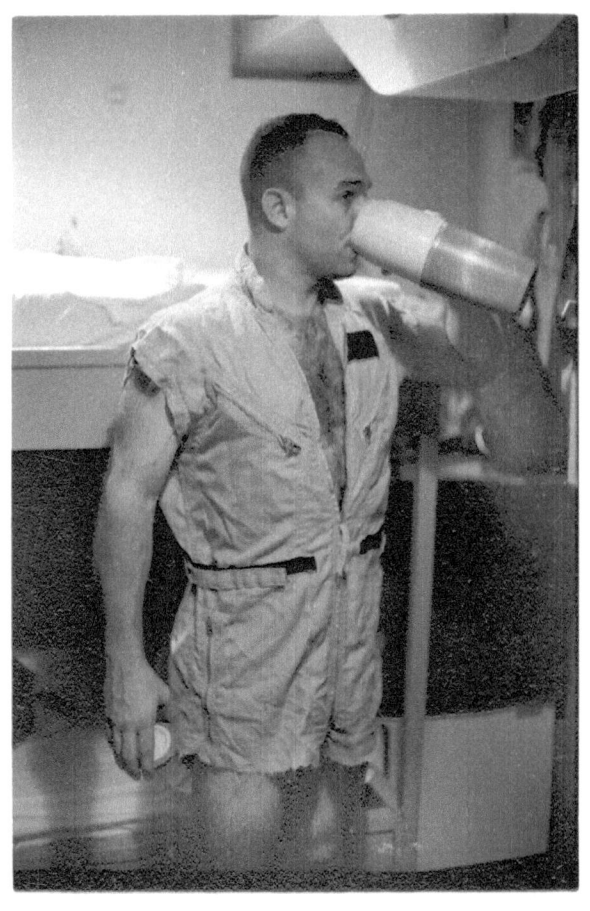

<u>LT Ashton "BOO" Langlinais in his new modified flight suit!</u>

LT Bud Watson

VA-152, A SPAD SQUADRON IN VIETNAM

PREPARED B Y LT J.M. WATSON USNR

DECEMBER 1967

INTRODUCTION

As 1967 closes Attack Squadron ONE FIFTY-TWO is completing its third and final combat cruise with Carrier Air Wing Sixteen aboard the USS ORISKANY (CVA-34). It will also be the squadron's last cruise flying the A-1 Skyraider, as the aircraft is being phased out of the Navy's inventory after twenty-one years of service. This narrative will summarize VA-152 operations in the Vietnam conflict.

At the onset of the war A-1's participated in the strikes against major targets. The aircraft proved too vulnerable to concentrated anti aircraft fire and during VA-152's 1965 and 1966 cruises it was utilized for armed reconnaissance over North Vietnam. By 1967, emphasis has shifted from armed reconnaissance in the southern route packages (Nam Dinh and southward) to major strikes in the Northeast Triangle (Hanoi, Haiphong and the northeast rail line). Air defenses in the latter environment precluded A-1 operations overland and only coastal-armed reconnaissance was conducted in 1967.

By far the most important role to emerge for the A-1 in Vietnam, however, was in Search and Rescue (SAR) operations. The Spad's mission was called Rescue Combat Air Patrol (RESCAP) and consisted of locating downed pilots, thwarting capture attempts, suppressing ground fire and escorting pickup helicopters to and from the rescue scene. Assistance of jet aircraft overland was necessary in the more heavily defended areas.

RESCAP stations were located near the SAR destroyers, on which the helicopters were based, and A-1's were held on station continuously during carrier flight operations. Normal two plane RESCAP handled cyclic operations in the lower route packages. When ORISKANY launched major strikes, VA-152 was in the habit of launching a Special RESCAP to augment the SAR forces.

When relieved on station, after an uneventful RESCAP, a secondary armed reconnaissance mission was carried out. If aircraft were available in addition to those required for RESCAP or when another carrier had the RESCAP commitment, flights were launched with a primary mission of armed reconnaissance.

DET ZULU

In April 1964, a portion of the squadron, called DET ZULU, was ordered to Vietnam to train South Vietnamese pilots. This mission was competed in November 1964 and the detachment returned to NAS Alameda in December.

1967-67 COMBAT CRUISE

By the middle of July 1967, when the squadron arrived on Yankee Station, the complexion of the war had changed. No longer was the emphasis on armed reconnaissance of line and communications in the lower route packages. Pressure had been shifted to the Northeast Triangle, specifically Haiphong, Hanoi, the routes connecting them and the northeast rail line. Heavy antiaircraft defenses in this area precluded A-1 operations overland except as SAR forces and in company of the jet aircraft. The first few days of the initial line period were intended to be warm up and consequently Air Wing strikes were assigned to the more southern route packages.

The first day on the line was 14 July and squadron activity was directed against Water Borne Logistic Craft 9WBLC) traffic along the coast. A four-plane flight consisting of LCDR Harmon, CDR Willson, LCDR Wolfe and LCDR Baker sank six WBLC's. In the afternoon LTJG Selkey and LTJG Jaehnig sank six more. ON the 15th LTJG Cassell was shot down and killed by antiaircraft fire from Hon Ne while attaching WBLC's.

On 16 July LCDR Verich from VF-162 was shot down and ejected in the karst southwest of Phu Ly. CDR Headley and LCDR Sharpe were called in to direct the SAR effort. At this time darkness put an end to the search and it was continued on the morning of the 17th. On scene SAR commander was LCDR Harmon. CDR Willson, LCDR Wolfe and LTJG Guenzel made up the rest of the RESCAP. IN spite of heavy ground fire, MIG's and SAMs in the area, the RESCAP, under the cover of the Air Wing jets, was able to find LCDR Verich, escort the helicopter (Big Mother 69) to the area and pick him up.

Tow days later, on a strike at Phub Ly, LCDR Hartman and LTJG Duthie of VA-164 were shot down. The Special RESCAP composed of LCDR Harmon, LTJG Langlinais, LCDR Baker and LTJG Miller was joined by several A-1's of VA 215 from the USS BONNE HOMME RICHARD. Under conditions similar to the Verich rescue, LTJG Duthie was picked up by an Air Force Jolly Green helicopter and evacuated to Udorn, Thailand. During this action, Big Mother 67, a Navy H-3, was over LCDR Hartman, ready for pickup, when ground fire critically wounded a crewman, The helicopter was forced to depart the area and the crewman died in flight. Clementine 2, a UH-2 from the southern DSAR destroyer, was then ordered to the scene, escorted by tow VA- 215 A-1's.. Like Big Mother 67 he took hits from ground fire and he had to be escorted back to the ship by the VA-215 A-1's and by CDR Headley and LCDR Sharpe, who had been backing up the other SAR forces.

The rescue attempt for LCDR Hartman continued on 19 July. During the night the North Vietnamese had rushed troops and guns into the area. A six plan Special RESCAP composed of CDR Willson, LTJG Ward, LTJG Selkey, LTJG Jaehnig, LCDR Sharpe and LTJG Sehlin escorted Big Mother 67 into the area in the company of Air Wing Sixteen jets. CDR Willson, on scene SAR commander and LTJG Ward, his wingman, circled LCDR Hartman while LCDR Sharpe, LTJG Sehlin and the Air Wing jets suppressed ground fire in the area. LTJG Selkey and LTJG Jaehnig escorted the helicopter. Once the helo was in the area the on scene commander marked LCDR Hartman's position with a Zuni rocket. At the same time a cluster bomb dropped by one of the other A-4's failed to open and exploded intact in the center of the heavily defended valley adjacent to the karst in which LCDR Hartman was hiding. The helicopter mistook the cluster bomb for the Zuni and flew directly over the flak sights in the valley. They opened up and the helo went down in a ball of flames with no chance of survival for the crew.

After the loss the SAR forces retreated to regroup. In the afternoon, LCDR Harmon, LTJG Langlinais, LCDR Baker and LTJG Miller took a helicopter into the area but the risk was considered by then to be too great and the SAR effort was discontinued.

On 20 July LCDR Wolfe and LTJB Benson directed by Clementine 1, a Navy UH-2 from the northern SAR destroyer, in the pickup of CDR Wittmore of VA-212 off the BONNE HOMME RICHARD. The Commander had been shot down in the islands near the Chinese border.

Electronic search in the Phu Ly area indicated that LCDR Hartman was still evading capture in the karst. LCDR Harmon and LTJG Selkey dropped him supplies on the night of the 20th and were rewarded for their efforts with a SAM lobbed into the area. On the 21st

LCDR Harmon flew to Udorn to coordinate the rescue attempt with the Air Force. Buildup of forces now precluded rescue attempts from the seaward side. Rescue attempts from Thailand proved equally unsuccessful.

During the relative calm that followed, squadron efforts were directed largely toward destruction of waterborne logistic craft, The remainder of July netted 16 destroyed and 17 damaged. In August and September, squadron pilots claimed 30 destroyed and 65 damaged. Principal WBLC hunting areas were around Cape Mui Ron and from Brandon Bay north to Cape Dang. On 28 July, LCDR Harmon and LTJG Lindsay destroyed a North Vietnamese PT boat in the islands east of Haiphong.

On 1 August a RESCAP composed of LCDR Wolfe, LTJG Jaehnig, LTJG Selkey and LTJG Lindsay directed rescue attempts for a Navy pilot from the USS Intprepid, down in the islands east of Haiphong. LCDR Wolfe and LTJG Jaehnig located the pilot and provided cover for him while LTJG Selkey and LTJG Lindsay escorted Clementine 1, a UH-2, from the northern SAR destroyer, for the pickup. In the process one North Vietnamese boat attempting to pick up the pilot was sunk. Also, on 1 August, LCDR Harmon and LTJG Langlinais sank a North Vietnamese PT boat I the islands west of Haiphong. Three days later the pair duplicated the feat.

Throughout the cruise spotting missions had been flown in support of Seventh Fleet ships engaged in bombardment of targets along the North Vietnamese coast. Targets had been WBLC's, suspected supply dumps and areas called Choke Points, in which transport arteries were made vulnerable by terrain and exposure from the sea. While damage was mostly in the form of harassment, some targets were destroyed. During these missions ordnance was held until completion of shore bombardment, in case coastal defense units engaged the ships. If such an engagement did not occur aircraft were released to perform coastal-armed reconnaissance, just as squadron aircraft had always been in the habit of doing when released from an uneventful RESCAP.

Firing upon gunfire ships was sporadic until early September when, while supporting offensive operations in the Demilitarized Zone, ships for which the squadron was spotting were taken under fire each day during the four day period beginning on the 1st. After this period, such firings again became sporadic as operations again moved farther North.

RESCAP never again entered the picture as importantly as during mid-July. As the Air Wing became more experienced and the air war further escalated. Targets became increasingly closer to the focal points of the Northeast Triangle. Potent air defenses and scarcity of terrain suitable for evasion in this area precluded SAR operations in most instances. On 26 August CDR Willson ad LTJG Ward rescued an Air Force F-4 pilot just north of the Demilitarized Zone. On 5 October LCDR Baker and LTJG Miller located ENS Matthene of VF-111 in the karst southeast of Quang Suoi but heavy ground fire made it impossible to get a helicopter to the scene. The following day CDR Headley led a division of aircraft inland north of Hon Gay to conduct electronic search for the downed Air Force pilot. Contact brought a survival radio was obtained but it was judged to be a hoax. On 26 October CDR Headley and LTJG Spiegel searched for several pilots down in karst areas southeast of the Red River.

On 9 October a detachment of three aircraft and four pilots was sent to the Marin Corp Air Station at Chu Lai. Under command of LCDR Sharpe the detachment operated with the southern element of Seventh Fleet ships engaged in shore bombardment of North Vietnam. The detachment returned to ORISKANY on 1 November just before the ship left the line.

The month of October was lucrative, netting 64 WBLC's destroyed and 75 damaged. From the end of October on the weather over North Vietnam worsened. Low overcast, clouds, showers and poor visibility predominated with only a few brief periods of fair weather. No further SAR operations were conducted and spotting for coastal bombardment was minimal also, as these missions became secondary and coastal-armed reconnaissance primary. In November and December 21 WBLC's were destroyed and 34 damaged. Marginal weather also greatly diminished logistic effort by the North Vietnamese and the cruise, which had begun with such fury, was ended quietly.

ADDENDUM

The Squadron returned to Alameda on 31 January 1968 and almost immediately began transitioning to the A-4 Skyhawk. All of the A-1 pilots were ordered to new squadrons. Pilots took their places from VA-146 and VSF-3. On 14 February Commander Willson was relieved by Commander Philip E. Johnson, the former commanding officer of VA-146. At that time VA-152 became an A-4 squadron though for a while the Spads still remained awaiting transfer.

Spads on run-in Route Package Six north of the DMZ. Bombs Away!

Vietnam – an Introspection

The project consists of the juxtaposition of images depicting the recollections of war with those of combatants and innocents - spouses, lovers, sons and daughters. I shot all images using a Nikon FA and Nikormat FT with 20mm, 50mm, 135, and fisheye lenses. The only exception is one depicting a Vacation Bible School class held at the First Baptist Church, Opp, Alabama, circa 1950. The images coincide with the title and poem I composed about the Vietnam Memorial, better known as The Wall. The poem titled, Touch Me – a Soliloquy, is an integral part of the project. It is copyrighted, as are the images.

By digitally layering one images with another I intend to project images of how I, as a participant, remember those situations affected me emotionally. The pilots and ships crew became one as brothers working closely for the safe launch and recovery of aircraft flying missions over Vietnam. The loved ones who remained behind and the lovers met along the way were integral to the emotional impact of not only this project but, additionally, to the war effort itself. These remain vivid impressions of daily operations and recreation during the seven months while USS Oriskany was deployed in Southeast Asia, 1967.

The title piece is an image of an aviator prior to flying his last mission before he was shot down and held prisoner by the North Vietnamese. He was my roommate. The other individuals were shipmates and lovers met along the way. We consider ourselves family. I love them all.

Title Image

An Attack Pilot standing in front of his A-4 Skyhawk prior to launching an Alpha Strike over North Vietnam. He was my roommate, Dave Carey, an Annapolis graduate, and this was the last photo taken prior to his capture. He was held as a prisoner of war for five and one half years in the Hanoi Hilton. The year - 1967.

The overlay of the Red Cross is my artistic interpretation of not only medical assistance but, additionally, a symbol of crisis, of emergency, and of the Rules of the Geneva Convention as they apply to war.

TOUCH ME - A SOLILOQUY
BY
HANK MILLER

Bar Scene

Aviators of Attack Squadron 152 on liberty in Sasebo, Japan.

Tokiwa Stand Bar was favorite spot for this squadron's personnel.

The women are prostitutes under the watchful eye of "Mama san" who is inside managing the store!

The overlay is our squadron insignia for VA 152. Our call sign is Lockett. Our slogan is "Non Hankus Pankus."

Dear Friend

Sue Slusher, wearing my flight jacket, is staring into space. A Berkeley graduate, we met in 1966 at the 39 Main, a bar in the San Francisco Bay area, and remain close friends today.

The aircraft behind her is the A1 H/J Skyraider, better known as the Spad. It is being catapulted off USS Oriskany for a mission over the coast of North Vietnam. Most Spads were utilized in close air support with helicopters to rescue downed aviators on station. The Spad remains the most formidable attack aircraft used over both South and North Vietnam.

My Wingman

LCDR Jack Baker, my wingman and section flight leader, pre-flighting his Spad prior to launching for a mission over North Vietnam. We made a pact the day we departed Alameda for Vietnam – to get out of the war alive. We both succeeded.

The overlay is a photo I took on the day we returned to our homeport of Alameda just as we passed under the most beautiful sight in the world - the Golden Gate Bridge. The weather was cold, the sky was clear, the wind was howling. The sailors, in their winter blue uniforms and white hats, were on the flight deck in anticipation of greeting their loved ones after seven months absence. A day I'll never forget – 31 January 1968.

My Girl

Cindy McNutt is one of four young ladies sharing a flat in San Francisco who I knew during the Summer of Love, 1967. She is sitting in my MG-B. The scene behind her is of a mission I flew over Route Package 6 just North of the DMZ – North Vietnam. On that day, we supported the Air Force aircraft flying strikes out of Da Nang.

Cindy wrote me a letter every single day for seven months. Not a day went by that I didn't have at least one from her to read, and appreciate, with the news from home along with the love displayed in her written words.

Rescue

Cher Mole, a TWA flight attendant and the roommate of Cindy's, and I were in the Japanese Tea Garden, Golden Gate Park. I found her gazing into space with a wonderful expression. Afterwards, Cher, Cindy and I hopped into my MG-B and sped towards Sam's Anchor Cafe, in Tiburon, CA, for more fun. This was four days prior to being deployed with my squadron and air wing - June, 1967. Those fun filled days will never be repeated.

The image of the pilot is one of his rescue shortly after being shot down over North Vietnam. The helicopter crew returned him safely to USS Oriskany. The squadron's Commanding Officer shakes his hand and welcomes him back to the safety of the ship, if for only one or two days. He returned to fly more dangerous missions.

Dear Friends

Diane and Fran are two Peace Corps volunteers I met while on liberty in Hong Kong, Christmas, 1967. My roommate and I toured the Oriskany to show them how we lived and worked in contrast to their volunteerism in the barrios of the Philippines. Diane and I are the only two out of our foursome alive today. We remain very close friends.

The overlay is an image taken of the author while standing in front of the Spad.

Dreams of Home

Sailors on the flight deck staring out towards the San Francisco skyline. Coit Tower and Telegraph Hill can be seen in the background. Dreams of home always a reality while away from loved ones, and the city or farm.

The overlay is one of an underway replenishment and the seas are rough. The destroyer's crew is wearing life vests during the maneuver as an added precaution in case of falling overboard.

Dejection

Two members of our squadron after returning from a failed mission attempting to rescue a downed pilot somewhere over North Vietnam. Our pilots provided close air support for the helicopters who, through sheer bravery of their crew, flew at low altitudes in dangerous territory to bring those downed pilots back to safety. This was one of disappointment and dejection.

The overlay is an image I took of my wingman while we attacked a target on the coast of North Vietnam.

Flight Deck Officers

Flight Deck officers serving aboard USS Oriskany and Carrier Air Wing (CVW) 16 during the 1967 Cruise to Southeast Asia. Both men were not only co-workers but also close friends. Theirs was a most dangerous job- launching and recovering combat aircraft 24/7, in rain, fog, and pitching decks.

The aircraft landing behind them is an A3 Skywarrior – the largest aircraft based aboard a United States Naval aircraft carrier. We nicknamed it "The Whale". It was used mainly for in-flight refueling of the fighter and attack aircraft.

Fighter Launch

An F-8 Crusader is heading towards the bow for a catapult launch to eventually engage the North Vietnamese pilots in aerial combat. His aircraft is armed with 20 mm guns and air-to-air heat seeking Sidewinder missiles.

The overlay is a silhouette image of a lone flight crewman relaxing by the jet he helps to maintain. It is sundown and the feeling is eerie. Night operations will commence only too soon.

Pondering Pam

One of the flight deck officers in a rare moment relaxing between launch and recovery of aircraft. Their work gave an entirely new definition to the term 24/7 - in rain, fog, and pitching decks.

The overlay is one Pam Bush, a friend living in San Francisco, having a picnic at a beach on Pt Reyes seashore, Marin County, California, while toasting someone somewhere!

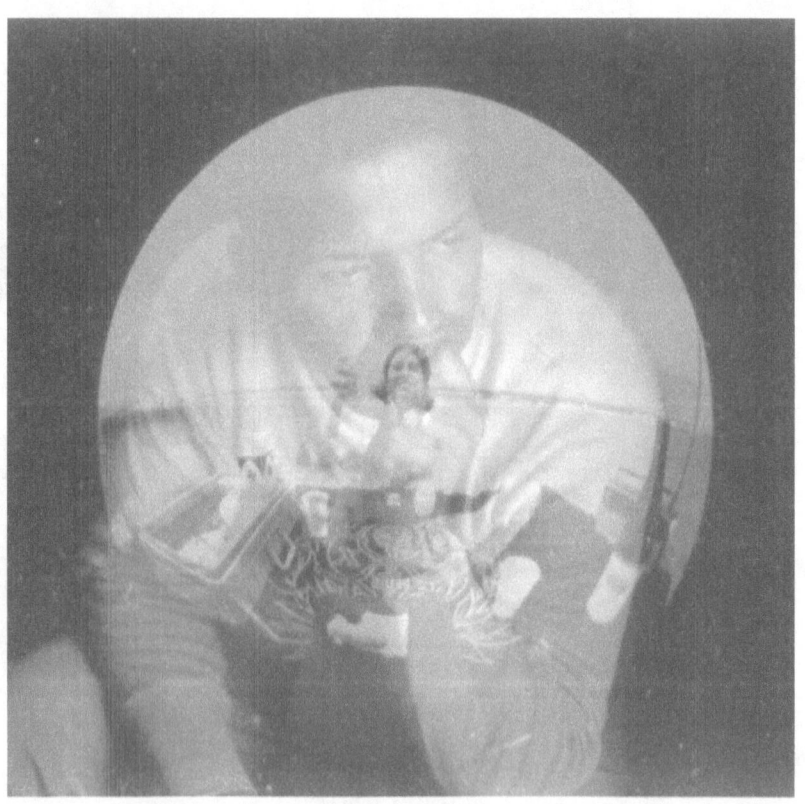

Cold Cat Shot

An F-8 Crusader suspended in space after a failed catapult launch. The pilot ejected but his parachute failed to deploy in time. He landed in the catwalk on the starboard side of the ship. He died immediately.

The overlay is one of those crewmembers who maintain the aircraft to ensure the safety of the pilots and crew. What a sad moment for them.

No Answers

This is an image of children taken during Vacation Bible School, Opp, Alabama, circa 1950. Opp is my hometown. My cousin and I shared many a wonderful summer with our maternal grandparents and friends, in south Alabama.

The superimposed image is one of the cemetery at the Presidio, a former Army installation, near the Golden Gate Bridge. If you look closely you will notice a ghost image walking between the headstones.

The Wall

The photo was taken in my grandmother's backyard, Opp, Alabama. I am on the left, my cousin is in the middle, and our best friend is on the right. We all remain close today.

The Vietnam Memorial, better known as The Wall, is an image I took during my trip to Washington for my father's burial in Arlington in 1993. He was a Navy Rear Admiral, a hero during three wars, and is buried just a few rows behind that of the father of Penne Poole, my high school sweetheart. She and I still reflect today on the meaning of The Wall as millions have since its inception.

All images and content protected under United States Library of Congress Copyright Laws.

Geisha House, Sasebo, Japan

The Perfect Ending!

www.ingramcontent.com/pod-product-compliance
Lightning Source LLC
Chambersburg PA
CBHW021959160426
43197CB00007B/185